Don't Rain On My Parade
My Coloring Book
Sam, You Made The Pants Too Long
Gotta Move
Why Did I Choose You
He Touched Me

THE
WAY
WE
WERE

Barbra Streisand

My Name Is Barbra

SONGBIRD

Barbra Streisand

Sorry,
couldn't find a bird!

Barbra
Streisand's
Greatest
Hits
Volume 2

Barbra
A Biography of
Barbra Streisand

Donald Zec and Anthony Fowles

Barbra
A Biography of Barbra Streisand

NEW ENGLISH LIBRARY

Copyright © 1981 by Frandon Ltd.

Design: Ian Hughes
Picture research/Editorial consultant: Romey Fullerton
First published in Great Britain by New English Library
Limited,
Barnard's Inn, Holborn, London EC1N 2JR in 1981

All rights reserved. No part of this publication may be
reproduced or transmitted, in any form or by any means,
without permission of the publishers.

Typeset by The Yale Press Ltd, London SE25
Printed and bound in Great Britain by Pitman Press Ltd,
Bath

The pictures in this book are reproduced by courtesy of the
following:
Rex Features – pages 6, 76, 95, 99, 133, 136, 141, 146, 149,
163, 213, 227, 233, 247
Syndication International – pages 15, 48, 59, 111, 113, 115,
116, 197, 205
Camera Press – pages 10-11, 160
Keystone Press – pages 81, 119, 123, 128, 169, 172, 179, 245

ISBN: 0-450-04857 8

ACKNOWLEDGEMENTS

Research into the life and career of such an internationally-discussed star as Barbra Streisand is a constantly expanding task. For each fact established a dozen more appear on the horizon. It is impossible to acknowledge here all the assistance, whether written or spoken, we were given. Nevertheless certain people were particularly invaluable as major sources of information and opinion. We would like to express our formal thanks for their kind and perceptive help to the following; Mike Frankovich, Muriel Harris, Irwin Kershner, Howard Koch, Walter Matthau, Vincent Minnelli, Jason Monet, Sydney Pollack, Otto Preminger, Jerry Schatzberg, George Segal, David Selby, Omar Sharif, Harry Stradling Jr. and Peter Yates. We owe special thanks to Elliott Gould for his characteristic and good-humoured frankness. In the media field, Lawrence Grobel's incisive interview with Miss Streisand in *Playboy* provided valuable supporting artillery to our own assault on some of the myths surrounding the star, a process notably assisted by Al Coombes, *Ladies Home Journal*; Shana Alexander, *Life*; Lawrence B. Eisenberg, *Cosmopolitan*, and of course writer-director Frank Pierson in *New West*. Author Clive Hirschorn was most helpful in comparing notes with us over the *Hello Dolly!* saga and also in allowing us to quote references to it from his excellent book *Gene Kelly* (W. H. Allen, 1974). George Crane and Daily Mirror Newspapers Ltd were, as always, most helpful.

Finally we would like to express our appreciation to author, Rene Jordan, whose accomplished book *Streisand* (1976) skilfully encapsulates the actress's early life and career.

Donald Zec, Anthony Fowles, London July 1981

'Barbra Streisand is the complete reason for going to a movie . . . as Garbo was.'

Pauline Kael

'She's a man-eater. A regular ball-breaker. A female Orson Welles. She wants to control the picture. The timing, the editing; she wants her own hairdresser, her own wardrobe, her own director – she wants it all. And I have to tell you, I'd give it to her. If you want Streisand you have to bite on the bullet. You did it with Marilyn. You do it with Brando. And you do it with Streisand. Period.'

A mogul at MGM

ONE

THE FACE is familiar in five continents and is, triumphing over all early predictions, in part her fortune. The name is more than a household word. In an era where there is no studio system, no longer even a 'star' system, she has been described as alone constituting 'a complete reason for going to a movie'. The innumerable facts of her career, long since chronicled, require continuous monitoring and up-dating as, like an eccentric moonshot, she courses erratically through a firmament she outshines. Rumours, myths, legends, suppositions, have been assiduously documentcd. The slanders, too contentious to be repeated publicly, enjoy a seamy half-life at private dinner parties, trade receptions and other familiar salt-licks where the smart-mouths barter second-, third-hand anecdotes. Living at the core of the most plastic community we know today, she is not only charismatic in herself but the cause of fleeting charisma in others.

To drop her name on however thin a pretext is to command attention and ambivalent respect. The name, of course, is Barbra Streisand.

To isolate the truth behind the person enveloped by such a career and fronted by such legend is perhaps, finally, as impossible as it is fascinating. There is no single truth. Streisand is protean. By choice. Ferociously opposed to the cliché of having an 'image', she changes hers at will, defying the neutering of easy categorisation. She is, in one respect at least, not Paul Newman but Marlon Brando, the actor she is on record as most admiring, as most wanting to play opposite. Newman, it can fairly be said, has largely spent the past twenty years repeating himself. He has parlayed his lithely impertinent charm into a position of – in Hollywood terms – fabled bankability. Brando, his one-time young lion rival has, by contrast, continually gone out for his shots. *Julius Caesar* and *Queimada*. *A Countess from Hong Kong* and *Last Tango in Paris*. Napoleon and Fletcher Christian. The attempt to throw his best shot has more than once ended with Brando dumped on his butt on the canvas while the crowd boos. Indeed, his artistic hubris (all the world loves a losing loud-mouth) has often seemed to cue derision. But his range of performance has been prodigious and, at its best, on a level matchlessly transcending technique. Barbra Streisand can legitimately claim credit for swinging toward the Brando end of the scale. She has positively rejected stereotyped reprises of an easily-arrived-at, easily projected personality. Why? Sound, long-term commercial sense? Impatience with going through old motions? A sense of the fastidious? Yes, all of these, no doubt. But also, surely, from motives distinctly deeper and more complex.

To try to catch the truths behind the phenomenon – to discover what makes Barbra run – is a challenging enterprise. It touches not merely upon the superstars the public hungers for, but on the darker mystery – what can drive a member of this not always happy breed to pursue the status with sometimes pathologic relentlessness.

Ask any Eighties New York taxi-driver to take you to Pulaski Street in Brooklyn's Williamsburg district and, if it's at night, the possibility is he will gun his motor, leaving you at the kerbside. Ask by day and perhaps show him your money and, yes, what the hell, what's he got to lose, he'll chance his arm and a leg and his neck. As he pulls to a halt, you'll already have appreciated his point of view. You'll be tempted to ask him to wait and keep the engine running. This isn't strolling territory.

Now, in the 1980s, the district is the depressing sum of all the cancers that can blight a city centre that is forsaken, run down, strapped for cash. Garbage blows about as in an emptied, windswept stadium. Or stinks in the sun. Barbra Streisand has done well. Pulaski Street, where she was born, has not. Deserted buildings stare at you through cadaverous eyes. The graffiti on their walls is just as lack-lustre. Obscene, four-lettered, it is spiritless and second-hand. It lacks the wit of the vitally defiant. Some of the buildings are such ruined shells, such desolate, skeletal façades, you think of Berlin, Dresden, where the desolation may have come more instantly, more lethally, but scarcely less completely. And Warsaw. This is ghetto territory. But not Jewish. Not now. Puerto Rican. Blacks. The whites who remain on this street, behind the cracked windows, yellow-ochre walls, are resigned to minority status. A few people stare at you now with furtive aggression as they pass. You become aware that you are on a block whose idiosyncratic places of worship attract congregations that might just be as militant as their gospels. Step cautiously over the shattered sidewalks, the discarded hubcaps and anybody's garbage, and note The Holy Name Assembly of Yahshua The Messiah. And The Church of the Solid Rock. See, in fact hear, the odd one out, the Hasidic School bus taking Jewish children to their Hebrew studies, as it rasps smokily and fast past the Hot Gospel emporiums as though uneasy at being found loitering in such company.

So, of course, it was not to any Jewish school in this neighbourhood, but to one in Venice, California, that in the spring of 1980, Barbra Streisand made a prophet's ransom of an endowment – on condition it take her father's name, the late Emmanuel Streisand.

You get back into the cab and believe you have solved the mystery. No wonder, you consider, born and raised in an environment like this, who wouldn't be motivated to climb their dedicated, clawing, endlessly self-improving way up to the top of the heap; to the degree of status that invited you, along with Isaac Stern, Sinatra and the rest to perform for Presidents at the White House. As the relieved driver speeds you back toward your Hilton your thoughts inevitably turn to another legendary female entertainer, a guttersnipe who also rose, by some reckonings, to become the highest paid female performer in the world. Piaf. Yes, you have it. Pleased with your detective work, you settle back against the vinyl upholstery. In error. You are wrong on three levels. You should have thought more about that endowment.

Hungry fighters are the best fighters. But for every ghetto or Dust Bowl-born champion, how many sank into emaciated oblivion? Hunger is not enough. You need talent. Let us allow that at the outset. But talent is not enough, either. If you are to become a real-life King of the Mountain and worshipped, but also make your name synonymous (for some ill-wishers) with Queen-bitchery and ego-tantrums,

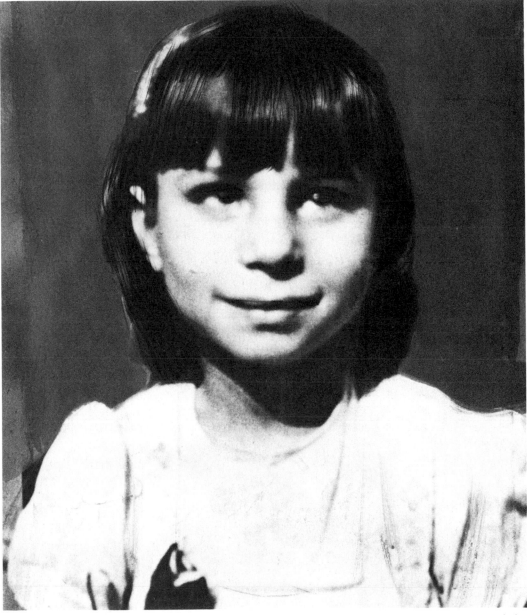

Barbara, still with three 'a's, aged six

then other compulsions must drive your talent remorselessly. In the early Forties, Flatbush Avenue ran through an area that was not New World Hispanic but predominantly Old World European. Overwhelmingly Jewish. In taking an apartment on Pulaski Street for himself, his wife Diane and their first-born Sheldon, Emmanuel Streisand was aligning himself with the comfortably off, indeed the rising middle-class. With a Ph.D. in Education from Columbia, his star was rising and he was winning golden opinions for his English and Psychology

15

classes. The birth of a second child, a daughter, was a joyously attained milestone on a broad sunlit avenue stretching toward a fulfilled and prosperous old age. But the scenario went awry. Fifteen months later Emmanuel Streisand was dead. With an appalling lack of warning, brain haemorrhage struck from those clear blue skies to make the daughter – as the world knows, she had been named Barbara Joan – fatherless.

Therein surely lies a deeper clue to motivation than locality. For a while, her mother withdrawing from the world into almost catatonic mourning, Barbara Joan was to experience a poor and deprived childhood. But it remained safely above the stark, starvation realities Piaf endured. Literally born on a sidewalk, Piaf by the age of six was singing on that same sidewalk not for a supper but for a crust. It is easier to grow up as a tiger from the gutter than, however indifferent, from a parlour. In a famous throwaway that offers an authentic-sounding voice behind the calculated alliteration, Barbra Streisand dismissed her teenage Brooklyn as made up of 'baseball, boredom and bad breath'. Boredom in its deadly, enervating way, is a killer of young talent and its aspirations. Barbara Joan's did not die young. They did not die even though, on graduating from PS 89 to Erasmus Hall, she became just one unit in the student body of the world's biggest high school.

With the incisive intelligence she inherited from her father, Barbra Streisand nailed Erasmus Hall as an institution dedicated to teaching its young ladies to marry dentists that they might bear them three sons. You can understand what she's saying. But it can hardly be the whole truth. Erasmus Hall allowed Barbra Streisand as a young lady to take giant strides towards the getting of wisdom. She was a loner from the outset. Her studies provided an area she could control. It was an area blessedly free from the spiteful, confusing cross-current of other people. She was very much the intellectual father's daughter. She emerged from the school with a straight A, 93 per cent average and the first of the not inconsiderable number of awards she has since won, a medal for Spanish.

Her father's daughter. Straight As. Barbara, it is scarcely a secret, dropped one, became Barbra. If Emmanuel Streisand had lived it's doubtful if his daughter would have dropped that letter. But then she might never have been the Streisand the world knows. Imagine, as she must have done, Emmanuel Streisand alive, with the intellectual's contempt for the spurious, the Sammy Glick side of the trade. How would the scenario have read then?

Wrapped round with love and reassurance, a strong father's presence in a prosperous household, Barbara with the 'a' would have been nearly as outstanding a student. She would have mastered an instrument – the cello perhaps. She would have gone to college, widening her interests into . . . you name it. On campus she would have fallen in love. Perhaps a little pregnant (we are hypothesising a conforming life), she would have married a boy named, like her brother, Sheldon. Or Barry. He would be studying to be a dentist. Later, living in Nassau County, Long Island (site of junior partnership), she would look after their three sons and still find time to play in the local orchestra. A touch bored no doubt, as the Seventies closed, she would be increasingly into Women's Lib, high on Baryshnikov, low on Reagan, and the most strident voice at dinner parties in favour of everything in the Jane Fonda catalogue. Eventually, in her fortieth year or thereabouts, she would insist on going back to college in pursuit of higher knowledge which she felt somehow she'd missed . . . Only, her father died. In the crude colours of pop psychology, Barbra without an 'a' can be painted as an over-compensator.

There are, arguably, many such in show business. Gwen Verdon, for example, made a mockery of polio with a technical precision only a handful of dancers could begin to lay claim to. Another dancer (originally) determinedly proved to the world as well as herself, Shirley MacLaine, that her ear infection had not unbalanced her cornucopia of talent. Another star, Billie Cassin, confounded a country doctor's prediction by overcoming a severed tendon to grow up as a third dancing daughter and, under her final choice of name, Joan Crawford, achieved a towering reputation and an Academy Award. And here we come nearer the Flatbush home. Joan Crawford was one of the stars whose image Barbara Joan carried home from the darkness of the neighbourhood Loew's; whose very gestures and lines she would copy, work her own variations on, hour upon private hour before the family bathroom mirror.

Like David Niven, whose autobiography records the fact, Barbra has no conscious memory of her father. But subconsciously the beloved Emmanuel Streisand, Ph.D., *her* father, would be there on the rostrum, setting standards. If the degree of perfectionism she now strives for seems impossibly severe – pathological to some – don't overlook the legacy from the late dedicated Mr Streisand. His shining image, perfect in death, defined his terms and standards in absentia.

And then, from seven on, his daughter was caught up not only with equalling an ideal, but more prosaically, 'showing' him.

In 1949 Diane Streisand married again. The step-father to step-daughter relationship didn't take. Her mother's new name was Mrs Louis Kind. Only, for Barbra, he wasn't. To this day she tends to dismiss the (in fact) realtor as 'some kind of second-hand car salesman'. Maybe she compared the idealised portrait she carried in her head, to the new head of the family. On those uncompromising terms, the unfortunate Mr Kind never had a prayer. No fault of his. Hard at the best of times, to use a showbiz analogy, to follow a great act. To follow in the hallowed footsteps of an idol constructed out of a daughter's dreams, was too much to expect of Louis Kind or any other mortal. By osmosis, or design, Barbra Streisand had to be a winner. Losing sucks. Elliott Gould married her knowing this. Eventually he retired hurt, offering rueful good wishes to his successors. Significantly her lovers, lieutenants and celebrated escorts in the Pierre Trudeau mould, have all been winners. Though Ryan O'Neal, to date, has won no Oscars, it has not been refuted that briefly, as her lover, he well earned his spurs. Jon Peters, the street-smart, archetypal Streisand 'man' has lasted the course as her lover and protector, precisely because he wins all his fights, some by knockouts, others well within the distance. And as the girl from Pulaski Street lands Robert Redford as her co-star, Trudeau as her date, Golda Meir as her friend, and Queen Elizabeth II as her royal handshake, allow her a muffled sob in the night . . . *'Look, poppa, we've come some ways from Flatbush Avenue.'*

When shooting ended on *On a Clear Day You Can See Forever*, the director, Vincent Minnelli, presented Barbra Streisand with a painting of Sarah Bernhardt. With it was a note expressing his clear belief that she, Barbra Streisand, was the

Erasmus High

only actress who could ever play that role in a film. Minnelli could not know that Barbra Streisand had long shared the notion. It germinated in the New York Public Library where the then sixteen-year-old Barbara Joan sat, solitary, absorbed, reading the nineteenth-century dramas which Duse and Bernhardt had brought to life. In one respect Streisand as Bernhardt is not so fanciful. Old photographs reveal a not inconsiderable likeness between Barbara Joan and Sarah-Henriette-Rosine. Certainly she looked more like the Frenchwoman than did Glenda Jackson whose portrayal of Bernhardt could not survive a vapid screenplay and mechanical direction. It would not have happened to Streisand. France would have fallen before she allowed such mediocrity to slide out of the studios under her name.

Which brings us to another handicap area abundantly compensated for, triumphantly turned to advantage – Barbara Joan Streisand's looks. The snide references to ant-eaters and Durante – we all have a share in the guilt – died no natural death. They were killed off by Streisand's living proof that beauty has damn all to do with the plastic symmetry of assembly-line idols. In the days when Barbara Joan was growing into two simultaneous awarenesses (that in this life people were often judged by their looks; and that she had drawn an 'ugly duckling' outfit in the handout) the image men yearned for in their dreams owed plenty to the World War II pin-up, Betty Grable. Virginia Mayo, the young Janet Leigh – they were on the screen largely by virtue of their 'girl from *Esquire*' looks. More subtle talents – Lana Turner, Rita Hayworth, say – still launched their performances from a basis of a traditional, Max Factor-advertisement conception of the beautiful. Flatbush Avenue might have said of Barbara Joan, 'a young Ingrid Bergman she is not.'

Time and again the embryonic superstar brought home images from the movies and tried them on for size. That sharp intelligence must have told her they didn't fit. Whatever essential flash of characterisation she could duplicate through make-up or mugging – now Mildred Pierce, now Scarlett O'Hara's younger sister, now Stella Dallas – Flatbush was right. The sense of the gulf between wishful thinking and reality must have been corrosive. There must have been many despairing moments when she might have taken a pick-handle to the bathroom mirror. Or maybe not. Streisand has bypassed superlatives by being Streisand. Even in those days, for all her impressionist period, she was true to herself. She has never subscribed to the 'if you can't lick 'em, join 'em' school. There is the recipe for true mediocrity. Despite her having long since clocked the shrivelling fact that she was someone her classmates preferred not to be seen with over-much, a blazing integrity inside Barbara Joan steered her clear of Erasmus Hall's sub-industry for 'homely' students – the routine nose-bobs by which Sadies or Rebeccas were transformed into Cindys or Candys.

Eventually, famously, she was to turn necessity to advantage. To triumph. Gutting thrift shops, out-topping her last outlandish make-up, she parlayed her (then) offbeat looks into a 'look-at-me' death or glory press-ganging of the attention. You could hate. You could adore. You couldn't ignore. In the unlaced, post-hippy, post-punk scene of today, the stylish tatterdemalion tactic seems commonplace. Not then. Barbra Streisand was not quite the first (she admits to admiring and imitating a kooky pioneer spirit at Erasmus) but it was she who made it incandescent. She threw the fashion book away a further distance than most. Look at the Beach Boys as they first appeared. Look at them now. If Bette Midler, New York Jewish and all, pushes her considerable fleshly and intelligent talent to the degree of fame Barbra Streisand has achieved, it will be due in some part at least, to the second lady having cracked a mould.

Barbra Streisand can appear beautiful by acting beautiful. She becomes beautiful by projecting the Streisand charisma. The ugly duckling has not needed to change into a swan. What has a swan ever done anyway, except die in the last act? Without the aid of a surgeon's hammer or plastic-remoulds, Streisand has succeeded on her own merits, attesting to 'the profile, and nothing but the profile, so help me!'

Even film-makers at the sharp end of Streisand's obsessive perfectionism concede, as we will see, that she *achieves* a kind of beauty that is unique on the screen. As Rex Reed was to say after *Funny Girl*, 'It took the combined efforts of God knows how many people to do it but I'll be damned if they haven't made her beautiful. In the most remarkable screen debut I will probably ever see in my lifetime, the toadstool from Erasmus High School has been turned into a truffle!' Producer Howard Koch says, 'She has the ability to walk into a place and make it light up.' Sydney Pollack, that most articulate of talents, who endured bizarre studio pressures and other nightmares directing *The Way We Were* says, 'Streisand is great and looks great. She's not like anybody else and nobody else is like her. She is absolutely unique. That's a blessing, and a curse for her.'

Part of that curse is living with the newspaper headlines and the almost daily gossip in the 'trades'. Thus Hollywood at least, manages the adroit art of dissecting a body that's still alive. With a gnawing lack of originality it presumed love affairs where there were none, missed out on such intimate liaisons as really existed. Certainly Omar Sharif and Ryan O'Neal figure prominently in the anthology.

Pierre Trudeau, the distinguished statesman who squired her on to the front pages of the world, might have wryly considered Barbra to be a more penetratingly observant soul-mate than the beautiful, pop-oriented will-o'-the-wisp he married. Headlines, yes, but all grist to the mill. To the boys back on Flatbush Avenue who were reluctant to take this long-nosed Cinderella to the Ball, Ms Streisand could legitimately chortle, 'Up yours!' And maybe did. Love scenes, bed scenes with the WASP fantasy lover of millions of women, Robert Redford. Ditto with one of the most sexily adroit actors in the cinema, George Segal.

'Tell me something,' queried the one aged Streisand-era momma we unearthed in Flatbush, 'is it true she's paid *$4 million* to make a movie?' 'True', we said. 'Good luck on her!' she replied. 'Nobody buys what they can't sell.' But nobody directly concerned with the 'property' would claim that the selling was easy. The squally stories of the so-called 'Streisand ego' and rank-pulling began with *Funny Girl*, blew hard on *Hello Dolly*, reached gale force on *A Star Is Born*. It is likely that the sour, critical responses to *A Star Is Born*, sub-consciously at least, must have been fuelled by the media's general hostility to Streisand and her who-does-he-think-he-is producer-lover Jon Peters. In essence, the indictment against Barbra Streisand resolves into the collective charge that her ego is so huge, she wants to do it all, control it all, decide it all, assuming responsibilities way beyond those accorded to a star no matter how talented, or powerful. Further, that hardly before the ink is dry on the contract she is an infuriating *kibbitzer*, 'leaning on' writers, composers, the producer and director, when not tangling with the hairdresser and the make-up person. Item: is it true William Wyler, the veteran director of the film *Funny Girl* walked off the set after a short demonstration of the Streisand School of Directing? Was she – as writer-director Frank Pierson asserted in an extraordinary piece about the making of *A Star Is Born* – as ferocious and insufferable an ego as he makes her out to be? If we accept his version of that ill-fated affair – the rows, the screams, the in-fighting and the four-lettered soundtrack – then the St Valentine's Day Massacre may have been sorely misunderstood. It should be noted that Streisand's spirited counter-argument is no less persuasive than the accusations. Likewise the *Hello Dolly* affair and that short, exquisitely venomous confrontation between Streisand and Walter Matthau. His censure of the actress ('a pip-squeak who didn't have the talent of a butterfly's fart,' etc.) has mellowed considerably over the years. Matthau, a kindly genius, revisits the scene of the 'crime' and chivalrously accepts much of the blame. Streisand's frequently expressed admission, 'Okay, so I'm a perfectionist,' is said with a weary resignation knowing that some read that perfectionism as a neurosis bordering on paranoia. If so, it started early.

In August 1963, already caught in the slip-stream of success, she made this pained observation to a writer friend: 'It's so scary the way they're all knocking me. People who don't have success, hate success.' Perception, or paranoia? Today, a thousand light years and a zillion dollars on, she could write the script on success, Hollywood-style. But the fear remains. Physical as well as psychological. A fortress home shielded by electric barriers, Dobermans and Jon Peters, with the lover the most formidable of the three. Then there is the fear of a huge talent hugely uncertain of itself. Sydney Pollack, better than most at understanding the torment, tells of the ceaseless night phone calls from Streisand during the filming of *The Way*

We Were. Eleven p.m. every night, asking, suggesting, worrying. The fear inside Barbra Streisand is significantly underscored in the informed assessments of many of her friends and associates we talked to.

We know from her own frank admission that before a live performance she is consumed by adrenalin-saturated terror; that in the midst of a major movie production she is a prey to doubts and fears which are way beyond the familiar first-night agonies. She is able to hide it, of course, the way all good troupers do. Olivier for example has managed a prodigious output of film after film despite the pain of a serious illness. Streisand's pain goes deeper. Her success at overcoming it at crucial moments was not achieved without extraordinary tenacity – and a kind of native *chutzpah*. Was it *chutzpah*, or a determination not to fall into the customary inanities that led her, on being presented to the Queen of England at a premiere, to ask Her Majesty why women have to wear white gloves on these occasions, but not men? A slightly embarrassed Queen Elizabeth fell back on a pleasantly vague reply citing tradition, custom. But the exchange registered. Pushing 'convention' towards its limit, the girl from Flatbush was claiming the right not to have her own identity swamped by protocol any more than by Pulaski Street. Perhaps too, she was intent on discovering for herself just what that identity was.

It happened once that the film director Otto Preminger paid a visit to a Brooklyn high school for the purpose of casting juveniles. During his interviewing he was told there was a woman on the premises who insisted on seeing him. His business done, Preminger was taken to the office of the school secretary, a plump lady of middle years who immediately proceeded to berate him. It seem he had had the gall to reject her daughter whom she had brought along when Preminger was searching for an unknown to play, yes, St Joan. The gall and the bad judgement. The plump lady was a Mrs Diane Kind, *née* Rosen. In between times, of course, she had been Mrs Diane Streisand.

Preminger listened with contained politeness. He sighed, shrugged. 'It seems,' he said, 'that in turning your daughter down I did her one big favour.' What *chutzpah* there. The mother who had once vehemently protested against her entering show business, now proffering her daughter, the nasal quintessence of Flatbush Paddy Chayevsky maidenhood, for the role of a French Catholic saint. As fanciful a notion as, say, casting an internationally known Arab screen actor as a New York Jewish gambler.

But Preminger boxed his draw only by anticipating events. A decade or so later, at the staggeringly unprecedented age of twenty-seven, Barbra Streisand had accomplished an unheard of, indeed, undreamt of feat. She was the only person, male or female, to have won every major entertainment award: the Tony for the theatre, the Grammy for recording, the Emmy for television and the Oscar for film.

The amiable Mrs Kind, formerly Streisand, now living in condominiumed security just outside Beverly Hills, could today inform Otto Preminger that her daughter asks, and receives, $4 million for a picture. The same as Robert Redford. Particularly Robert Redford. Dollar-for-dollar with the most powerful box office draw of the decade. There, at the top. Perhaps 'The Greatest Star' – as she herself has sung. The road from Flatbush Avenue to becoming 'the complete reason for going to a movie' was cut through lush, dangerous, sometimes hostile territory.

It is that territory we now explore.

TWO

On Friday, 9 May 1980, the *New York Post* ran the following item on an inside page:

> **Devout Barbra is answer to Jewish school's prayers**
> Barbra Streisand, who has shown a new interest in her religious heritage since becoming involved in the Jewish film *Yentl*, has just forked over a small fortune to keep a seaside synagogue school afloat on the West Coast.
>
> She donated the undisclosed (but reportedly *very* substantial) sum to an orthodox synagogue in Venice, Cal. The cash will supply 20 percent of the congregation's budget for its 44-student day school center for the next five years. In return for the gift the school will be renamed for the star's late father, Emmanuel Streisand . . .

Not exactly a riveting item. But the essence of it reveals vital clues to what, as the Streisand saga swirls into the 1980s, drives her, makes her run. Bequests by the famous, notably in Hollywood, occasionally have an earsplitting stealth to them, anonymity in that village hardly being the name of the game. But this endowment by Barbra Streisand was way above that class of highly audible generosity. It was not only public witness to the fiercely affectionate picture she constructed in her mind of the father she was too young to know. She had also come full circle to a tradition which she had conformed to, kicked out against, but had never ignored.

Barbra Streisand was born on 24 April 1942, in a five-storey brownstone apartment house in the prosaic Williamsburg section of Brooklyn. As she is fond of wryly pointing out, the difference between Williamsburg, Virginia and *her* Williamsburg was huge enough for a belly laugh. Pulaski Street, with its immigrant burlesque – Irish cops, Sicilian enclaves, hot bagel stands and shared poverty – was a long way from the Colonial-type gentry of Virginia whose replica homes and streets still delude the innocent tourists. Flatbush Avenue which intersects with Pulaski Street, began, architecturally, to die from birth. A World War or so earlier, P. G. Wodehouse had been able to pen the praises of the area with lovey-dovey, young-married simple-mindedness:

> *When it's nesting time in Flatbush*
> *We will have a little flat*
> *With a welcome on the mat*
> *Where there's room to swing a cat . . .*

But by the war of '41, love's young dream had been supplanted by the seething harmonies and discords of the tenement symphony. Williamsburg in Emmanuel Streisand's day, conformed with the classic immigrant syndrome, a landfall in the

New World where Jews, Italians, Irish fervently swore allegiance to the United States while clinging tenaciously to their own identity and richly human traditions. No people nurtured those traditions more fiercely than the Jews. The scene could just as readily interchange with London's East End of the period, or the Cheadle district of Manchester. In the winter cold and darkness Williamsburg saw its pallid kin-folk leaving for the garment districts of New York or the tenement workshops where cabinet-makers worked sweat-shop hours for starvation wages. And God walked hand-in-hand with privation. On Flatbush Avenue, Pulaski, Nostrand and the other feverish arteries leading to the heart of Brooklyn, the Talmudic scholars in dark kaftans, round black velour hats framing ashen faces, proclaimed their rigid orthodoxy, sustained by the handouts from many who could ill-afford to support them. But somehow they found the cash to send their children to religious schools where as, Chaim Potok and Isaac Bashevis Singer have depicted, history went back 5000 years, and lives interlocked visibly and audibly with each other. No coincidence, surely, that it is Singer's *Yentl* which Barbra Streisand chose as her first personal statement in movies. If *A Star Is Born* came uncomfortably close to her professional life, then *Yentl*, peripherally at least, projected her back to the deeply-affecting rituals of her earliest years.

The Streisands, Emmanuel and Diane, ran an orthodox home. On Friday evenings, the approaching Sabbath, those treasured heirlooms of Jewish orthodoxy, the silver candlesticks, stood on starched white tablecloths ready for lighting and Emmanuel's blessing of the Sabbath. With his Ph.D. in Education from Columbia, teaching Psychology and English in high school, perhaps a glittering career ahead of him, he still clung to the tradition and identity which has so enriched the mainstream of American culture. His wife had been born Diane Rosen, the daughter of a garment cutter who was also a cantor in the synagogue. Her intelligence was not unworthy of Emmanuel's. She had graduated with straight As. But not, her bad luck, in an era of equal sexual opportunity. The function in life of a 'nice Jewish girl' was to get married, be a good wife and have babies. Diane Rosen took a secretarial job in Manhattan. But for a while – and this was to prove crucial in her attitude to her daughter – she nurtured dreams of performing on a stage, not styled as 'showbiz' in those prim years on Pulaski Street. She had a lovely singing voice. People admired it; they encouraged her to 'do something with it'. She dreamed her dreams of operetta and musicals and went so far as to record a test show-piece record of Romberg's 'One Kiss' – the choice telling us everything about the voice. But no Broadway or even Pawnee, Oklahoma career ensued. Instead, she married Emmanuel Streisand. The event may well have come as a relief. American entertainment had waved goodbye to Sigmund Romberg. Diane Streisand was cast in a more compelling role maintaining the strict home for the husband she adored and revered and, from 1935, for their first-born, Sheldon. Now all that was needed to round out the happy family was a daughter.

But seven years of exemplary orthodox existence was to pass before the professor and the doting Diane were to realise that dream. When the daughter was at last born, both parents for all their joy, must have had their private misgivings. The child, Barbara Joan, might have been described (not in the Streisands' hearing) as 'unusual going on freakish'. Sleeping little, crying even less, she stared silently out at the world with wide-open eyes. Her head, even for a baby, was clearly far too disproportionately big for her tiny, even puny, body. She was born hairless, and remained so for the first two years of her life. When her mother told her about it in later years, Barbara Joan, with typical Brooklyn humour, figured that maybe the Martians had done a piece of smart cradle-swopping. By the time her hair started to grow only her mother was around to rejoice at the fact.

Without warning, like a twig being snapped, Emmanuel Streisand, at the age of thirty-four, was dead of a cerebral haemorrhage. The family's happiness, security, had been shattered like a mirror. Pulaski Street, the Jews, the Irish, the Italians as always closing ranks in tragedy, rallied round Diane Streisand. In the seven days of ritual mourning she sat on a low stool, crushed by grief. Each person's death diminished all on Pulaski Street. Everybody had admired and respected Emmanuel Streisand. But no one, nothing could console his prostrate widow. From her favourite perch on the living-room sofa, the baby Barbara Joan stared solemnly, uncomprehendingly at all the comings and goings. All these milling shapes, strange noises, her mother just sitting there swaying from side to side. And yet one shape, one solid form against the light, seemed not to be there any more.

The Depression was over. World War II altered little in the life of Brooklyn, except that garment makers were switched from pin-stripes to khaki. Barbara Joan had an uncle overseas, human enough to have his Army paychecks diverted to the Pulaski Street apartment. The family could eat. Just. Later Barbara would not quite quip with Groucho Marx, 'I've worked myself up from nothing to a state of extreme poverty.' As she remembers it, 'We weren't *poor* poor, we just didn't have things.' She was not to have 'things' for some years. The war ended. The uncle came marching home with all the rest of the boys and the paychecks dried up.

Diane Streisand, with two younger children to feed and rent to pay, secured a job as a bookkeeper. Barbara Joan became a classic infant type, farmed out with grandparents, relatives, neighbours for the endless hours until, overtime finally completed, her mother returned exhausted, to claim her. Observing other children with their fathers brought home to Barbara what she had lost. But tenement life contains its own powerful antidote to grief. As she played on the sidewalk outside her grandfather's tailor shop she became aware of the bonding element which heals all pain, adds a special lustre to simple joy. The births, deaths and marriages of Brooklyn, of Williamsburg at least, were everybody's affairs. People who need people . . . Barbara Joan's concept of the good life, according to the gospel of Emmanuel, was beginning to form. Articulate now, with the keen intelligence she inherited, she could sense the exciting undercurrents which, as she would soon learn, take Brooklyn talent surging on to Broadway. Out of such boisterous, urban ferment has come not only Groucho Marx and his brothers but the likes of Moss Hart, Milton Berle, Jack Benny, Danny Kaye, Lorenz Hart, George Burns and, a generation off, Stephen Sondheim. And Fanny Brice, a Streisand heroine of some significance.

Who knows what tricks of phrasing, gestures, and *shtick* the future star absorbed sitting on a tenement step, as with big grave eyes she watched Pulaski Street laughing, crying, arguing, fighting, clowning, throwing confetti or walking behind its dead? Her mother at work all day, sometimes late in the evening, she had a sense of being deserted by both parents. She was rapidly learning that to be a survivor you needed plenty of 'street savvy'. It came easy. And stayed with her, according to movie moguls at the sharp end of her demands today.

When hungry she patrolled the corridors of the apartment house on the doleful-eyed lookout for a snack from some kind-hearted neighbour. Snacks seldom came kosher. But sweet or savoury, hot or cold, Italian or Irish, Barbara Joan was not one to quibble, even if years later as a pretend 'Second-Hand Rose' she might voice a muted *kvetch*. 'I'm not hungry, Momma' was as near as she could get to telling her fretting mother that she'd had a quick, furtive nosh at, say, Mrs O'Shaughnessy's un-kosher cookies. Later, she was to be more positively 'sinful'. Like all of the deprived children about her, she became a dab hand at swiping candy, fruit and, before long, school supplies. Precociously self-reliant (she was once told she was 'born forty') she became a survivor at the earliest of ages. And 'lost her innocence' just as early. She learned, and later declared it, that nothing got what you wanted as much as going straight out and getting it for yourself. She acquired the live-off-your-wits nerve, the survivor's *chutzpah* and self-reliance that may well be the basic raw material, plus talent, of a superstar.

Little seemed to faze the child, Barbara Joan. At four and a half she was walking to, returning from PS 224 by herself – several months up on the little girl whose maturity ('I'm five!') she would characterise in her *My Name Is Barbra* TV special. And she loved school. It was *directed* time away from the dreary apartment with its few home-made improvised toys. It was a place where her bright wits began to show her how they could compensate for not having 'things'. This was stuff she could do!

And in the afternoons she had discovered something else. Living in the same apartment block was her friend Irving. His parents owned a mid-Forties miracle – a seven-inch television set. It was an early window on to the beaming anarchy, graceful ineptitude, the expertly deployed slapstick of Laurel and Hardy. Howling with laughter Barbara and Irving imitated the peerless pair, switching roles. Streisand's gifts as a comedienne go back to those afternoons before the seven-inch screen, miming Ollie's balletic 'business' with an imaginary tie; and also the strident, 'Funny Girl' humour of Fanny Brice. (Pauline Kael, that most perceptive of critics, was to recognise Streisand's gifts as a comedienne faster than most. She wrote, after seeing *The Owl and the Pussycat*, '. . . She can ring more changes on a line than anybody since W. C. Fields . . .')

If television gave Barbra Streisand an insight into the art of performing, grabbing an audience, school was to add other elements to the source material. In that very good and driving LP of some twenty-five years later, *Stoney End*, Barbra sings:

I was raised on the book of Jesus.

And as she sang it, the joke would not be lost on the girl who once attended the Brooklyn Yeshiva where the 'book of Jesus' was hardly required reading. But the later Streisand could sing the line as blithely as she rejected the whole reach-me-down tradition of the stern, unquestioned rituals of the classroom.

She did not yet have the nerve to do it to his face but, after the rabbi had left, she would yell the one word summarising her protest at force-fed religious instruction. 'Christmas!' she hissed. Her classmates recoiled, expecting if not the wrath of Jehovah, then bad 'vibes' from Above. And when the heavens did not open up, or thunderbolts fall, the girl who shouted 'Christmas', followed it with a defiant, 'and a Happy New Year.' Probably through this childish yet liberating non-conformism Barbara Joan was learning something about herself. She would learn that no matter how prodigious her leap to the stars she would never entirely escape the gravitational pull of her heritage. She would live Croesus-rich behind electronic gates, with notices reading: 'Beware! Guard Dogs Trained To Attack.' She would share bed, board and business with a half-Cherokee ex-reform school character named Jon Peters; but she put her soul as well as her money into Bashevis Singer's *Yentl* and her father's name to a nearby school.

So, Christmas or not, Barbara Joan spent long periods of her young life being a credit to the rabbi.

'I remember,' she has said, 'a whole life when I was five and six in Williamsburg. My friend Rosalyn Arenstein was an atheist – I was always trying to convince her there was a God – and my other friend, Joanne Micelli, was an Italian. Joanne went to St Joseph's and I went to the Yeshiva of Brooklyn. Joanne used to say, "The Jews killed Christ." And I'd say, "No they didn't." Meanwhile, I had this fascination about wanting to be Catholic – the nuns, the fathers, the costumes, the whole thing. I'd always go "Hello, Father" and curtsy. I thought it was great. Also, to have a father, that there was a guy named Father who sort of loved his people.'

The aching awareness of loss implicit here, the longing for a substitute father, is obvious. For all her rebellious flashes, Barbara Joan, knowing now she had once been an alien, a Martian, felt herself more rejected than rejecting.

Her thoughts, as she has frequently expressed them, ran this way: 'I felt like a victim asking myself, why did it happen to me? I wanted to be like all the other kids whose fathers came home every day. Mine never did.'

Perhaps the most poignant expression of this sense of loss, however, is to be found not in direct statement but obliquely in Barbra Streisand's work. If 'obliquely' is the word. The 1965 album, *My Name Is Barbra* is a prime example of her life and art inter-penetrating openly. A portion of the material is indifferent. 'A Kid Again' and 'Where Is the Wonder' are very much poor man's versions respectively of 'Penny Candy' – from the 1952 *New Faces* – and 'When the World Was Young'. But when, between these, Barbra turns to a song from an all-but-forgotten musical *The Yearling*, 'My Pa', the feeling of sorrow, of regret for what has never been, is utterly moving. Barbra Streisand, the twenty-three-year-old singer, momentarily assumes the role of any child who securely knows they have the greatest father in the world.

> *My Pa can light my room at night*
> *With just his being near:*
> *And make a fearful dream all right*
> *By grinning ear to ear.*

the song begins. And it ends:

> *My Pa's the finest friend I ever knew:*
> *I only wish that you could know him too.*

As the song dies away one is left with the awareness that for Barbra Streisand the central pronoun of the last line is incorrect. Or as she herself has expressed it in an interview with *Playboy* magazine: 'When a kid grows up missing one parent, there's a big gap that has to be filled. It's like someone being blind, they hear better. With me, I felt more, I sensed more, I wanted more . . .'

And 'wanting more' and wanting it badly enough, she got it. The question her achievement poses today is: would she now settle for knowledge that having no father had its enormous plus in her ferocity to compensate? A fair question if being fatherless was the only way the growing child felt inferior and deprived. She soon knew otherwise when the kids at school started taunting her with 'big beak' and 'crazy Barbara'. She was bright enough to recognize that with her large nose, skinny frame, and a hint of a squint, she was fair game for this familiar brand of juvenile blood sport. She was different, *visibly* different. And, by classroom rules, 'different' is bad. When some of the girls in the neighbourhood started ganging up on her, making a circle round her, poking fun, she cried and the fun over, they ran away. She wondered then what made them do it. And still does. The difference now is that people have got something to hate, if we accept her conviction that those who don't have success hate success. It was less easy for a nine-year-old, albeit a physically gauche one, to accept that Nature having slipped a little in designing her, gave a special dispensation to make her suffer for it. If she had been as healthy as the average Brooklyn tearaway with a father as an antidote to 'Jewish Mother' overprotection, she might have come through to her teens unscathed. But she was anaemic, prone later to asthma attacks. She remembers being sent, at the age of five, to a health camp. Scrubbed, washed, her hair disinfected against lice, Barbara Joan was finally put into the camp uniform. That kind of antiseptic conformity was as soul-crushing as Siberian exile is to a Soviet dissident. She was homesick. She cried. And when the other inmates mocked her for weeping, she claimed she wasn't, pleading a 'loose tear duct'. Her possession, her identity, her sense of self, resided totally, she recalls, in a maroon sweater with wooden buttons which had been knitted for her by the lady who took care of her while her mother went to work.

Still concerned about her daughter's health, her mother sent her to a Hebrew summer camp, hedging her bets on both healthfulness and Godliness. She didn't stay the course. The camp cooks attempted Jewish home cooking in bulk – and failed. Barbara Joan, a superstar in the making, showed her distaste by tossing her portion down to the other end of the table. On visiting day when her mother arrived with Barbara's future stepfather, Louis Kind, she told them, with stubbornness more finely honed today, that they'd better pack her bags because she had no intention of staying a day longer. They gave her no argument. In the car going back to New York, Louis Kind was silent. If, as his step-daughter claims, he was 'allergic to kids' then her own allergy to the man who dared to take her father's place must have been ill-concealed. Cue then to the little girl with the psychic hole in the heart as expressed by Louis Kind, the 'wicked step-father'. Of course, the 'used car salesman or something' as Barbra referred to him later on (in reality a real estate dealer) was demonstrably not wicked. Understandably Diana Streisand, *née* Rosen, had a need to start a new life with another man. But walking in on a loaded situation, the middle-aged beau never had a chance with the daughter of Emma-

The corner of Newkirk Avenue and Nostrand Avenue, where the Streisand family moved after the death of Emmanuel Streisand.

nuel Streisand. It was an affront, perhaps, to Barbara Joan. It was also cruel to be Kind.

The resentment did not flare into open hostility even when, in the autumn of 1949 the widow Mrs Diane Streisand became Mrs Diane Streisand-Kind. Pulaski Street accepted the merger with characteristic sympathy. The daughter did not. Her rejection of him was not entirely out of loyalty to Emmanuel Streisand. Her mother began having her own misgivings fairly early on in the marriage. Although never divorced, the Kinds separated in 1954. But what he did do for his step-daughter was to take them all to a new apartment, a shade better than the one in which she had been born. It was on the corner of Nostrand and Newkirk Avenues. Not exactly going from the Bronx to the Barbizon Plaza. But new paint, new furniture, even in this box of an apartment, was exciting to her. The urban environment hadn't changed, of course. It was as nondescript as ever, the family environment even worse. On the night they moved in Barbara slept with her mother. She awoke to find she had developed clicks in her ears. Two years later the soundtrack had changed to a high-pitched ringing. It has stayed with her all her life. To the average child this complaint (*tinnitus* is its medical name) was no major hardship. Who complained of a ringing in the ears against kids' screams and the raucous noises of the streets of Brooklyn? But imagine that insistent, high-pitched interference to a music talent as subtle and fine-tuned as Barbra Streisand's. She has become accustomed to it and never speaks of it. But as a child she remembers it vividly, remembers never hearing 'silence'. And wearing head scarves, which her well-intentioned mother believed would effectively 'shut out' the noises. This wrapping of a scarf around her head had to be endured in New York's sweltering humidity. The total visual effect, the unsymmetrical nose, the dominant centre-piece in the oval frame of the scarf, did not, in fairness, stop the traffic. But people looked. They passed remarks. She ignored them. Okay, so she was different. She had this face, and this ringing in the ears. Already a loner, the scarf proclaimed the fact. An 'ugly duckling' with a ringing in the ears – who needs it? Sammy Davis, Jr's historic response to a golfer, 'My handicap? I'm a one-eyed Jewish nigger!' encapsulates Streisand's own wry, tough acceptance of the bad cards she'd been dealt.

Some girls in a similar situation might have been too dumb to notice, to think, to care, or developed complexes which, years later, might have required full-time sessions with a shrink. Emmanuel Streisand's daughter, out of tune with her home life, out of step with her classmates, had one great plus – brains. Between classes at Erasmus Hall High School, she took herself off to the library. It gave her privacy as well as vastly widening her knowledge. At nights, in her cramped corner of the living-room, she burned the hours out in frenzied study. It brought speedy dividends. Her average shot up into the 90s. She had proof now that, when she set her mind to something, she could win it. This kind of competition she had time for. Competing socially and sexually was 'for the birds'. So at any rate reasoned this 'ugly duckling' who was revealing no outward indications of becoming a young swan. Instead, the bones stuck out like coat-hangers from the feminine and frilly operetta-chorus dresses that her mother – and Sigmund Romberg – considered the acme of teenage fashion. To clinch the point she would often put a 'little shepherdess' ribbon in her daughter's datedly styled hair. And just as often Barbara Joan would turn the corner and remove it. This was a post-Dick Haymes, Sinatra bobby-soxer age. A hair ribbon had to be the stuff of ridicule at Erasmus Hall where the atmosphere of fraternities, sororities and fourteen-year-old dating was giving her rejection problems. She was one of nature's wallflowers. She worried herself physically sick to avoid the formal sexual context of a junior prom.

And yet, in her other classic flight into herself, the ugly duckling was beautiful. The seven-inch television screen of her babyhood had expanded into a new visual ecstasy – the huge screen of Loew's Kings Theater on Flatbush Avenue. Barbara Joan discovered the magic, realler-than-real fantasy world of the Saturday matinee when she was around eleven years old. Hollywood movies were at their commercial peak. The onslaught from television was still to come, but for the moment the studio system poured out its cornucopia of the excellent and the banal; the pretentious raised to Art; kitsch and Katharine Hepburn. The cigarette smoke swirling in the projector beam, the frayed plush fretting at the back of her knees, Barbara Joan watched with increasing critical discrimination. The intelligent daughter of E. Streisand, Ph.D. could discern junk from quality. Sitting up front was not the best location for maintaining critical judgements. The alternating babel of jeers, cheers, and booing was policed by white-coated basilisk-eyed supervisors

The Loew's Kings Theater on Flatbush Avenue where young Barbara Joan dreamed of being on screen

stabbing the darkness with accusatory torch-beams. 'Hey, which of youse brats is makin' a ruckus – is it you wid der nose?!' Immune to all that, she sat through her favourite programmes twice round. The gestures, bits of business, that Ida Lupino, Anne Sheridan, Crawford and Hepburn were silkily deploying, were not lost on her. Like every impressionable girl-child of her age, she played out her secret dreams of stardom in the privacy of her room. Except she now had glimmerings that this could be real. Her mirror became her coach, her co-star. She gave it Bette Davis's stare, Joan Crawford's pursing of the lips, Vivien Leigh's classily flirtatious smile, Rita Hayworth's mussy-haired sexiness. She went through the catalogue of Loew's Kings, the Hollywood gamut from A to B.

'It was *me* up there,' she told author Rene Jordan. 'Men were pursuing *me!*'

For the moment Barbara Joan was mugging in front of a mirror. But she had a growing conviction of where the future could take her.

Meanwhile it was still today. With only one bathroom in the apartment, Barbara Joan's rituals in front of the mirror created problems. Mrs Streisand-Kind and her husband occasionally had needs more urgent than their daughter's, involved in a scene from, say, Joan Crawford's *This Woman Is Dangerous*. Driven out, she would slink in sulky silence, boredom and resentment up on to the apartment building's roof. There, in that cliché set of smoke-stacks and fanlights, she could revive her dreams, spiting the world, smoking the illicit cigarette of the early teenager. We can imagine Mrs Streisand-Kind enacting the role of a stern Jewish mother in relation to her daughter's dreams of stardom. 'Such ideas she had! All these notions they put into a girl's head. Instead of spending all your time at the movies why don't you . . .' The 'sensible' alternatives suggest themselves. Now thirteen, the young would-be Rita Hayworth began forgoing school lunches, spending the money instead at the cosmetic counter at Woolworths, buying garish lipsticks and a variety of mascaras. This way she could really resemble, well almost, the flame-haired star of *Gilda*. She experimented in endless combinations of conventional and outrageous shades. But how would she look on film? Objective analysis was required. She took herself off to the nearest penny arcade photo booth. Curtained off in front of a different mirror, she applied the paint, the powder, and the eyeshadow with speed, four minutes beng allotted to each customer in the booth. Thus Technicoloured, she then struck up a variety of exotic poses with Hayworth, Crawford, Bette Davis in the top seeds. In between each pose the machine would whirr and click. Finally the images, sticky and with their poor, passport-type contrast and flat lighting, would slide into her hand. Tiny. Paper dreams one-and-a-half-inch square. One ten thousandth the area of the screen at Loew's Kings. Pulaski's early verdict ('a Rita Hayworth she's not') was unlikely to be overthrown by a higher court.

What was missing? Props maybe! Costume! It was now that, tentatively, she began to dabble in a habit that has never left her and which, at a crucial period, contributed to her blast-off discovery. She began roaming neighbourhood thrift shops, squeaking the wire hangers along the rails hunting out thirty-year-old dresses, feather boas and floppy hats. They were 'effect' ensembles; a striking sartorial *mélange* of Mac West and *My Fair Lady*.

Any analyst's textbook on 'A Plain Girl's Behaviourism in Compensatory Activity' might find this early Streisand archetypal material. When you are not beautiful you have to *seem* beautiful. Or, as Rex Reed said, you need to *achieve* it. Some years, and maybe $20 million onwards, a friend of hers, Muriel Harris, tells us about her freakish wardrobes stacked with rail after rail of outlandish, 'Second-Hand Rose' pick-ups. A traipse back through the Twenties to that elaborately fringed and bugle-beaded era. Festooned like that, you stand out from the crowd. On one occasion, her friend recalls, the now-famous Barbra Streisand arrived at her home with one colour nail varnish on her left hand, a totally different colour varnish on her right. (When we saw her in her freaky New York apartment during the triumphant Broadway run of *Funny Girl*, she received callers like an African queen, a jewelled turban over exotically mascara-ed eyes, a flowing ivory caftan and sandals beneath. She looked ravishingly dramatic, needing only an asp clasped to her bosom to complete the effect.) Effective, and different. The teenage Barbara Joan made certain of that from the outset. Despite the gulf which manifestly existed between her looks and the bland, production-line beauty relished at the time, she was more and more convinced she could be, would be, an actress. There had been straws in the wind.

At the age of seven, in 1949, she had made her first public appearance as a performer – singing at a local PTA meeting. Sick all day with a severe cold (in the light of future experience we might wonder if it was psychosomatic) she had argued with her mother and had won. She had gone on. The applause had been more than a short-term cure. It had planted a seed. A seed, incidentally, which might have sprouted into an unexpected species. Shortly after the concert and the move to the Nostrand and Newkirk Avenues apartment, Barbara Joan announced she was going to be a ballerina. It may well have been an anti-Kind, get-me-out-of-the-house diversionary tactic. But initially, it worked. She was enrolled with her mother's consent at Miss Marsh's dance school. The consent was soon qualified, removed. A check-up by the family doctor revealed the skinny-lizzy eight-year-old to be positively anaemic. 'Delicate' would once have been the word. With no foreknowledge of the roller-skating scene in *Funny Girl* to modify her opinion, Mrs Streisand-Kind removed her daughter from the dance school. Barbara Joan protested shrilly at the time. Hindsight has probably convinced her that her talents were more likely to cast her opposite Redford than Baryshnikov. She might also have ended up no ballerina, married to a dentist. In limbo now, no dance school, no first step on the road to becoming Rita Hayworth – an event took place which turned out to be crucial. On a Saturday afternoon in April 1956 she was taken to the Cort Theatre, Broadway, to see a production of *The Diary of Anne Frank*. Broadway! To the girl from Brooklyn this was Loew's Kings writ large in Cinemascope on the scale of the Grand Canyon. And the play . . . the play was like nothing she had seen before. Yet something she knew intuitively.

The girl could have been herself. The intelligent, far-seeing father on the stage was clearly the role her own father, had he lived, had they all lived in Holland, might have assumed. The orthodox background – even the confined and cribbed apartment! She knew these people! And yet, the actors, she decided, most of them anyway, weren't that hot. The bright high-school student in Barbara Joan was well able to discern heart from head. That visit to the Cort Theatre had refuelled her determination to become an actress. She announced it unremittingly virtually every hour on the hour. Her resolve had acquired a cutting edge which scythed through her mother's now half-hearted objections. At this stage she acquired a useful ally, a kind of surrogate parent in the unlikely form of Muriel Choy, who with her husband ran Choy's Orient, a chop-suey establishment close to the Streisand-Kind apartment. 'A Chinese lady yet!' Barbara's real mother might have exclaimed, as her daughter moved more and more into the Oriental couple's orbit. No doubt that Barbara Joan found Muriel Choy's background and values a stimulating corrective to those she battled against at home. The relationship began with Barbara baby-sitting for the Choys' children. Mrs Choy remembers the period with affection. 'She began at the age of twelve and quit when she was sixteen. In between baby-sitting she'd act as cashier on Sundays. I thought she was a nice kid, otherwise I wouldn't have had her as a baby-sitter. We all knew of her ambitions.'

Working at Choy's enabled Barbara to play both ends of the gastronomic gamut against the middle. She stuffed herself on wantonly un-kosher won tons and moo shu pork, then returned home to toy adroitly with the mandatory chopped liver. But her interest in the Choys went further than baby-sitting or punching the cash register keys. This she could do standing on either of her ringing ears. She was able to identify with this tiny pocket of minority culture, and feel at home with it. That same quick ear, the talent for mimicry, allowed her to pick up a smattering of the language, enhancing her sense of cross-ethnic solidarity. 'It was the world against us at Choy's Orient,' she once said. With egg roll you may get wisdom.

Mrs Streisand-Kind's recording of Stromberg's 'One Kiss' was the perfect musical illustration of a mother-type – the kind who warns her daughter that 'one kiss' could lead simultaneously to a social disease or unscheduled quadruplets. 'My mother said that babies come in bottles,' sings the disbelieving child who leads off *My Name Is Barbra* with a plangently cynical flavour of straight autobiography. She learned better from Muriel Choy. As she told writer Lawrence Grobel, 'Muriel Choy used to tell me about things. About love, and life, and sex. I would ask her things that my mother never told me. Just about being a woman.' (One of the questions the innocent baby-sitter raised with Mrs Choy was 'is the man always on top?' The reply, 'not necessarily', was Chinese inscrutability at its best.)

'Us against the world.' Believing it, the fifteen-year-old Barbara decided that the secret she shared with her bathroom and photo-booth mirrors – the movie-star make-up and the wild hair dos – should now be revealed. She began turning up like that at school, with the clothes to match. A kook was born. Since nature had perversely fixed her so she couldn't join 'em, then get a load of this, she would beat 'em! She was the odd one out, and if outwardly she was more defiantly confident than she inwardly felt, when it's you against them, you have to look like you're winning.

Significantly one of the few fellow pupils she felt drawn to at the time, (they would sit together at lunch) was also an un-lovely-looking eccentric who found it hard to run with the herd. He was a gawky odd-looking boy who wasted good learning time burying his head in copies of *Mad* magazine, occasionally emerging to laugh hysterically. Though he sat with Barbara, he would largely ignore her. He was manifestly a brainy odd-ball destined for think tanks, or oblivion. Well who today hasn't heard of Bobby Fischer? Their fellow students would glance across at their table, nod and wink; two of a kind, they deserved each other. Even their noses matched! That was the gibe but it says much for the target at which it was aimed that she refused to take the panic route to the nearest plastic surgeon. The pressure, the propaganda was formidable. 'When you gonna have your nose done?' the girls at Erasmus Hall High School wanted to know. They'd had their Nilotic jobs hammered into standard snubs, retroussés or Hedy Lamarr look-alikes, why not she? 'They wanted me to cut the bump off,' Barbra Streisand recalls with some amusement. 'But I wouldn't. I love my bump. I don't like pug-noses or little tiny ones.'

It happens that Barbara Joan's instinct, living with, making the most of what she had and was, was flawless. Had she conformed, re-styled her nose in accordance with the profile of the week, the chances are that it would have significantly altered her voice. The unmistakable timbre, the idiosyncratic resonance that make a Streisand recording as instantly recognisable as her kook wardrobe once made her, derives not only from the heightened awareness that tinnitus lends her ear; it owes plenty to the unique configuration of the septum of her nose. Surgery might have changed all that. Of course, Barbara Joan would not have known that at the time. Her objection reflected a fierce individuality. It has been called other things since then. At that time it blew up into her first major confrontation with her mother.

She was intent on enrolling in Malden Bridge Summer Theater near Albany in upstate New York. Mrs Streisand-Kind was equally determined that she should not. Her daughter had the money – a touchingly modest sum of $150 left to her by her grandfather. $150 was the enrollment fee.

Ruth Gordon (who had played the part of Dolly Levi while Barbara Joan was still discovering Loew's Kings) had had a father who, believing 'everyone should have a chance' had staked his daughter's dream of a stage career with his life's savings – $400. Mrs Streisand-Kind, the evidence suggests, was not in the same mould. Her resistance, probably based on admirable motives, argued: why squander her grandfather's money on a passing whim, an adolescent fantasy? One look told you she didn't have it in her to become an actress. Better she should spend the money on practical things. Like the cosmetic dentistry she needed. Then maybe some nice reliable boy . . . Barbara Joan raged against the counter-offer. It offended her flaring sense of personal integrity. Besides – dentists! What a sell-out! The archetypal marital goal for an Erasmus High girl. She *would* go to Malden Bridge.

Inevitably Diane Streisand-Kind made a strategic withdrawal. Okay. So all right. She would find out from someone with know-how and authority that it wasn't so easy. Then they'd all be spared this nonsense and her daughter could start to learn shorthand and typing. Her honest comments a dozen years later make clear how totally she underestimated her daughter's ambitions and talent. 'She decided to be an actress when she was fifteen. It's a very hectic life and, well, I couldn't figure this out. But I was the breadwinner and had a lot to do.' An understatement; she endured real hardship but kept it to herself. 'That summer I wanted her to go with me and her sister to summer camp but she wanted to go to Malden Bridge Playhouse with a friend. So – I gave her $300. As long as she'd be happier there and doing something she wanted. I was in the Catskills and she was in the Adirondacks. I had to contact the director to find out how she was.'

'How she was' was great. She was having a ball. Part of her mother's agreement to let her go there was the hope that her 'emaciated' daughter would happily fatten up during her stay. But she'd only put on a few pounds by the time she got home. Privately Mrs Streisand-Kind rated that a disaster. They didn't even have a cook there? How do you do Shakespeare, Chekhov or Thornton Wilder without a cook!

Her daughter was relishing something more delectable than her mother's recommended fare of kosher pot-roasts, million-calorie potato pancakes. The smell of the grease-paint in her original-model nostrils; the roar of the crowd just a few rehearsals away. She toted flats, marked up the stages she'd just swept, and painted scenery. That might have been enough for any stage-struck girl lucky to be in the heady atmosphere of summer stock. Not this one. She told everybody how they could improve their performances. Obligingly getting lost, as requested, she returned, with more suggestions. Take note William Wyler, Sydney Pollock, Ray Stark, Frank Pierson, you were not the first.

One of her suggestions, out there at Malden Bridge, is interesting in its revelation of Streisand's intrinsic totality of forwardness, determination, desperation even. The big production that summer was *Teahouse of the August Moon*. Barbara Joan Streisand, scene-painter, gofer, publicly coveted the role of Sakini. Sakini is the leading role in John Patrick's play. It is a male part. She had her reasons: he was supposed to be a five-foot nothing of an Okinawan peasant. A wily runt of a survivor. None of the guys in the company – conventional leading men to a man – could get that, right? Whereas she . . . right? Wrong. *Chutzpah* is not infallible. It can't take you everywhere. As she didn't win Preminger's nod for St Joan, so she was firmly nailed in her place now. Her place was on the back of a goat that in a wordless cameo she had to ride across the stage. But almost literally, she had the last laugh. At every performance her Okinawan Paul Revere brought her a big hand. And on applause like that she could live for a year. Who needs chicken soup?

She returned to Brooklyn still 'emaciated' but with precise goals. Next summer she would have to serve out her time in school. Then it would be back to Malden Bridge. After that summer – the world. But first things first. She had to raise the money to stake her another session at the theater. The cashier's job at Choy's Orient was okay, but would it ever take her to the hand-embossed pavement outside Grauman's Chinese Theater? Now she took a cliché out of the classic rags-to-stardom scenario. She became a cinema usherette, re-entering her childhood palace of dreams. She was not, apparently, the best usherette in the circuit. And for a fascinating reason. 'When I directed people to their seats,' she says, 'I hid my face because I knew I'd be famous one day and I didn't want the embarrassment of having any of them think later, "Oh, yeah – *her* the star . . . . she used to be an usherette at our neighbourhood theater." ' This usherette, at least, was carrying a torch for something more than a weekly wage. So the battle between her ambitions and Mrs Streisand-Kind's Jewish-mother caution raged on and on. Her mother brought out major artillery. She enrolled Barbara at a typing school. Secretaries had status. Status was halfway towards a nice marriage.

Mrs Streisand-Kind was not being malignant in discouraging all thought of a stage career. Lacking vision, and in the classic pattern, she was acting from the best of intentions. (It is ironic that the mother would one day herself take a position as a school secretary, having years before, as Diane Rosen, cut a disc and harboured her own dreams.) By a blatant stratagem Barbara Joan let her fingernails grow tiger-lady long . . . and flunked typing school. Let others be secretaries. She knew where she was going.

Probing her 'all or nothing' ambitions and motivations produced a curious phobia. Fear of early death. Maybe it was the subconscious reaction to her father's sudden passing at a cruelly early age. But the story goes that at the age of nine she came across a booklet on cancer and discovered she had nine of the symptoms listed. She woke up one morning with a pressure on her chest. Convinced it was cancer she went secretly to the doctor. She climbed the stairs, rang the bell. There was no response. He had no surgery that day. She returned home. The pressure disappeared. 'It was my first psychosomatic illness,' she said. It was at this time that her half-sister, Rosalind Kind, was born. The event, apparently, did not throw Barbara Joan into ecstasies. Nothing personal. Merely that it seemed to confirm Louis Kind's permanence in the household. This distancing of Emmanuel Streisand's daughter from the child of Mr Louis Kind has persisted, though without rancour. Both parties recognise that, if it is tough to be Barbra Streisand, it's maybe tougher to be her half-sister.

In the event, Rosalind Kind was to experience no objections from her mother when she elected to follow a singing career. But the battle between Barbara Joan and Mrs Streisand-Kind had hit crisis point. Finally, worn down by the clash of wills, recognising that there was no way she could crack her daughter's steely determination, the mother gave in. The summer of '58 saw Barbara Joan back at Malden Bridge. No lead roles, yet. She played the heroine's tomboy sister in *Picnic*. And in *The Desk Set* she played the office flirt, with such Marlene Dietrich overkill, the audience laughter extended into cheers. Recollections of that summer suggest that the emaciated apprentice deployed inspired talent, but always undisciplined, and wilfully over the top. Critics were not slow to make the same sort of comment as her career blazed on.

The summer ended. But the academic year that now commenced was unique in Barbara Joan's life. In January 1959 she was graduated. She was legally free to take on the world. She'd paid her dues to Mrs Streisand-Kind. She would now make a scintillating gesture to the memory of Emmanuel Streisand.

Within five superlative, shining years she was to achieve a position from which she might consciously lament: look what you missed by dying so soon.

THREE

PALAMOS IN the Catalonia region of north-eastern Spain was a long way from the 'deli's', the raucous, multi-ethnic Babel of Brooklyn. Or Broadway. The proving grounds of Barbra Streisand. Robert Ruark in *The Honey Badger* had already looked ahead to his own death with the level, unwavering stare, the intrigued fatalism of a bullfighter. And if it is true that, in the contemplation of imminent death, people experience a kaleidoscopic reprise of the significant events of their lives, then Robert Ruark's musings, sharpened by the tequila of the morning, are interesting. He had, in his reporter's role, been everywhere, seen everything. When accordingly, we asked him to expand on the famous men and women he had known, praised, admired, despised, his settled response came as a surprise.

Initially he threw out a few somewhat predictable names – presidents, dictators and such. But speedily what came to dominate the variegated territory of his reminiscences was the recollection of a singer he'd seen and heard long ago at a nightclub in New York. The club was the Blue Angel. And just as Dietrich had held Hemingway's fascinated attention, so the girl who as a drama student had parodied *that* blue angel now drew a like admiration from Ruark. With the heightened recollection of a man with only a finite time left him in which to look back, he remembered the occasion and Barbra Streisand as if it were yesterday. 'She murdered 'em!' he recalled with a low chuckle. 'And I tell you I was the first to alert everyone how great she was going to be.'

That last is a heady claim. By the time of her second appearance at the Blue Angel in January 1963, Barbra Streisand's star was distinctly rising. The rocket of her talent had ignition and, quivering with building power, was close to blasting upward from the launch pad into the rarer atmospheres of stardom. For two years a huge growing network, Greenwich Village its nexus, had grapevined the word about that, beg, borrow or steal the price of admission, you just had to go see this knock-out kook with the trick of transmitting the throb in her voice into your own pulse. She had already garnered rave reviews from the likes of Walter Kerr, Howard Taubman. These were for her performance in a Broadway show that had seen her nominated for a Tony and secured her the New York Drama Critics' prize as 'Best Supporting Actress in a Musical'. But if by 'telling everybody' Ruark meant writing perceptively, prophetically, his own iron-hot first impressions of a talent that was to shake New York, capture America, orbit the world, then we may excuse his exaggeration. He was among the first journalist-critics with reputations of their own to stake his professional opinion in the black and white commitment of a column. Published in the now defunct Los Angeles *Citizens News*, Ruark's perceptions are worth recalling. Not only do they substantiate his rare prescience (informed by years of experience clocking the world's best) as a talent spotter, they constitute a near-to-definitive piece on the genesis, the emergence at a precise historical moment, of a talent soon to be fabled. But not yet. Sitting at his Blue

Angel table, Ruark was being wise neither before nor after the event but *at* it.

Her nose [he wrote] is more evocative of moose than muse, and her eyes at best could be called Nilotic only by way of mascara but about 2 a.m. when she sings 'Any Place I Hang My Hat Is Home', she's beautiful, even if home is only Brooklyn.

Her name is Barbra Streisand. She is twenty years old, she has a three-octave promiscuity of range, she packs more personal dynamic power than anybody I can recall since Libby Holman or Helen Morgan. She can sing as loud as Ethel Merman and as persuasively as Lena or Ella, as brassy as a Sophie Tucker or as little-girl-tiny as a memory of Margaret Whiting, and she has a professional expertise that is second to nobody this side of Lee Wiley.

She has a fine, dry comic style, when necessary, and this knack of making herself beautiful in your ears. She is the hottest thing to hit the entertainment field since Lena Horne erupted and she will be around fifty years from now if good songs are still written to be sung by good singers . . .

Only the Blue, I should say, with its combination of a Streisand inside and a Bobby Short outside in the lounge, would stay crammed in a hungry month at best . . . If you make it at the Blue, you've got it made.

And so Miss Streisand – who you might as well start remembering now so you can tell people you knew her when – fits the pattern of the only saloon in the city I frequent with any regularity. Only Miss Streisand can sing a cornball like 'Happy Days Are Here Again' and make it emerge as a torch song which collapses the house. Only Miss Streisand can make an international event out of a song called 'I'm in Love with Harold Mangot' which is pure garment-center-Bronx-fashion humor.

And only Barbra Streisand, at this moment or in the past, can turn her head back so you can count her tooth-fillings, swell her vocal cords like a flamenco singer and turn 'Cry Me a River' into something comparable to Enrico Caruso having his first bash at Pagliacci. When Streisand cries you a river, you got a river, Sam.

Streisand came into the singing business more or less accidentally – she says – as an unsuccessful actress. I'm inclined to doubt this offhand approach to success, because at the age of twenty she threads her way through some of the more intricate Cole Porter and Harold Arlen stuff with the deftness of a Sarah Vaughan or a Peggy Lee on a good, hard-working night when nobody is making private jokes with the sidesmen.

Barbara is too impossibly skilled to be only twenty, but twenty she is, and already a two-year veteran of the big time. She was an overpowering smash in the recently folded musical *I Can Get It for You Wholesale* and was moonlighting on the side until the show folded. Now she's full-time big time on her own, and the next musical she makes will see her name over the title.

Once in a while I like to rave, so I can brag about it twenty years later. If the world lasts another twenty years, Barbra Streisand from Brooklyn's Erasmus High School will still be around, rocking the rafters and getting more beautiful as the night grows later.

The world did last another twenty years although, unhappily, not for Robert Ruark. Still, his review, written in 1963, was a triumph of style and canny judgement. It sits well alongside his later and more serious works which underscore what the writing business has lost.

January 1963! Four years almost to the day since Barbara Joan had graduated from Erasmus Hall. Little more than three years since she had cut out from her mother's Newkirk Avenue apartment, walking blithely along on the swaying tightrope from Flatbush Avenue to Broadway.

But first she had to quit school, and this she did the day, the minute it was legally permitted. Having proclaimed with strident fortissimo, her determination to become an actress, the immediate goal would seem to be a place in a drama school. But that required the power-base of hard cash. The girl with a 93 per cent average on high school graduation went out and promptly secured a job – as a switchboard operator. It was, of course, a nothing post. The best it could do for her was to give her the chance to try all manner of assumed voices on for size. Innocent callers in, say, Vassar, Detroit or Juarez may just have imagined they had Rita Hayworth or Vivien Leigh on the line. But the position did afford two tangible benefits. It paid. Each week she could salt away half of her ninety dollars salary. And the job was in Manhattan. End of the rainbow. She was still slugging it out toe to toe with boredom. But during office hours, at least, she was rid of the 'bad breath and baseball' aura suffusing Brooklyn. And Manhattan had the one thing Brooklyn lacked – Drama classes. She went out to grab a place with the same try-and-stop-me tenacity that buttressed the Barbra Streisand we know today. Don't stand on the side-lines rubber-necking, Barbara, get some! Zig-zagging a frenetic course across the island she tried four different drama classes. One of these was the acting seminar conducted by Eli Rill. A seminar is supposed to be a group of students meeting under the guidance of a tutor or professor for the exchange of information, to discuss theories. The irresponsible girl from Brooklyn upgraded that scene with a deluge of questions. How? Why? What's the motivation? And supposing we did it this way? Her time in the class was characterised by a running difference of opinion with Mr Rill. Perceptively he saw in this dynamo of a screwball a great potential for poised, off-beat comedy. Not so his pallid apprentice. While recognising she didn't have the face to launch a thousand cover stories – who needs it! – she knew, soon the whole world would know, that she was cast for more serious work. Camille, Medea, Phèdre – Mr Rill could take his pick. 'I kept telling her,' he said, 'that she had to develop what she had and not try to be somebody else. She would make it clear that my role was to make her a tragic muse.' With hindsight we can say that perhaps both Rill and his pupil were right. Angelina Scarangella has since counter-poised a Katie Morosky (The Way We Were) against her Dolly Levi and, in portraying Fanny Brice, combined the two.

Who? Angelina Scarangella? Indeed. It was under that unlikely stage name that the bright, hungry-to-learn student first presented herself to the drama class. The name – halfway, in feel, between an Italian melodrama and a contagious skin disease – was an alias that cold-bloodedly Barbara Joan had lifted from the Manhattan telephone directory. But why the camouflage? And why choose a name so overtly exotic? (At one point she had book-matches personally inscribed with the name). One answer would seem to be that in these early days Barbara Joan coyly decided that she would need to succeed first before revealing who she really was. It was as though she were hedging her bets – and, anyway, wasn't Angelina Scarangella so much more groovy? Ponti's Sophia, who changed her name from Scicolone, to Lazzaro, then to Loren, may understand how she felt. Loren's argument that 'Scicolone' might not have been the most seductive name to put on the billboards, especially against the name Cary Grant, applies with equal force to 'Scarangella'. Then again, the theory is that, even under that name, Flatbush's heroine would have made it just as big.

The second of her drama coaches was more than a mentor. He was a friend. Alan Miller, who had come into Barbara Joan's life by way of her hanging about the Cherry Lane Theater. A revival there of O'Casey's *Purple Dust* had included Miller's wife, Anita, in its cast. Anita Miller had an eye for talent and was prepared to be impressed, moved even, by eagerness and dedication. She introduced Barbara Joan to her drama teacher husband and, no less impressed, he found a place for her in his acting class. Two vastly significant spots in New York for Barbara Joan now became Alan Miller's theater workshop on West Forty-eighth Street and the Miller apartment on West Seventy-fifth.

Several pointers to the shape of things to come emerged from the workshop. One occurred when Miller asked his students to depict an inanimate object of their choice. Student Streisand chose to be a chocolate chip cookie melting in an oven. Given Marcel Marceau's celebrated impression of a rasher of bacon finding itself being fried in a skillet, this was not an earth-shakingly new concept but a neatly compact exercise. One that was brilliantly executed. A fellow student (and contemporary room-mate) still remembers how brilliant. 'I had never seen anything like her expressiveness before,' she says. 'She was a limp and passive blob until she was put in the oven. Then she began huffing and puffing as the dough expanded. Then she was wheezing and collapsing as she got toasted.' 'The whole point,' Streisand explained later, 'was to experience something organically, to lift it from an intellectual level and give it a physical life.' A little heavy, perhaps, for a melting chocolate chip. It is Miller's recollection that is important. 'Her portrayal was beautiful – so tender. We saw Barbara not awkward and unsure but as she felt in her imagination.'

She could accomplish this on a larger, more formal scale as well. In an excerpt from *The Rose Tattoo* she portrayed the sexual awakening of the daughter (played in the film by Marisa Pavan) with unstructured physical spontaneity that the handful of fellow students present still remember. Abruptly she had leapt on the back of the boy playing the young sailor. She was clawing at him one second, caressing him the next. Her eyes shut she was exploring his face with her fingertips as he spoke. She was conveying all the trembling intensity, uncertainty, that lies in the first tactile experience of a lover's body. It was wild and awkward and brilliant and all from out of an improvising left field. Once again, flying by instinct, Barbara Joan had responded to interior signals. They were not signals crudely restricted to one message, one key. They were beginning to persuade her of the virtues, the strength of restraint – of just *being*. She would watch fellow students go up on stage and sense intuitively that they would never make it. It was not merely that they lacked all charisma. Self-conscious, they would twitch, get visibly nervous, be awkward in a way that worked against them. Barbara Joan watched them intently and absorbed the inference.

She was learning other important lessons too, outside the drama class. The Millers took over the Choys' surrogate role. They were to exert a profounder, more crucial influence in her development. Their uptown apartment was mildly Bohemian, casually civilised. She came to know it well, baby-sitting for their son Greg. The tot sleeping, she took in the Schubert Alley ambience of the apartment, rinsing the drab Flatbush sediment from her mind. There were books, records, paintings. It was a place where people slept when they were tired, ate when they were hungry. After the straitjacket life on Pulaski Street, this was Elysium. And she was paid for it too, making her tuition fees less of a hassle. Barbara Baby-sitter played disc after disc on the hi-fi (as it would then have been styled), picked up book after book. She was beginning to comprehend what she needed to learn. What she was missing. The Millers' apartment had plenty of sustenance to feed her hunger for culture. And what she could not find in the Millers' apartment she ran to ground in the New York Public Library. We know that she did not take the familiar route into classical literature. Sure, she latched on to *Anna Karenina*, basic to the diet of an aspiring young actress. Likewise *Gone with the Wind* and Chekhov, which no student could ignore. But then she parted company with her young contemporaries. While they were into Tennessee Williams, Arthur Miller, Odets, O'Neill, she was smouldering through the musty editions of nineteenth-century French drama, Dumas fils and *La Dame aux Camélias*. If they were good enough for Bernhardt, Duse, Garbo, then it had to be right for Angelina Scarangella soon-to-be Streisand. Determination. Doing it her way. Some months after the seventeen-year-old Barbara Joan had landed the switchboard job, she discovered she'd salted away the giddying sum of $750. Riches. A fortune like that made the long subway journey back to the drabness of Newkirk Avenue doubly depressing. That's where the action wasn't. Anticipating the title of one of her earlier tracks, Barbara Joan announced to her mother that she had 'gotta move'. Her place, she determined, was somewhere on the world's richest island.

This proposed Manhattan transfer was the final, decisive confrontation between mother and daughter. It was Mrs Kind's last stand. The immovable object hadn't a prayer against this irresistible force. We can understand, even admire her last-ditch resistance. She genuinely believed her screwball gamine of a daughter had zero chance of making it as a performer. 'Fiasco' was the word that Mrs Kind used to describe her predictions. Also there was a secondary, perhaps, deeper reason for her opposition. Living alone at that age in a place like that! That was something a nice Jewish girl brought into the world to have babies didn't do! What would the neighbours think! It would never have happened if her first husband was still alive. But he wasn't – and it did. The determination was total.

Total but not heartless. A diplomatic, face-saving compromise was achieved. When Barbara Joan Streisand finally moved, lock, stock and a barrel-load of theatrical bric-à-brac into a minute apartment on Thirty-fourth Street, it was not to live alone. She agreed to shack up with a flatmate her mother had vetted. The scene was set for archetypal situations – the odd couple within, the Shelley Winter's momma outside just happened to be passing and is everything all right, are you keeping warm and having enough to eat? And just happening to have two jars of chicken soup here in her outsize bag. Privacy, shmivacy. One does not have to go far to trace the source material for the knock-out nightmare fantasy in *Up the Sandbox* where the larger than life monster mother, toting a similarly outsize pair of cutters, is not at all deterred by a chain-locked door.

Overall, however, it must be conceded that Barbara Joan carried the day. She never again lived for any sustained length of time under the same roof as her mother. She has looked after her well. Today Mrs Streisand-Kind lives in an all-comforts-provided-for condominium in Beverly Hills. It is close enough for Barbra to recognize her mother is within kibbitzing distance. But it is sufficiently detached to prevent Brooklyn intruding on Jon Peters and Ramirez Canyon.

For Barbara – still with an 'a' – the move to a new, her first, pad at the start of the new decade, the Sixties, was no kind of a wrench, outsize or otherwise. And looking back, the whole scene must have been fun, fun, fun. Freewheeling through New York! The Big Apple! Wow! The drama classes, the Greenwich Village spots, the movie houses all there on your own doorstep as well as your employers! Wow again! The reality, in sober fact, was anything but fun. There was the constant changing of apartments; changing (walking out) of jobs; being unemployed. All standard stuff for the opening reels of a cornball, rags-to-riches showbiz bio-pic. But not so cornball when you already owe two weeks' rent, and your current room-mate announces she's throwing in the towel; when your twenty-five-hour days are wearing you to a frazzle; when the chance you're aching for catches you out of the running. Barbara came to know the sad, drab, institutional decor and minds of the Unemployment Bureau. She stood in line to collect her checks in that spirit-killing atmosphere of loser's apathy. When officials discovered she had not been following up on the telephone operator vacancies they steered her towards, but on the contrary (and she had the gall to tell them so!) had been goofing off trying to get work in the theatre, they threw the whole bureaucratic book at her. And stopped the checks.

When things go wrong, nothing goes right. It was at this time she experienced one of her very few clear-cut turn-downs in the theater. After performing a test piece she was rejected by the Actors' Studio. Then, of course, the Actors' Studio was the holy of holies and Strasberg was its guru supreme. Barbara knew this as well as anyone. In her commuting days she had whiled away her time on the subway writing long letters to the great man expressing her thoughts on 'the actor's life'. One, she remembers, was about her feelings on hearing a fellow student proclaim he wanted to play parts 'like myself'. Her reaction was scornful. 'Can you imagine this actor wanting to reduce the level of art to himself?' she wrote. But Lee Strasberg was to remain unedified by these letters from an unknown woman. Girl. He never received them. Having purged the thoughts out of her system Barbara had had the sense, and style, to tear the letters up. She may well have wanted to do the same to the questionnaire they gave her when she applied for a place at the Actors' Studio. One of the questions asked her to name her favourite actress. She avoided the good, very good Strasbergian disciples currently in vogue, like Eve Marie Saint, say, or Geraldine Page. Instead she doubled up with genuine enthusiasm, two candidates, Mae West and Rita Hayworth. There was no bridging that madness, and The Method. She lost points there as she did in the test scene. She went into it like a demon, and over the top. Overwrought at the cool reception, she burst into tears. Streisand and Strasberg were not meant for each other. Her tears dried, she was right back out on the street again. Hindsight suggests it was just as well. The potential clash of styles, egos and personalities, would most likely have proved destructive. She consoled herself with the knowledge that were thousands just like her in New York, L.A., London, Rome, wherever, clamouring for recognition. And out of them, some stars would be born without the assistance of the Strasbergs and their Method.

Drama classes, in a sense playing at play-acting, were not enough psychic, let alone economic, nourishment. Both Alan Miller and Eli Rill were emphatic in telling Barbara that, however humbly, she should try getting into the game proper: she should start doing the rounds of the casting directors and agencies. She did. And was not discovered. It was she who made the discovery. She was a leper. The trudging walks towards Times Square, the entrance into dingy, dated office blocks, the approaches along mean, dispiriting corridors to the wearying, stale, cigarette-fume-laden air of outer offices and their endless waiting, all led to the tired, careless repetition of the ultimate put-down cliché: 'Don't call us, we'll call you.' It was the very boredom with which it was delivered that withered hope the most.

'It was degrading, humiliating,' she has since said. 'Nobody should be forced to beg for work.'

And yet one has to see it from the other side of the desk as well. Here she was, walking in looking like the kicked-around half of a rag-doll act. Her photo had as much relation to cheesecake as Eleanor Roosevelt's passport picture. Her resumé – where the hell was Malden Bridge? – was no more than a short stringing together of wishful thinking. It was the classic new-girl-in-town dilemma. She had no right to expect work because she had no experience; when she'd gone out and gained experience by getting work then she could get work . . . Come in Catch 22.

One of the most poignant of these don't-call-me rejections was when she put herself forward for a walk-on part as a beatnik. Type-casting for sure, enhanced by the old raincoat worn over black tights. Her come-on-strong 'Look, you'd better sign me up, I'm terrific!' was met with a yawn. Her angry protest that a walk-on with no lines hardly demanded a track-record as thick as the Manhattan phonebook earned a nod toward the door. Barbara blew her stack. In Brooklyn street-language. She wouldn't beg! And they knew what they could do with their smart-ass suggestions she should get her nose fixed, buy a decent dress. She was herself and she would make it with what she had. From here on – well, one day – they would have to come to her.

Tough talk. It was a way of saving face as she got out of a kitchen where she couldn't stand the heat. Except, cooling off, she didn't get out. Told by the bureaucrats she was down to her last ten weeks of unemployment entitlement, she hung on in there. Between classes, auditions and maternal deliveries of chicken soup, Barbara was making contacts across the network. She was meeting characters who had at least got to first base. One such person was a young artist, Terry Leong. Introduced to this walking thrift shop with two-tone hair, he saw excitement and potential. It was Leong's design skills that steered Barbara's inherent sense of style from slam-bang primary shock towards more thought-through ensembles. Accompanying her on her bargain basement scavenging of the thrift shops, he built on what they bought. The effect was still offbeat, but stunning. He designed the costumes for the first production that Barbara appeared in in Manhattan. He probably had a ball; the play was Josef and Karel Capek's *The Insect Comedy*. The production had been thrown together by a bunch of out of work actors whose description of themselves as a 'non-profit group' was as much historical fact as a declaration of intent. Frank Aston's review in the *World Telegram and Sun*, May 1960, was probably intended to be kind. He admitted he was typing with kid gloves on because 'no one in it claimed to be anything like a pro'. It damned with tolerance and shattered the struggling young cast. The play died after a three-day run at the Jan Hus Theatre. In the cast was a talented young actor who was about to become the next crucial figure in the evolution of the star. Their relationship began as an exercise in mutual admiration – it turned into, or on to, something much deeper. Barry Dennen took his place in the line of father-figures who played Svengali to Barbara Joan Streisand's Trilby. As regards the immediate future, his influence was to be more than crucial. It was decisive.

Dennen initially perceived his fellow 'insect' in the play as being 'hysterically funny, endearing and exceptionally serious about becoming a great actress'. Off-stage they traded reminiscences of Marx Brothers and Mae West and Laurel and Hardy movies, working their own variations on the classic gags. The private progressed through the personal to the same address. Not long after the play closed, Barbara Joan moved into Barry Dennen's apartment. Mrs Diane Kind's Flatbush-oriented protests, compounded of tears, traumas and more chicken soup, cut no ice with her daughter. Dennen's pad was easy enough to find. It was in Greenwich Village just across from a gay nightclub called The Lion. The two room-mates were not of a piece. She was randomly self-educated, dominated by a powerful will and an uncanny instinct. He was intelligent, formally educated, with a sharp analytical mind. She sensed that he knew what was best for her. And was right. It was Dennen who redirected her bright, unrecognised promise towards singing.

Barbra Streisand had always maintained – still does – that she is an actress first and a singer, a performer, if at all, a long way second. But for some months now, events, and the pangs of poverty, were pushing her on stage behind a microphone. An acquaintance had come back to her previous pad for an after-a-show coffee. He had produced a guitar, she had started to sing along. Her current room-mate, another aspiring actress named Marilyn Fried, had been knocked out by the quality of her voice. Was it for real? Was it a one-off fluke brought about by the late hour, the room's acoustics, a magic combination of coffee and relaxed togetherness? From the back of a closet Barbara produced a demonstration record that she had made half-a-dozen years before. The quality of voice was constant. So was the response of her two listeners: she had set her sights on the wrong career. She was born to sing.

Barbara was sceptical, diffident, embarrassed – and intrigued. Coyly she returned to the incident the following day. Should she maybe consider auditioning. As a singer. Like, was she good enough? Not that she was a singer, you know. She was an actress. Right? Right. Only . . .

Only she did have, she knew privately, the chance to audition as a singer – for, of all things, *The Sound of Music*. It had come about via a typically offbeat photograph she had pushed around the casting offices. Barry Dennen has recalled his impression of it, and how it worked for her: 'She was all swathed in cloaks and veils and earrings and chatchkalas, looking like Ruth Draper in a moving moment. It was so hilarious that Eddie Blum of the Rodgers and Hammerstein casting office called Barbara just to see what kind of girl would send out a picture like that.'

In the event, Blum kept her singing for a three-hour stint – a long time for a girl with an untrained voice and not much in the way of a 'book' of prepared audition pieces. But Blum could see beneath the rawness. 'He took her to lunch, then to dinner. He spent the whole day talking to her. He was fascinated with her talent and her intelligence. Around ten-thirty that night he brought Barbara back to our apartment.' Then, Dennen recalls, Blum administered his pay-off to the long day: 'He told her he couldn't put her in the chorus because she was something special and there was nothing in *The Sound of Music* for a talent like hers.'

Lose some, win some. In the period after *The Insect Comedy* but before she moved in on him, Barbara had called up Barry Dennen and asked whether she and a guitarist could come over and make use of his sophisticated recording equipment. As one friend to another, Dennen replied, 'Of course.' It was a response which carried some weight in their mutual, her long-term, future.

The informal, try-things-on-for-size session duly took place. In between setting his levels, Barry Dennen all but flipped his lid. He was more than ecstatic. If there was one thing he recognised, it was great singing. Not just the subjective judgement of a man turned on by the female behind the voice. As a small boy in California and continuing steadily on ever since, Barry Dennen had built up a formidable personal record and tape collection of the stand-out American female vocalists: Ruth Etting, Helen Morgan, Lee Wiley, Ethel Waters, Mabel Mercer, Billie Holliday. Here, in the rough, was a voice to match them. With polishing . . . Bluntly he told the owner of this voice to forget playing insects in plays and set her mind on one objective: singing. Morning, noon, night, she should concentrate on that and nothing else. The reply ran according to form.

'I'm an actress,' Barbara Joan Streisand insisted, in a voice that dug its heels in. Years of self-conditioning, a genuine uncertainty as to the quality of her voice, couldn't be shrugged off that lightly. Dennen considered. Right on his doorstep was The Lion. Each Thursday the club held a talent contest. Often it was destroy-your-neighbourhood-victim night. But equally, the audience was knowledgeable, sophisticated, able to recognise genuine talent and not grudging in their appreciation. He would make The Lion the focus of the challenge. Okay, if Barbara the actress would go so far as to walk in and sign up for the contest, he would help her choose a set of songs, work with her and direct her act. Broke, hungry for recognition, still Barbara hedged. The compromise she offered was a significant pointer to the perfectionist in the making. The incident has since become legend.

She was undecided, insecure, reluctant to surrender one inch of the territory of her ambitions. She was also scared witless of being roasted alive for daring to test-fly an untried talent in public. She decided to arrange her own pre-contest audition. Not in a theater, not in a recording studio, but her kitchen. Even there she was too nervous to face the handful of friends gathered to give her moral support. (Perhaps *especially* the handful of friends – how many potential talents shrivel under this too personal scrutiny?) She turned her back on them. Fixing her gaze on the calendar on the wall, she sang the subtle, musically complex 'A Sleepin' Bee'. She finished. And waited. There was no applause, no comment. 'Well, am I any good?' she was forced to ask. Still nothing.

'I remember, when I turned round,' she recalled later, 'I couldn't understand why they had tears in their eyes.'

If you can move people to tears in a kitchen when you're not slicing onions, you must have chances. Barbara got back to Barry. Yeah, sure, what the hell, why not . . . she'd put herself down for the talent contest. He was delighted. She was a shoe-in. There may have been one other factor which tipped the balance in favour of Barbara Streisand deciding to compete. The Lion offered its winning contestants not only fifty dollars and a week's engagement, but a hefty evening meal. The faint aroma of all the dinners she had copped at Choy's Orient may have drifted back to Barbara's memory. This wouldn't be the first time she had done a deal for a meal. Except, if she blew it, there in The Lion's den it might be she who came close to being eaten alive . . .

FOUR

STREISAND'S DEBUT at The Lion is legend shading into the apocryphal. It happened all right. She was there. As Barbra Streisand, now defiantly without the 'a'. But if all the people who claim to have seen her there *were* there, then the proprietors were breaking the New York Fire Department's capacity regulations by about half a million. In the first summer of what were soon to be called the 'Swinging Sixties', The Lion was a favored nightspot for gays. In those less humane, less understanding days, 'coming out' took a lot of nerve. It also took a brave man to get tagged as a regular there. You could get clocked by the law or whoever. Hence there was always the inevitable gay over-reaction. In the small, crowded brothel-red front bar, in the larger piano room in back, the atmosphere teetered towards the hysterical. Bitchiness saturated the smoke-filled air particularly on a Thursday, talent contest night. Then, if some poor no-hoper of a schlemiel had the temerity to pretend he could entertain, the collective derision from the assembled queens was murder incorporated. This was the audience at The Lion which Barbra Streisand, just turned eighteen, faced one hot and heavy midsummer New York night.

Even before she opened her mouth her appearance had triggered a reaction. Giggles, deliberately not suppressed, accompanied her walk to the microphone. This was freak time. The beanpole of a trainee had made up her face like a blind fugitive from a Noh play. Her multi-colored hair was impersonating a schizophrenic traffic signal. Winks flicked from table to table, eyebrows were overkillingly raised to heaven. But at least there was silence. This 'look-at-me' get-up was the sort of compensatory camouflage to insecurity many in the audience could identify with. It wasn't the appearance that outraged them. It was the choice of song. The fledgling witch stepped forward and announced she was going to sing Harold Arlen and Truman Capote's 'A Sleepin' Bee'. It was bad news. The freak was profaning sacred ground. 'A Sleepin' Bee' was Diahann Carroll's song: hers by right of a first-come stake-out on the first night of *House of Flowers*. And hers, anyway, by virtue of the magical flawless way she delivered it. The excellent and beautiful Diahann Carroll was – still is – what the trade knowingly calls 'a singer's singer', 'a performer's performer'. In the style of the Colosseum, Streisand was being thrown to The Lion.

She stood before the microphone in the unflattering pink-red spot facing the affronted silence of the audience. And she dismissed them. She shut her eyes. Body motionless, arms at her sides, she began to sing. Abruptly, magic suffused through the hostility.

For the first two bars the smart guys who had exchanged knowing leers raised approving eyebrows: this kid had something. Then she had them – as individuals. Each listener had latched into a personal communion with the singer. Only great performers can command that. They could hear now that the voice was beautiful and – the second miracle – that, as she became the song, the kid was beautiful too.

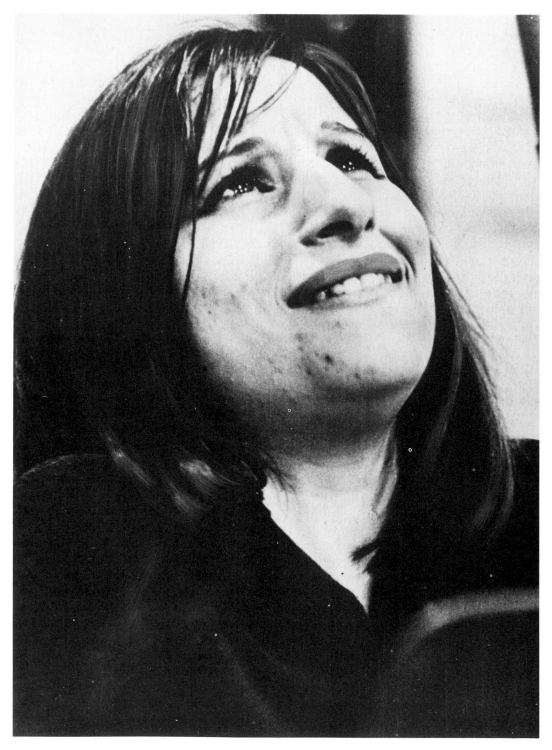

Aged eighteen rehearsing for her night club debut

The story goes that in accordance with the lyrics Barbra Streisand held a bee cupped in the palm of her hand as she sang. Legend errs. It was the audience she held there. Halfway through the performance she opened her huge blue eyes and stared at them, in a kind of ravishing hypnosis. She had devoured The Lion.

How to describe the Streisand voice – the *sound* of it? You don't, of course. You can't. There is that unique timbre, yes, that individual resonance which lyrical or torch song seems to vibrate with its own built-in echo. But *duplicate* that sensation in words? Pointless. Insulting. The best that critics have ever managed is a sort of evasive approximation. 'Her voice takes off on smooth gravel and soars about in some previously uncharted musical land of sweetness,' someone once tried. 'Sweet as molasses, tart as lemon juice' has been offered up. Almost all attempting to pin down the voice, whether from adoring or hostile viewpoint (we'll come to that later), have spoken of the drive, the exuberance, the ability to convert each song into drama. Above all, compelling. Barbra Streisand has the charismatic, siren's power of grabbing all attention. She possesses that extra dimension all great entertainers share of annihilating small-talk, the rustle of programs, the tinkle of ice-cubes. It focuses all concentration, dares you to cough or have cardiac arrest until the final note is sung. Streisand's last note faded on the heavy backroom air. To silence. Nothing. The song finished as it had begun, in total quiet. But what a difference in the quality of the two silences. The first had been prelude to bitch-mouth put-downs. The second was that awed moment when, from a psychic decompression chamber, an audience emerges from the spell suddenly to locate itself in the everyday world. Then The Lion roared. It was that kind of self-exciting ovation it is a privilege to be part of and which is impossible to fake. It had been deafeningly demonstrated to the actress Barbara Streisand that, despite her best endeavours to the contrary, she was a singer. She had sung for her supper and earned a week's engagement. The ecstatic Barry Dennen was proved right. In the euphoric aftermath they behaved like archetypal Neil Simon lovers, swapping smart gags, upstaging Broadway. The star-spangled Streisand walking barefoot through Central Park.

Starting from zero in terms of having a 'book', Barbra needed to work up an act fast. And, preferably, cheaply. Music publishers give nothing away free – to unknowns. Barbra now mined gold from those countless lost hours at the switchboard. Reviving her talent for telephonic mimicry, she called the length and breadth of Tin Pan Alley, nasally impersonating Vaughn Monroe's secretary. The songs came within the hour by private messenger. With carefree insolence she was singing in the evening the number she had 'got down' that afternoon. She still stopped the show and the clatter of cutlery. And as the underground word mushroomed upward, an extraordinary new chapter was added to The Lion's crowded history. When they'd packed the place to its tiny limit and still admitted thirty more, people were lining up on Ninth Street and back around the corner to Sixth Avenue.

There were gags, and some that stuck. Like the case of the missing 'a'. In terms of clothes, make-up, Barbara Joan Streisand had turned herself into a look-at-me psychedelic experience. Part of her yearned to do the same with that label we all get tagged with – her name. The ear-grabbing title of Angelina Scarangella tinkled enticingly. Try forgetting that, buster. Except . . . who the hell along Flatbush

Avenue, which usherette at Loew's Kings, would know that local girl was making good? The sight of her given name painted glitteringly on a Lion sign clinched the compromise she needed. She'd never liked the heavy stressing of her first name's second syllable. So lose it! And anyway, maybe she could have her cake and eat it. Or rather fig. One evening on the way to the club she stopped at a fruit stand on Eighth Street and saw a box of Smyrna figs. 'Smyrna . . . isn't that in Turkey?' she wondered aloud. That evening she introduced herself as Barbra Streisand from Smyrna, Turkey. Now the world was her natal oyster. 'I was born in Madagascar,' she was later proclaiming but sensing a descent into the commonplace, added the exotic plus, 'but I was reared in Rangoon.'

And there was work. The one week at The Lion stretched to three (and at fifty bucks and as many french fries as she could handle – such riches, yet!). But Barry Dennen knew with professional certainty that even so rare a gift as hers was nothing without the solid foundation of a sure technique. He worked Barbra harder than any drama coach had ever pushed her. Each evening he lugged his recorder along to tape her act for a sometimes merciless autopsy. By day he played for her benefit dozens of those Lee Wiley, Ethel Waters classics that placed him alongside the later pole-axed Robert Ruark. There were still the in-gags, the Mae West, Marx Brothers by-play, but he worked ceaselessly, maddeningly on the running order of the numbers she would do. Perhaps above all – and it may prove the one strike against him as a mentor – the actor in him encouraged the actress in her to approach each song as if it were a play in miniature, a dramatic statement.

'I'm not a singer but an actress who sings,' she would declare. 'But a song is like a three-act play, right?' Well . . . maybe.

Certainly it was an approach that paid off handsomely for a time. The rapturous ovations each evening were reverberating where it mattered. Barbra, with her toughened, polished act earned herself an engagement a block along the street at the Bon Soir. It was not a spill-over of enthusiasm that swept her to this straightly orthodox, more chic nightspot. It was an audition performed cold before the Bon Soir's experienced Burke McHugh. He needed an act to warm up the house for his top of the bill – Phyllis Diller. It wasn't quite the 'can you start tonight?' of the conventional musical. McHugh was cautious. Finally the nod came through. Barbra had two weeks at $108 per – more than double her Lion rate.

Phyllis Diller was by all accounts more than warm towards Barbra. Seeing the second-hand collage Barbra intended to open in, she growled 'Oh no!' and offered the newcomer the run of her own wardrobe. Barbra was embarrassed, reluctant to make a fatal compromise with the persona she had created. Perceptively Phyllis Diller read the signals. 'Forget it,' she said. 'Just go out and do your stuff. And when you come into big money, which you will, save it in Hong Kong and Tokyo banks.'

If there was a flicker of hesitation about the way she looked, Barbra wouldn't yield an inch over the way she sounded. The Bon Soir had doubts about her choice of material and its running order. Who the hell ever heard of 'Who's Afraid of the Big Bad Wolf' being dished out to a nightspot audience? The unwritten rule book demanded that a singer opening the bill came on with a belter to stun the audience into attention. So what was all this smart-pants stuff opening up with 'A Sleepin' Bee'? Barbra was adamant. She would do it the Dennen–Streisand way. The Bon

Soir told her it was the hard way, but shrugged. If that was the way she wanted to learn, okay with them. Egg on her face would hardly worry Phyllis Diller. In the event, it was the Bon Soir and not Streisand, who did the pratfall.

It was the Lion experience over again. Barbra was not concerned to woo the audience. She made them come to her. Standing at the microphone in the single spot, she began the quiet, contemplative unfolding of 'A Sleepin' Bee'. Well before the middle eight the smalltalk had subsided to silence. The clatter from the bar had stopped. The power to compel attention was more potent than ever. The applause at the end of the song, and at the end of her set, was proportionately louder. Nobody would have guessed one of this bright new talent's backstage secrets. The hard-edged authority with which she manipulated lyric and audience, masked a performer's classic fear of going out to meet an audience eyeball to eyeball. Nerves racked her rigid. Bats, rather than butterflies, looped inside her stomach. Some nights she had to be virtually dragged on stage. But as, each night, the ovations persisted, her confidence grew. Barry Dennen assured her that, look, what they had evolved really worked. Yet though her stage-fright diminished, it never completely disappeared. The core of insecurity has never totally vanished. The bravura star of *Funny Girl*, the fiercely insistent co-producer of the embattled *A Star Is Born* has dragged herself on stage, on to the set, sick to her stomach at the prospect of confrontation with audience or director. At the Bon Soir this inner tension never showed. The two-weeks' engagement was extended to eleven and her money increased.

Perhaps only one customer during those eleven weeks went away from the nightspot less than totally pleased. Mrs Diane Streisand-Kind had been a guest the night after the opening. Barbra (who? what kind of a way to spell your name is that?) was wearing a lace 1890s peignoir, on Terry Leong's advice. Okay, so maybe she was mistaken about her daughter. All these people must be shouting about *something*. But what a daughter! Mrs Kind went home shocked and ashamed. How could she be so shameless to appear in public in a nightgown!

There is no way now, of course, we can experience again those early, yet amazingly assured sets at The Lion and the Bon Soir. The tapes that Barry Dennen recorded both in rehearsal and live performance were, naturally, sub-professional. Many were erased by later versions or experiments. Others were wiped on grounds of sub-standard acoustics or performance. Some were retained, and there is a tale (shortly to be told) about them.

Nevertheless, leaping forward some two years and more, it is possible to form an impression of how Barbra must have come across at those historic sessions. The core of titles laid down on her first solo LP are those that were the armature of her Dennen-influenced opening career. The disc, overweeningly titled *The Barbra Streisand Album*, was released in March 1963. This might seem a surprisingly long delay for the solo debut of an artist who had created a furore among 'in' New Yorkers in the summer of 1960. But unlike her instant club success, Barbra's recording career did not zoom from zero to light-speed in nothing flat. Her predilection for the offbeat had the conservative moguls of Capital Hill (RCA and Columbia) running scared. Her appeal was dismissed as 'too limited' – and Jeez,

Barbra at the Bon Soir

Harry! what'll that nose look like on the sleeve? It was not until after her vitally important agent tie-up with Marty Erlichman and significant contributions to two cast albums that she was able to persuade Columbia president Goddard Lieberson that she was worth the gamble of a contract. Even then he was sceptical. 'He said I wouldn't sell records,' she has since remarked, 'that I was much too special, that I would appeal only to a small clique.' Still, Lieberson had the courage of his shaky convictions. In June 1963, just four weeks after the disc's release he and Columbia had the gratifying surprise of handling the number one bestseller on the long-playing list. And Barbra, as thousands rushed to buy, had the satisfaction of a racing start in beginning her collection of gold discs. It was well reviewed by the professional critics. John F. Indcox in *High Fidelity* said: 'Miss Streisand is a remarkably accomplished singer of popular *Lieder*, with a voice of pure and rather unusual timbre which she uses quite brilliantly in a repertoire running all the way from torch ballads and show tunes to novelty numbers.'

And Stanley Green in *Hi Fi/Stereo Review* echoed this appreciation: 'The eagerly awaited Barbra Streisand album . . . turns out to be a fascinating package. Miss Streisand is a compelling stylist with a full, rich vocal quality that may give you goosebumps when you hear her more dramatic arias. She has a sure control and knows what she is doing at all times. There are few (if any) better versions of "Cry Me a River" and "Soon It's Gonna Rain" . . .'

The most fulsome appraisal of all appeared over the facsimile signature of Harold Arlen, but since this appeared on the sleeve notes and Mr Arlen contributed one of the album's titles and no less than five to the follow-up disc, we may perhaps discount his rave as being, if not ballooned out of proportion, a touch subjective. Of more abiding interest are the reactions of the fans who rushed to buy, and the singer herself.

The fans (at last!) rushed to buy. They brought home both more and less than they had bargained for. This was not easy listening, music to *half* listen to as you fixed drinks or arranged details with the neighbouring Joneses about your joint vacation. These were intense, demanding, edgy tracks. Perhaps now began the

inescapable further variation – and pun – on the given name as Barbra Strident became born. A family delving back into early Sixties nostalgia for an early Eighties party is more likely to reach for Dionne Warwick, say, or The Supremes. As for Barbra herself, she refuses to listen to the stuff, explaining it this way in the extended interview she granted *Playboy* in 1977: 'Sometimes when I hear that first record of mine where I'm *geshreying* and getting so emotional, I think, "Oh my God! How did they ever like me?" I'm embarrassed by it.' Judgement at the distance of two decades suggests that, as so often, her instinct may be correct.

The record, to begin with – and in common with all her subsequent LPs – is superbly recorded. (And like some of her subsequent LPs at eleven tracks to two sides, it comes close to giving penny-pinching short measure.) At any given *single* moment, the arrangements by Peter Matz are superb. For example, the strings in 'Cry Me a River' are deployed over a marvellous range, insistently deep, sinisterly shrill; the piano floats shimmeringly over the broad velvet river of brass. Track by track the voice is all these things. Lyrically thin, gutsily fat, the combination of vibrant purity is never quite submerged at either end of its spectrum. You can grasp at once what The Lion regulars heard and saw in her. And yet . . .

Barry Dennen would tell the privileged few to hear those early tapes of his, that it wasn't the real thing: you had to go see her. Sound on vision, that, of course, must have been part of it. These tracks, by the highest standards, won't do. They are – harking back to The Lion – too perverse. Something of the club's febrile ambience, it seems, is crudely and arbitrarily imposed on the songs' natural themes or attitudes. The Bon Soir was more right than not. 'Who's Afraid of the Big Bad Wolf?' seems now not a wittily original variation of a childhood theme but far too close to a precocious brat showing off: 'Hey Momma, look at me!' The lyricism of 'Soon It's Gonna Rain' is overwhelmed by tugged-voice Garland pastiche. The held-back tempo of 'Happy Days Are Here Again' is too unmotivated an attempt to pour a new whine into an old bottle. And the Streisand 'Cry Me a River' in its fierce 'now I'll have my pound of flesh' selfishness is as inferior to the Julie London version as, on her follow-up album, her belted 'When the Sun Comes Out' is

53

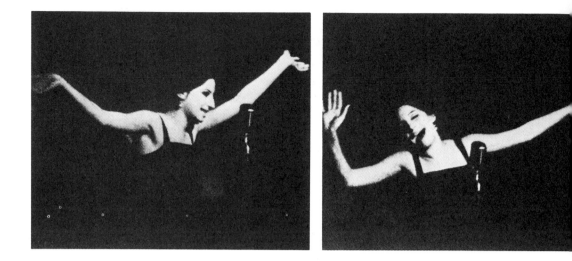

inferior to Mel Tormé's. Even the celebrated 'A Sleepin' Bee' disappoints. Capote's self-consciously ingenious-to-inept lyrics hinder rather than help. The best track on the album (and arguably the best crafted song) is 'I'll Tell the Man in the Street'. It is treated in the straightest way of any, the ballad's spiritual key-signature observed and the voice not forced through too many dramatic detours along the line. Yet even here the unforced echo of Ella Fitzgerald, hinting how *she* might have handled things if she'd slotted it into her Rodgers and Hart, drifts into the mind.

There were not only errors of strategy throughout *The Barbra Streisand Album*. Tactical foul-ups litter each track at every maladroit turn of phrase. It isn't just a question of the overly 'arty' tag to 'My Honey's Loving Arms'. The phrasing is not just out of step with the lyric. It doesn't come within a mile of it.

The reasons for this betrayal of the voice by the mind are not hard to find. In the first place, it is the vocal equivalent of the 'look at me' dress sense. Do anything, no matter what, so long as you get attention! And this approach, understandably enough in a newcomer, was plainly exacerbated by the 'I'm not a singer but an actress who sings' attitude. Encouraged by Barry Dennen ('Who's Afraid of the Big Bad Wolf?' was his idea) this determination to find dramatic nuance at every turn of phrase explains a lot. It has to be mainly inversions, crescendos and diminuendos; the breaths, the catches in the throat. It is not drama, but melodrama. Yet even this is understandable. Barbra Streisand did not walk into Columbia as a singer with a creditable track record. She was not someone who, over years in the clubs, had got down a body of material she was utterly at home with and who had evolved a defined singing persona. Her claim was correct. She *was* an actress. She stepped up to the mike determined on 'being' as much as singing. Style mattered strongly to her, but it is largely dictated by the material at hand. You don't sing 'The Battle Hymn of the Republic' in the same manner as 'We Shall Overcome'. The most enduring recordings have always been those where, with magic, a performer's own style has fused totally with the material. This does not happen with *The Barbra Streisand Album*. The instrumental ability of the voice is unmistakable. But one senses that here is an artist with the same crucial problem of an early Sammy Davis, Jr – prodigious talent married to an enfeebling lack of artistic tact.

All ancient history, of course. Barbra could now cry a river all the way to the bank.

Some comparisons are worth making in the light of two network television appearances she was to make some two years later when her recording career had been firmly established. One was on the *Judy Garland Show* where she sang not only with Judy, but also with the Force Ten *chanteuse*, Ethel Merman. Experienced, secure, with a dreadnought ability to impose her own style on numbers tailored to suit it, Merman could, can, never be upstaged by guest talent no matter how pushy. Garland occupies a unique position in American entertainment. Many of Streisand's fans and virtually all her detractors see Barbra as a direct, lineal descendant to Judy. Their critics linked them as a couple of earth-mothers belting out when all else fails, in defiance of all musical values. In the year that Judy Garland died (the award-laden Barbra was twenty-seven), Ralph J. Gleason, a 'pop music critic', offered this bleak reaction to the younger artist:

> She's untouchable? Well *I* wouldn't touch her, but it's got nothing to do with her talent. She is the last gasp of the New York Broadway Musical. And so is rich, successful – boring. She's the only one under thirty who can listen to the stuff she does. At least she's better than Judy Garland who is the worst.

This over-heated assessment by the less-than-gallant Mr Gleason contributes nothing to the Streisand argument and nothing to the marvel that was Judy Garland. But yes, with all her assurance and sky-high bravura it is plain fact that Barbra Streisand has probably never won the warm public response that poor Judy, her frailties worn tremulously on her sleeve, inspired.

The other show Barbra appeared on at that period was the *Dinah Shore Show*. It is a relevant compass-bearing in the landscape of Streisand's development. The Shore style, gimmick-free, unforced, perfect pitch, timing and phrasing, was a lesson to any singer. All that, plus a willingness to subordinate her own self to the song. Her recordings reveal her as a vocalist able to 'get inside' a song, become not its manipulator, but its medium. Later, a maturing Barbra Streisand must have realised that she too could learn from Dinah Shore how to avoid the short-term imposition of 'self' upon material. But that 'tutorial' was still to come.

There is one particular reason for the vindictive counter-attacking of the Streisand 'Cry Me a River'. She herself has indicated what it was: 'I realised each song is another play, another character. When I used to sing 'Cry Me a River' I had a specific person in mind. I tried to re-create in my mind the details of his face.' She names no name, but the 'specific person' was Barry Dennen. As the initial eleven-week engagement at the Bon Soir drew to a close, there were straws in the wind that Barbra, 'born in Madagascar, reared in Rangoon', might be growing tired of playing Trilby to Dennen's Svengali. The carefree couple who resembled offbeat types straight out of a Neil Simon play were now drifting towards the disenchantment of the later reels of *The Way We Were*.

There was a third character common to both scenarios – the go-between, tag-along, friend and confidant. He was played in real life by Bob Schulenberg, an artist and designer and a long-standing Californian friend of Barry Dennen's. Arriving in New York he was introduced to Barbra that same evening. They were both knocked out. She by the then novelty of air travel making it possible to have lunch in L.A., dinner in New York. He by this incandescent combination of uncertain defiance walking down Sixth Avenue tricked out like a Jewish Christmas tree. He was knocked out by her talent too. And he was excited by the conviction that he had the technical know-how to enhance it. He could do for her make-up what Terry Leong had done for her wardrobe. He examined that asymmetrical, sphinx face and marvelled at its infinite variety of possibilities. Already halfway under Schulenberg's spell, Barbra became an avid pupil for his experiments. Whose face is it anyway? Schulenberg evolved a curious 'workshop' method. He made up one side of her face. She, armed with all the paint, lipstick and powder in the catalogue, went to work on the other side, trying to duplicate the effect. The alchemy complete, she would sit under a small reflector and look in the mirror to see how she had made out. The exercise would be repeated until Streisand produced more faces than a disgraced President. Schulenberg has recalled: 'There were nights when she must have cleaned off her face six times. But she learned the technique very fast because she has finesse. She could have been a painter if she had applied herself to it.'

Ironically it was this preoccupation with the permutations he could work into Barbra's face that precipitated an incident which eventually led to her break-up with Barry Dennen. Striving for perfection, artists sacrifice many things to their art, friendships being high on the list. The ritual which did it for Barry Dennen occurred one summer when he was appearing in a Central Park Shakespeare series production of *Measure for Measure*. It was a big thing in his career. Naturally, he got (according to the records) his girl, his friend, tickets for the opening night. It happened that that was one of the nights when the merry pranksters, Barbra and Schulenberg got hooked on making Barbra over as an Audrey Hepburn look-alike. Pushing the gag out on to the streets of the Village took Barbra's mind off Shakespeare. She and Bob stood Barry up. It was ill-mannered and not a little callous. The mentor who had hefted his recording equipment into the Bon Soir time and time again had the right to expect her in his corner once in a while. It was no way to treat a guy who recorded your songs and kept you warm at night. Eventually that wound healed only to be opened again by Dennen this time, giving measure for measure. He had returned to California to visit his family. Due back on a certain date, Barbra and Bob Schulenberg stacked his apartment with goodies and deli-delights by way of a welcome home. He never showed on the day and night in question. Take 2, the following evening. Now he was standing them up. A week passed without any message. Then suddenly he was there. Her greeting was laconic, throw-away. It wasn't *that* nice to have him back where he belonged. Besides, she had professional problems of her own once more. She wasn't that sure, again, where she belonged.

The booking at the Bon Soir was over. She was right back out on the street again. Only a different street. A street of higher quality. A much tougher street – as

Elliott Gould was to discover in two years or so. Professional life, personal life, Barbra was in the cross-currents, without direction.

Curiously, the Audrey Hepburn persona confected by Bob Schulenberg produced an unexpected dividend. Impressed by the resemblance to Hepburn he had created, he did a sketch of her. Barbra had glossy copies made. These were circulated by Ted Rozar, the first agent Barbra had tied herself to. (Seeing what happened to his client may have made Mr Rozar wonder during his troubled sleep how the hell he let that fish get away!) As a result Barbra was offered nightspot bookings in Detroit and St Louis.

Edgy before, she was now apprehensive. A good way shy, still, of her twenties, she was genuinely nervous about doing something that, Malden Bridge apart, she had never done before – quitting New York. But she had to consolidate professionally. She needed time and space in which to think and breathe. Half-thrilled, half-terrified at 'going on the road' she accepted the gigs. Feigning culture shock – and small girl in big city humility – she psyched herself out of apprehension, drawing on that inner core of self-reliance again. Her act did not suffer. Both cities were wowed by it. She wrote back to say that she was lonesome and in a New York state of mind. But evidently this wasn't so all of the time. Sharing the bill were The Smothers Brothers. She found herself involved in a friendship, particularly with Tom, that was to be sustained all the way to Hollywood and into their respective super-tax brackets. In Detroit she went horse riding and took driving lessons. And, shades of Lee Strasberg, actually went up to meet the sometime idol of a few years back whom she could still impersonate in her sleep – Mae West. But she was still an entertainer in search of a style. She needed, the act needed, the booster shots of Dennen's actor-musician talents. She wrote him on a number of occasions. No doubt for old times' sake too. But on her return to New York the old times couldn't be reprised. By the time Barbra returned for a second run at the Bon Soir, they had stopped living together. *Finita la Neil Simon comedia.*

FIVE

BARBRA STREISAND'S second stint at the Bon Soir was early in 1961. It proved she was smart and quick to learn, adapt, take a hint of an idea, work it up into real substance. The paying customers who remembered the first engagement could detect that this time around her act was tighter, more polished, more thought through. The crews dangling lights and mikes were grudgingly impressed backstage. The directions she gave them were a pain, sure, but they made sense, you had to admit that. The perfectionist that later made grown men want to open the nearest artery, was beginning to emerge. This was the legendary period when the first track from her second album, 'Any Place I Hang My Hat Is Home' might have been a personal anthem. She no longer had the use of Dennen's place. She had no place of her own. Brooklyn was unthinkable . . . Lugging a bed-roll, a portable cot under her straining arm, she crashed out a night here at this friend's pad, a weekend there at that acquaintance's. There was no shortage of offers. She carried assorted keys around with her like a wardress. Some nights she was reduced to camping in some draught-ridden office in an empty, echoing commercial building. It rapidly destroyed the after-glow of a standing ovation awarded less than two hours before. And, inevitably, the time was coming round again when the Bon Soir experience would be over. She'd be out of work again.

But by now she had achieved some kind of breakthrough. She had some kind of grapevine going for her. Even before the closing of the Bon Soir run it gave her a first exposure on television. Phyllis Diller was booked for *The Tonight Show*. Generous again, she put in a word for Barbra. As a result, along with La Diller and Gore Vidal, Barbra Streisand made her television debut on 5 April 1961. It wasn't the greatest. She didn't fall on her face or walk into the scenery; she was, in fact, well received. But Paar wasn't there himself (Orson Bean was pinch-hitting), and it all happened very fast. *Variety* had other matter for its front page the next day.

Still, it was a credit, a straw in the wind. When Mike Wallace's talk show, *PM East*, was getting off the ground as a syndicated, yet poor man's rival to Paar's, Barbra was one name thrown up by the talent co-ordinator. After a tenuous first connection – how do you contact a person of no fixed abode? – she was found and asked to come down and audition for a singing spot. It now became the familiar story. The incredulous looks of the production staff and technicians when this fugitive third witch from a Brooklyn *Macbeth* walked in changed to a different kind of disbelief when she opened her mouth and sang. They put her on that night strictly – to her relief – to sing. On, and off. In this one quick spot she was better than ever.

Overall, the ratings sun did not rise over *PM East*. The programme suffered a sickly infancy. It needed some kind of zap to jolt it out of its 'me too' plastic rut. But the remedy . . .? Not so easy to devise. Except . . . Barbra's off-camera personality had knocked everybody for a loop with its combinations of wit and

Rehearsing her first album

chutzpah, bludgeon and intelligence sandwiched between Jewish rye. You couldn't ignore her. She wasn't an Identikit pretty face like . . . who was that broad last night, you know, the model . . . ? Barbra Streisand in the summer of 1961 became a semi-regular on *PM East*. Not just as singer, but talking yet.

And in the jargon of the trade she was a 'natural'. The alliance of her IQ and perception, with her Brooklyn-smart gift for repartee made her a perfect conversational sniper. She was no respecter of reputations. Then, or now. She turned on David Susskind in one well-remembered transmission when he was expanding on the theme of success, the sweet smell of, in a show business context. A victim of endless hours waiting in his outer office for the finally achieved interview, she gutsily accused him of having a vested interest in ignoring new talent. Susskind reeled in the face of a quality few of his subordinates had possibly shown him: honesty. Wallace, on air, suggested his own programme was itself a showcase for new talent. He received a stingingly realistic backhander from his side-kick. 'Now, let's be honest,' Barbra said. 'Those people don't watch television, not the ones that do the hiring. A show like this just gets the public interested in paying the minimum to see me at places like the Bon Soir.' A smartly calculated balance – honest appraisal and a plug!

PM East was in no way threatening to shade *The Lucy Show* in the ratings. But for Barbra it served the purpose of imposing her image upon the easy-come, easy-go consciousness of one section of the ad-mass sprawled out there before its Zeniths and its Panasonics. Supposing television had seduced her away from singing, reduced her to the level of a TV personality, and she had ended up being to Mike Wallace what Arthur Treacher was to Merv Griffin . . . where could she be today? Hostess of her own mid-afternoon, women-oriented chat show? Married to some harrassed TV executive? A name you couldn't quite put a face to until she showed up to open your new friendly local supermarket? Fortunately, the artist named Streisand is not that easily seduced. In the fall of 1961, Barbra landed herself the showcase, launch-pad of a spot in a brave new revue being staged, well almost, on Broadway.

The venue was the Grammercy Arts Theater. The revue was entitled *Another Evening with Harry Stoones*. The title was guilty of hubris. The revue ran only for one performance. Not able to claim it was ahead of its time (*Beyond The Fringe* was already the talk of London) the show was generally regarded as too long – it had, count them, thirty-eight items! – and too sophomoric. The show could hardly have been that bad. To begin with its eight-strong cast included, apart from Barbra, Dom De Luise and Diana Sands. The former, after twenty years of being rigorously, professionally funny, had inched close to a top-billing entertainer. Diana Sands in 1961 already has *Raisin in the Sun* under her gorgeous belt and would before much longer be the original Doris in *The Owl and the Pussycat* both on Broadway and in London. (The cat's cradle of coincidences linking Hollywood to Broadway would later have as one of its strands Streisand in the film version of that show.) A third cast member was Susan Belink. Not exactly a household name but ask Susan Belling, a highly acclaimed soprano at the Met, about her early professional career and her smiling answer might surprise you. So, there was talent enough on display. Martin Gottfried of the influential *Women's Wear Daily* gave a high rating to the whole project:

A brightly spangled, shiny-new package of talented people came tumbling into town Saturday evening, spilling a real evening's worth of entertainment on to the stage of the Grammercy Arts . . .

But Gottfried was filing a minority report. Joseph Morgenstern in the *New York Herald Tribune* stated the majority, dismissive, opinion:

The show is callow . . . when it deals with children it verges on childishness. When it deals with adults, the material plows but rarely bites the already fallow ground of jokes about psychiatrists, television and rock 'n' roll, turning up routines that are more antic than comic.

Goodbye Harry Stoones. You came and went and almost all of the entire universe never knew you'd been. But for Barbra, superficially, there were a few plums in the cake that had failed to rise. *Variety* can congratulate itself on a perceptively early bit of talent assessment:

Barbra Streisand is a slim, offbeat, deadpan comedienne with an excellent flair for dropping a dour blackout gag, and she belts across a musical apostrophe to New Jersey with facile intensity.

The Turkish-born graduate of Erasmus Hall High was pleased, and angry. Okay, a couple of nice mentions, but before the show stage-fright had caused her repeatedly to run off and throw up. Gone was the mordant incisiveness with which she could ad-lib her put-downs and side-swipes on TV. Confronted by a blocked-out show, the perfectionist in her shrank from parading her real or imagined inadequacies before a live audience. So she was repeatedly sick to the stomach. And for what? One night! One lousy night! Crushed, the girl who was 'an actress who sings' felt Broadway theater, Schubert Alley, fading from view like a mirage. She was cast forever as a singer, period. A *chanteuse*.

But she kept on trucking. Unthinkable not to at that age. If you hadn't made it yet, it's because you don't want it badly enough. Stay with it. Want it harder . . . Immediately there was some good news and there was some bad news.

The bad news was that, whatever stops Rozar might be trying to pull out on her behalf, she was at this time, the fall of '61, getting no place fast with the record companies. Not finding the phenomenon of a spell-bound audience hanging on every note of a live performance relevant to across-the-counter sales, they played safe. And foolish. She was too much out in left field for Mr and Mrs America. This by now familiar reaction almost prejudiced the good news too. She had auditioned for the Blue Angel some six months previously. A booking there rated. As far up from the Bon Soir as the Bon Soir was from The Lion, it was arguably New York's number one *boite*. Parading a large posse of producers and directors among its clientele, it had been the link to the unequivocal big-time of such names as Nichols and May, Dick Gregory, Belafonte. Incredibly, the management had had their doubts. Who would be willing to pay mid-town prices to hear what might have been Carol Burnett's ugly sister singing unfamiliar re-treads from the Cole Porter scrap-heap? The answer, of course, when the booking belatedly happened, was:

everyone in town who could finagle a reservation. The tough, professional audience rose to its feet. Barbra acquired instant honorary membership of their demanding inner circle – and Robert Ruark found a lady able to be to him what the original Blue Angel had been to Hemingway. To one loud-mouthed heckler in the show – 'Hey, ain't you from Brooklyn?' – Streisand was at her best: 'Aren't we *all* from Brooklyn at some time or another?' And all of this against an early-hours background of a bed-roll lugged from here to there and back to the clink of an expanding bunch of duplicate keys.

The *PM East* spots were continuing as well. They brought two benefits, one immediate, the other long term. The first was a place of her own. The production team heaved a great sigh of relief. Here they were, with this semi-regular whom they could never contact! 'Try Joe's . . . maybe she's at Pete's . . . last we saw she was down at so-and-so's pad . . .' The wandering Jewess was making it tough to make her a star. They were at least two moves too late behind every number they called. So here she was, finally, nailed down in a rent-controlled apartment on Third Avenue and Sixty-sixth Street. At $62.70 a month it was not to be sniffed at. Though you sniffed at your peril. The perch was immediately above the kitchen of Oscar's Salt of the Sea restaurant. Essence of halibut, fragrance of old fish-heads floated up through the floorboards. Someone close to the aroma in high summer likened the smell to the stomach lining of an alley cat. Barbara's immediate response was to try and dowse the stench under gallons of paint. She threw herself into painting and decorating the pad with the same frenzy she brought to decorating herself. The aroma persisted. You can't keep a high squid down. Recognising that not paint, nor all the perfumes of Arabia could kill the lingering alley cat, she decided she would need to 'psyche' them out of existence. It was mind over batter, and it worked. Now and again, however, she will look into the beady, accusing eye of a fish, and feel a rising sense of guilt.

The other valuable spin-off from working on the *PM East* was an incidental meeting with Marty Erlichman. Erlichman was then a promising young agent with a small stable of clients and, a rarity among the breed, a genuine interest in the development of his artists' work. Among his clients were the Clancy Brothers who were appearing in this particular *PM East*. By now the executive producer of the programme, the man, in fact, who had rescued it from its early ratings doldrums, was Mert Koplin. He judged that Barbra needed more vigorous, imaginative representation. He invited Erlichman into the audio booth and suggested he hang around with his ears open while she sang. Erlichman entered the booth, emerging later way beyond the ecstasy barrier. Having come, he heard and was conquered. In her dressing room at the Blue Angel shortly afterwards he declared his interest: given the handling of her career he would see she got the attention, the exposure, her talent deserved. Barbra hesitated. She had asked the faithful friend Mr Schulenberg to sit in on the discussion. His reaction was simple and to the point. 'Does he want to change your style, your name, your nose?' 'No, he only wants to take care of the business end and let me be myself,' was the answer. Schulenberg shrugged. 'So what have you got to lose?' he said.

So Barbra signed with the short, plumpish, dynamic Marty Erlichman. He was delighted, and had cause to be. He could sense he had struck gold, unlike Ted Rozar who – at the time – was not unduly displeased. He had already placed Barbra as someone who was right to consider herself hot stuff but was 'too undisciplined for big-time show business'. Well, the Russians sold Alaska and the British turned down California. And Mr Rozar has had ample time to revise his opinions.

Most agents would be delighted with their ten per cent of the Clancy Brothers' gross over the past years. But before long Erlichman had shed all clients except Barbra. Managing her would have to be a full-time job. Agents, of course, like mother-in-laws, are natural patsies for attack. John Gregory Dunne, the journalist and screenwriter, has a story designed to put Erlichman in his place. At the premier of *A Star Is Born* Erlichman kept staring at Dunne with intrigued respect. He was obviously trying to place him – and in a favourable context. Then, says Dunne, the supreme accolade was bestowed. Erlichman snapped his fingers and said: 'I know you. You must be someone's manager . . .' Well, supreme accolade or not, it at least reveals Erlichman's obvious conviction that a manager should be more than just a booker, gofer or hustler. And in recognising it, he took his place in the line of big-brother/father-figures that Barbra Streisand has consistently, irresistibly gravitated toward. To be her manager was not just a case of jousting with this producer, that chairman, for a bigger piece of the action. The biggest priority, as the Barbra Streisand industry flourished, was the need to provide a barrier between her and her own insecurity. Considering the size and depth of that insecurity, even today, Erlichman's success as a barrier-builder puts him in a class of his own. Dunne's implied jibe (that Erlichman had hitched his wagon to a star) is amusing enough at a cocktail party level. But given hijacker's pay-scale for all activities, writing included, Erlichman's efforts when costed out in man-hours, do him credit. Managing Barbra Streisand, like walking on hot embers, requires a faith, skill and a skin you can strike matches on. Erlichman had timed his takeover bid adroitly. Yelta Tessye Marmelstein was about to accomplish for Barbra Streisand what *Harry Stoones* had failed to bring about.

During her big number on the first night of *I Can Get It for You Wholesale*, Barbra's heart stopped when she heard 700 people stirring waspishly in their seats. Had she dropped dead, they would have had to bring in a verdict of 'death by misapprehension'. The audience were riffling through their programmes to check the name of the unknown girl who had taken this so-so show, shaken it by the scruff of the neck, and was on her way to stealing it.

Barbra's involvement in Jerome Weidman–Harold Rome's musical has become an anecdote that bears an uncanny resemblance to an old MGM musical. The story goes she was discovered at the Blue Angel either by the writer turned producer, Arthur Laurents, or by him in tandem with David Merrick. The reality is more appealing. The production team putting the show together had called for an open rehearsal and she simply walked in off the street. Once again she had to thank the always faithful Bob Schulenberg for a tiny assist. It was November. The day after Thanksgiving. The evening before, Barbra had celebrated at his place. He had sent her on her way the next morning with good wishes and turkey sandwiches. So Barbra, the food freak, was well sustained when she walked out on to the stage of the St James Theater to audition.

There is no place on earth more drearily dispiriting than a 'dark' theater during an audition session. The handful of shadowed sceptics out front intoning 'Thank you . . . next!', give the whole ritual sado-masochistic overtones. Barbra, in one of her Technicoloured rag-bag coats, emerged into the wan stage lighting. Director Laurents, composer Rome and librettist Weidman must have exchanged looks to match the lighting. Three minutes later they were embarrassed. Here was a blazing talent, and the book actually didn't have a spot for her! The major roles were cast and . . . well, there was the old maid part of Miss Marmelstein, the plain Jane Jewish secretary, and she had sung that comic love-lorn number from *Harry Stoones* that *was* kind of Miss M., but there was the age difference and while they figured if . . .

In the event they had Barbra in to audition five times. Their reasons were sound, and subtle. They had come to a collective awareness that to cast this star-burst of talent as Miss Marmelstein would be akin to casting Ethel Merman as an attendant to Ophelia in a production of *Hamlet*. The prince could die on stage during Act Two and no one would notice. Yet, not to use such talent . . . In the end professional long-sightedness overcame immediate local difficulty. The mountain would come to Muhammad. Marmelstein to La Streisand. The part would have to be rewritten and enlarged, of course. And tossing theatrical traditions into the wings, they told her so directly. Her reaction was as bizarre as her entrance had been. 'Goody, goody!' she squealed. 'Now I can pay for my new telephone.'

Anyone with no more than a call-boy's flair for talent-spotting could have seen that Barbra Streisand as Miss Marmelstein would filch the golden opinions following the Broadway opening of *Wholesale*. Perhaps a performance gains subtle yet significant points when the performer has everything to gain, nothing to lose. That was the unique position Barbra was in at the time. As one of the two newcomers in the show, if the show bombed she would not have been a major casualty. However brilliantly or crassly played – and she intended to be terrific – the role of Miss Marmelstein could not make or break the piece. That burden fell on the shoulders of the other newcomer, a young man of twenty-two that David Merrick had lifted out of the chorus of Broadway musicals like *Irma La Douce*, to play the juvenile lead. He couldn't really sing, as the original cast recording bleakly confirms. Playing the lead, he really had too much to do too soon, was in a shade too deep, to walk off with any honours. The seven or eight other players in the important roles, might fairly be described as old-timers. At any rate they were 'old' in the sense that, having been around awhile, they might now have had something to prove. Singer Lillian Roth, for example, cast as an archetypal Jewish momma, needed a success to prove that her rehabilitation from alcoholism (unerringly played by Susan Hayward in *I'll Cry Tomorrow*) was complete. Marilyn Cooper, a fine supporting actress, needed to show she could sustain a lead; Bambi Linn, having produced award-winning performances in Rogers and Hammerstein shows, was eager to prove she could duplicate the success a decade later. Sheree North, her talent trapped in the strait-jacket of movie glamor, needed Broadway to expose the shallowness of Hollywood's treatment of her. But none of them, not even Harold Lang who had had enough talent to straddle both sides of the Atlantic in the celebrated revival of *Pal Joey*, ever had a fighting chance. For all the excellence of its source (Jerome Weidman's own mid-thirties novel), *Wholesale* was an indifferent show. For all its good intentions and bright ideas, it fell short of what makes a great musical. It ran some nine to ten months. To listen to the disc is to feel that audiences – or the ticket deals – were unduly charitable that year.

As 'Miss Marmelstein' in *I Can Get It for You Wholesale*

Wholesale is set in the New York garment trade jungle (as Saul Bellow had it, 'just a flat-iron throw away from Broadway'). The main character is a con-man hustler who, young and brash, Sammy Glicks his way to a fortune in the rag trade – and then sinks beneath the weight of unpaid bills and promissory notes. Its title is condemnatory. People who know the price of everything know the value of nothing. It is a musical that, plus or minus a chord and attitude or two, begs to be bracketed with *Pal Joey* or, say, the Kurt Weill – Bertholt Brecht collaborations.

It doesn't make it. The score, clever, accomplished at good individual moments, lacks the spiky rememberability that Weill could manage. At its worst, when, because of the garment industry's ethnic background, it tries for middle-European yiddish melodies, it achieves only Potash and Perlmutter pastiche. The oblique 'syncopation' between dramatic moment and musical comment that Stephen Sondheim has made his hallmark just is not there. It is not a musical you can walk out of whistling the new tune you can't get out of your head.

With one scintillating exception: that, of course, is the 'Miss Marmelstein' number. It may have been reworked in her image, but Barbra Streisand had the good fortune to get the one stand-out number. A love-lorn spinster's complaint that she can't get to first name, first base with anyone, sung (intentionally) in a kind of rum-ti-tum rhythm, it is no musical masterpiece. But sung with attack, and seasoned by Rome's clever lyrics, it has to be, it was, the number you'd walk out whistling. It and Barbra were the combination that had the customers rustling their *Playbills*. John Simon in *Theater Arts* summed up her supporting role triumph:

> . . . stimulating is Barbra Streisand, who makes Miss Marmelstein, the secretary-factotum, a being all good nature and exacerbation. Miss Streisand possesses nothing short of a Chekhovian brand of heartbreaking merriment. Gifted with a face that shuttles between those of a tremulous young borzoi and and a fatigued Talmudic scholar and a body that, by way of protective mimesis, has assumed the shape of any other neatly sharpened pencil, she can also sing the lament of the unreconstructed drudge with the clarion peal of an Unliberty Bell.

It was, in a phrase, an actress's performance. Knock-kneed, pigeon-toed, Barbra embodied that type of wallflower in Life's dance who needs – to desperation – a man, to remedy her condition of mid-twenties virginity. A man, the man, no *any* man (almost) who, on every level can straighten her out. Sent carooming on stage in a castored, swivel typist's chair, her hair a disintegrating beehive that was no longer contemporary and had never been fashionable, she inspired this fine pen-portrait from Rene Jordan:

> Like a masochistic St Sebastian, she stabbed a pencil into her beehive hairdo and showed them Miss Marmelstein to the last bleeding ego wound. In three minutes she made the song into a character study, a psychiatric test, a fever chart of an ailing soul. She was alternately naughty and naive, defeated and courageous, furious and plangent. She muttered asides as if she were getting ready to be carted away to intensive care at Bellevue . . . Finally, exhausted after Miss Marmelstein's painfully hilarious orgy of self-revelation, she broke into a giggle, stifled a sob, and then gathered her voice like a clenched fist, ready to hit an unfeeling world right in the kisser as she pronounced herself ready to bust. It was like a cue for the audience to explode with her, releasing the tensions of the last three minutes of heightening amazement.

As always there are the 'what if . . .?' alternative scenarios. What if, in the casting,

Barbra Streisand and Marilyn Cooper (look-alikes enough from a few rows back) had been offered reverse roles? Barbra's initial delight at copping the lead would have faded swiftly at the realisation that Miss Marmelstein had the one sure-fire song in the show. Marilyn Cooper with her tendency to vibrato did not have Barbra Streisand's clean-edged vocal ability – or, indeed, agility. But she could put a song across fetchingly enough. Her big spot of the evening, the ballad 'Who Knows' just simply doesn't get past the qualifying rounds of the 'great hits' contest. Marilyn Cooper was asked to make *her* impact with a song that echoed her role – conventional and faintly boring. Barbra, however, got the firework display. Her success, that night of 22 March 1962 at the Sam S. Shubert Theater, was marred, however, by what emerged as a bad joke. After the performance, the audience, locked in bottle-necked confusion in the lobby, could now more clearly check their *Playbills* to clock who this new blithe spirit was. This is what they read:

Barbra Streisand is nineteen, was born in Madagascar and reared in Rangoon . . . She is not a member of the Actors' Studio.

The last capsuled biography in the programme, it resurrected an old gag from Streisand's earlier kooky days. Those *Playbill* readers not privy to Barbra's 'born in Madagascar, reared in Rangoon' routine, would not however have missed the barb in 'she is not a member of the Actors' Studio'. At first, *Playbill* had balked at printing the item. They did so only when, with Brooklyn-honed persistence, she twisted their arm. Three months later, when the nightly ovations carried the thundering hint that a star was born, Barbra Streisand took another look at the *Playbill* item. She realised that what she had going for her now could do without this kind of hokum. She changed it to the conventional, and the true. Not yet twenty she was only one role away from being, arguably, 'the greatest star'.

A fascinating appraisal of the Streisand of that time is given by one of her Erasmus Hall fellow alumni, Bob Fern. Reported in *On View* in 1969, it shows a rare insight into the talents of the pupil who was a year in advance of him at school:

It was 1957. *And God Created Woman* had opened at the Astor Theater next to Erasmus and next to that another opening had just taken place: that of the first kosher pizza parlour. Barbra Streisand was a product of the world's biggest high school, the most urban and crowded area in Brooklyn and one of the most middle-class Jewish communities in the world.

I remember her as average-looking, plump with a big nose and a great voice. Other girls described her as 'funny'. She mugged a lot. Also they described her as either 'nice' or 'a really great girl' which meant then what it means now, viz., she was no sexual threat to them. On the contrary she was that cliché of clichés, 'a nice Jewish girl'. And in her first big break she played 'the nice Jewish girl' in *I Can Get It for You Wholesale*. All New York loved her . . . girls her age loved her – she was on *Broadway* and was *just like them* – so Jewish, so *real*. In a school like Erasmus filled with Sandras and Sammy Glicks all trying frantically to make it, when all my friends hated that image, hated the mannerisms, hated the pronounced accents, hated the early balding and the plump matronliness and hated the lack of sensuality that the graceful non-provincial Brigitte Bardot was teasing us with next door, it is an irony that Barbra Streisand made her career on a stereotype from a dying culture. And she made the accent, the look, the forced sentimentality, the harmless mugging and the middle-class urban reality of a Brooklyn high school the trademark of a great star and created a wholly new 'in' style. Everybody else wanted to be David Niven and Deborah Kerr.

The past, then. And the springboard. The passport to the future with the old-fashioned stamp across the mug-shot. Granted that the *Wholesale* role actually demanded that kind of Jewish 'girl next door', Bob Fern's remarks are valuable. They explain why, on the harder rocks of pop music, avant-garde critics have always regarded her as *passée*. His words remind us of origins, a body of material she would one day, as an artist, need to react against.

One day. For the present her self-powered talent was up and away. It was her emotions that concerned her more immediately. The name of the twenty-two-year-old that David Merrick had promoted from chorus to lead was, of course, Elliott Gould.

Rehearsing *Wholesale* with Elliott Gould, her leading man

SIX

For the nine months or so of the Broadway run of *I Can Get It for You Wholesale,* Elliott Gould nightly sweet-talked his ingenue opposite number in a song which began:

> *When Gemini meets Capricorn,*
> *On her way for the IRT,*
> *Maybe coincidence*
> *Maybe astrology . . .*

When, however, the shiny new telephone in the fish-scented bliss over Oscar's fish restaurant shrilly rang one night, Virgo was calling Taurus with a definite end in view. On the occasion of her final, final, final try-out for *Wholesale* Barbra had toured backstage dealing out scraps of paper like a peripatetic blackjack dealer. Scribbled on them were her autograph and new phone number. 'I won't call you. You call me,' she said. 'I just want to hear it ring.' Listening in the wings to her audition, Elliott Gould had been knocked for a loop. He had swooped on one slip of paper as it was about to be pitched into the waste bin. He was now taking her at her word.

The phone rang and Barbra stretched across to answer it . . . Would she have lifted the receiver if she had known for what the bell tolled? That it was ringing for a mad-cap affair and marriage. For separation and divorce and life-long attachment. For a child. For a success–failure range worthy of a manic depressive. But right now it was just ringing for her. Barbra picked it up.

'You said you wanted calls, no?' a voice said. 'You were brilliant today. This is Elliott Gould.'

He hung up. Not bad for openers. Boy Two had met Girl. Barbra had got herself more than a part. She had got the leading man.

Reminiscing nearly twenty years later, relaxed and ramblingly candid in his Los Angeles home on Hutton Drive, Elliott Gould coalesced the two acquisitions.

'I really don't want any credit,' he told us, 'and sometimes I find where people are difficult, like Marty Erlichman discovered her! But I gave her the job. If she hadn't appeared in *I Can Get It for You Wholesale* . . . Arthur Laurents chose me and the first person they asked me to look at was Barbra Streisand. I am the leading person in that . . . They brought her in, all having seen her before, and said, "What do you think?" I said, "I think she's brilliant." So we gave her the part. She wanted to play my girl-friend. My secretary in the show is more important to us than my girl-friend. We made her my secretary.'

Given the soul-searching and mental rewriting that Messrs Weidman, Laurents and Rome imposed upon themselves during Barbra's string of rehearsals, this account is one-side-of-the-coin testimony. Due, perhaps to his wildly alternating graph of professional highs and lows, plus perhaps an analyst-inspired ambiguity, Elliott Gould is occasionally given to contradicting himself. Objectively, the Gould-Streisand 'going together' and marriage has to be seen as a meeting of people who were very, very young. Kids. They were in their early twenties when they met; not thirty when they separated. The welter of published comment about their joint relationship seems overwhelmingly to evaluate it in terms of the two very considerable and mature screen personalities they were yet to become.

Initially their problems were not with each other but with the rest of the cast. The supporting players were cool in their reaction. A kid from among the dancers encapsulated the general irritation. 'Where's Barbra Streisand?' the exasperated ASM was obliged to ask in all directions. 'Try Elliott Gould's dressing room,' the girl acidly snapped back. A 'bit' player only one step up from the chorus herself (as it then seemed) Barbra had somehow offended backstage protocol by apparently setting her cap at the leading man. Put him in her pocket. Moreover, both she and Elliott were looked on more than a little askance by the seasoned old guard in the show. If the leading man stole the notices, well, okay he had chances to and everyone wanted it to be the hit of the year. But if that pushy little newcomer with the nose and manners to match . . .

Barbra was, in fact, compounding the problem. In rehearsal and the pre-Broadway performances, the solo nightclub performer was proving herself a stubborn team member. Searching for improvement she would vary the interpretation of her Miss Marmelstein role, vary the inflection of lines, vary stage business. Good for the final gelling of her characterisation (it was her inspired idea to deliver her knockout song irrevocably trapped in a typist's swivel chair), but it was unsettling for the other players. It was said that she was frequently late. In part this was the familiar pre-performance paralysis at the thought of confronting an audience. But at rehearsals, revisions, the indictment was that she was obsessed more with the redecoration of her apartment which friends were supervising for her back in New York, than with the show. And maybe she was nickeling and diming a pay-phone to death as, while everyone waited, she issued a new order-of-the-day regarding the toilet-seat colour, stressing that they had to beat that painter down some. But the world of grease-paint and celluloid was going to have to learn to come to terms with Barbra Streisand's strict order of priorities. When Lillian Roth kindly and perceptively took her to one side and explained that a certain basic professional courtesy would help everyone and her own cause most of all, Barbra was polite but unresponsive.

A more serious problem Barbra was suffering – and causing – was her own brand of withdrawal symptoms. Faced with hostility from either audience or management as a nightclub entertainer, she had always retreated to that rock-hard core at the centre of her being. No! she would not open her act with the latest mindless up-tempo pop belter. No! she would not grin artificially from ear to ear cajoling, begging the audience to love her. She would stand quiet and motionless, willing the audience into stillness, into appreciation of quality – her quality. Always it worked and they were there, with the bee, in the palm of her hand. Fine. But such a 'grande dame' gambit could not work in the context of the ensemble-playing of a stage musical. In the final rehearsals, and even before paying audiences in Philadelphia and Boston she was clearly under-acting, under-performing. Miss Marmelstein was not coming across with the impact those original auditions had seemed to guarantee. David Merrick – perhaps he *had* actually witnessed that Susskind roasting on *PM East* – was openly talking about letting her go. Rome, Weidman and Laurents stalled, argued for her retention. They'd get her to deliver. But if they were going to make good on *their* marker, somebody had to have the whole problem of her attitude out with her. As director it fell to Laurents. It became a celebrated anecdote . . .

Laurents chose a public moment for his 'shape up or ship out' onslaught. It was before the whole company the flat morning after their near-fiasco opening in Philadelphia. Everyone needed something of a kick in the pants. But Barbra, who had failed to impress the audience to anything like the extent of her potential, was seeded number one as the whipping boy. Laurents, leaning on vast experience and an acerbic wit, blasted at her with all the articulate but indignant fury he could generate in the heat of the moment. Weidman and Rome, seasoned hands though they were, felt themselves blenching. Arthur was going too far. They looked doubtfully across at the isolated victim. She took it, head down, eyes fixed on the piece of paper she seemed to be using to take down these withering theatrical 'notes'. The ordeal over, the two separated. Rome approached Laurents to reaffirm his own belief that Barbra would devastate the audience in her own good time. When she had got her psychic balance. Weidman meanwhile, on the principle that there is always a mean cop and a nice cop, went over to Barbra to encourage, pick up the pieces. He expected to find her in tears. When, however, she looked up from her notes, her eyes were no more than distantly troubled. It was her apartment, you see, its layout. They were doing it right now while she was here – here was the floor-plan, see – and she wasn't too certain they were getting the best use out of the space . . . Weidman recoiled and then delivered a famous judgement. Then and there, he later told friends, he decided that the said 'sacrificial victim' had 'genius plus the one other ingredient necessary for stardom. She was made of copper tubing.'

Elliott Gould was also, of course, party to that grisly morning-after post-mortem. He recalls putting his own rehabilitating ten cents in. 'She'd been brilliant as Miss Marmelstein,' he remembers, speaking of the verve that had captured his attention and sparked his call, 'and then we'd come to rehearsal and she wasn't putting anything into it and she was ready to be fired. I looked at her from the wings and said, "Look, I'm here to learn. I think you're great and I'm going to save your job. I don't see myself having any future as a performer – I don't think I want to. This is the only way I can get myself across and keep working so I'm going to save your job . . . not knowing that it was my job she wanted. I basically gave her the job and kept the job for her, letting my position be taken away." '

Well! There are many things in that statement. The self-doubt and loss of personal direction. The curious implication that her dawn could be his eclipse. That he helped Barbra through this less-than-pleasing patch is probable. To what extent and to what degree she allowed herself to be helped only in directions she had already determined on, is something else. Memory had obviously derailed the leading man's estimation of his part in the drama. So his remarks bespeak caution. When it comes to any (remembered) incident on the Streisand–Gould axis there are four versions. The truth. The untruth. The Streisand recollection. The Gould reminiscence. And some incidental intelligence.

Through Arthur Laurents we have one historical and astonishing fact. At the time when Barbra's stock was lowest among the production VIPs she asked to see him. He imagined she was about to beg to be kept on, to apologise, promise improvement. Instead, pointing out she would be much better in the part, Barbra asked to be given Marilyn Cooper's lead role as the ingenue playing opposite Elliott Gould. He misread her motives, suspecting that being stuck with a lesser, fourth-rate part, she was angling for the better role. Laurents firmly ruled it out. His objections were both ethical and aesthetic. She was left stuck with the sure-fire role.

And playing it she vindicated Harold Rome's forecast completely. Elliott Gould may have provided valuable moral and practical support. The audience in Boston and Philadelphia may have been correct in feeling they had been short-changed. But Barbra had timed her run up to Broadway perfectly. She came to New York like an athlete who has psyched his preparation for the Olympics with hair-trigger precision. She came, she performed, she conquered. She stopped the show.

Gould's own remembrance of things past is an honest play-back of the way things seemed and felt. As *Wholesale* came together, it became obvious, to himself most of all, that he was miscast, too under-experienced to nail down the hustler role of the anti-hero. He wrestled grimly, honourably, heroically with the part but came off, at a charitable estimate, with a dubious draw. 'I was the star,' he now ruefully admits, 'but my work could have been better. I was terribly green and I was trying too hard.' Came the curtain call there was no doubt for whom the biggest, most spontaneous cheers were reserved.

Sardi's is New York's famous theatrical restaurant. Here the mandatory post-opening-night party hangs fatefully on the arrival of the early editions which may herald a triumphant run or read like a recital of the last rites. Well-wishers, the real and the bogus, gleefully table-hop, spilling 'darlings' with glass-eyed sincerity. The heady atmosphere synthesises *All About Eve* and *Death in the Afternoon*. Sardi's at premiere time may well confirm Streisand's dictum: 'people who don't have success hate it in others.' If the occasion, a sure-fire hit, calls for bouquets, when tossed at Sardi's they seem straight out of Eden. But if blood and tears has to follow all the sweat, there are plenty of shoulders on offer upon which to weep. That night, there was only one name on everybody's lips.

The $64 question was how would those established performers, the Sheree Norths, the Harold Langs react in public to being audibly relegated to the wings by an unknown. The $64,000 question – as her mother sat saying, 'That kid of mine. I'd never have believed it!' – was would this girl receive a bigger volume of Sardi applause on her entrance than the show's nominal star? We shall never know. Elliott and Barbra confounded the gossip columnists' copy by entering together, arm in arm. Loud cheers rang out. We can guess well enough for whom. As, in breach of the pre-arranged seating pattern, Elliott Gould led Barbra to the top table, those cheers must have echoed hollowly in his ears.

The two youngsters, she nineteen, he twenty-three, had begun going together immediately after that crisp, 'you-asked-me' phone call. By all accounts, mostly theirs, it was an idyllic romance where the question 'who is bigger than whom?' was lost under the avalanche of fish-scented rose petals. It is unlikely that either party can look back now without a pang or two of wistful thinking. Sharif, O'Neal, Trudeau, Jon Peters – all figure to a greater or lesser degree in Barbra's later relationships. Gould has also dealt himself other queens from the pack. But press both parties on the subject and their reminiscences will run like parallel lines, meeting at infinite ecstasy. They took long walks the length and breadth of New York City. They consumed kilos of popcorn and Hershy bars in cinemas, favouring midnight horror movies about mad scientists, werewolves and monsters rivetted at the temples. Barbra has claimed she fell in love with the nape of Gould's neck, one of the few conventional features in his dark, ugly-handsome looks. He displayed no special preferences for the Streisand anatomy on the sensible grounds that he was turned on by the whole package. Itemised, that covered a flawless skin, a good firm body, fine legs and beautiful hands. A fairly handsome return for a nape of a neck.

He remembers particularly one tender incident which occurred after he had taken Barbra to a late-night movie. 'When we came out it was early in the morning and as we walked home we went to the Rockefeller Plaza where there is an ice rink. We skated for a while and we must have had a snow fight or something. I remember pulling her down on to the ice and rubbing, very lightly, the snow on her face.

'Then I kissed her through it. It was something very tender and special to us. She was,' he declared, 'like a flower that hadn't blossomed yet. I think I was the first person she liked who liked her back.

'I must admit,' Gould has said, 'that the happiest memories I have of Barbra are when we were living together before we were married. We were very dependent on each other then. We lived together, not for any legal reasons.'

And a realist is entitled to point out that that was at a time when both were in work, both earning money. It was a time, being cruel, when both egos could pretend to possessing equal time.

But realists and cynics figured not at all in the young lovers' scheme of things as they pondered the age-old question, my place or yours? In Barry Dennen's (forgotten) case, it had been his. Now as *Wholesale* settled into a so-so kind of run at the Sam S. Shubert, Barbra was keen to make it hers. Elliott, a young bull not wishing to surrender territory, baulked at becoming a permanent fixture among the rapidly mounting acquisitions in the chicly bizarre apartment. As she had once bought clothes, so she now bought objets d'art and objets de junk. The pad might look like a shop but she had an eye. It looked like home, smelled like fish. But eventually, inevitably, he capitulated. Her place. And Neil Simon's spirit reappeared for some quick rewrites tailored to the personality of the new leading man.

'The bathtub was in the kitchen,' Gould remembers (and who could forget such a surefire premise for a situation comedy). 'One night we heard a gruesome squealing and scratching. It sounded like a rat the size of an elephant. I looked under the tub and I saw a tail about a yard long with notches on it, probably to keep score of all the people it had bitten. I closed the door and called the fire department. We used to laugh about it a lot. I look back to Third Avenue with sublime affection. . . and that includes the rat!'

So – Elliott and Babs, those crazy cut-ups, have fun in New York. Nathan's hotdogs. Horror pics *ad infinitum* on television and in popcorn-littered movie houses.

'There was also a lot of stupid talk about the refrigerator we kept in our bedroom that supposedly was loaded with blintzes and gefilte fish. That was bullshit. It was full of Breyer's coffee and cherry-vanilla ice-cream.'

But it was in the bedroom.

Meanwhile, the show had to go on. Eight times a week. The repetition got to Barbra. It was a drag – as the records show. During the nine months of *Wholesale's* run, she was late thirty-six times, an average of once a week. Twice she was reprimanded by Actors Equity. Often she was complained of by her fellow cast members for what she did on stage when she did show up. Unwilling, for better or worse, to stay in the blocked-out rut, she experimented with the Miss Marmelstein role, dropping gestures, adding business, intonations. Harold Rome remembers that she would throw the conductor by altering tempi and phrasing without a by-his-leave. Tiresome though she might find repetition, her solution was just as big a drag to the rest of the cast. She might have claimed to be 'an actress who sings' but she was in no way a born *stage* actress. That was clear if not to her, then certainly to Marty Erlichman. Shrewdly, he had already set up a highly lucrative nightspot tour. If she could just get out of that run-of-the-show contract . . . Forget it. Whatever else, David Merrick knew what was bringing the money in. At a considerably enhanced salary she was at the Sam S. Shubert as long as *Wholesale* retailed tickets.

Win some, lose some. The contender had certainly won that elimination bout with a clearcut knock-out. The New York critics ratified the decision in their *Variety* poll by declaring her 'best supporting actress in a musical'. It was to be, of course, the first award of many and though her nomination for a Tony was an immediate source of friction – none of the other performers in *Wholesale,* leading man included, were 'up' for one – the result was clearly going to be a formality. For Phyllis Newman in *Subways Are for Sleeping.* Barbra's was not the only talent in town and, as she would discover person to person, it never does to take lightly anything that Jule Styne has set his hand to. The Antoinette Perry Award would have to wait for a while.

The Blue Angel, however, could have her right away. Within two months of opening on Broadway she was back there quasi-moonlighting after the theatre performance. Here was relief from monotony. Here, the prematurely frumpish Marmelstein stepped aside for the vibrant, attacking Streisand. Every evening was a 'one off'. Different ad libs, different running order, different audience moods. This was the cut and thrust she had discovered and thrived on and, as she drove her voice over a wider range than the *Wholesale* score, a reminder to the short-memoried entertainment world of the original string to her bow.

Another one was being belatedly added. The original cast recording of *Wholesale* was to at least take her into a recording studio. A second Harold Rome score – or rather, the composer's obstinately loyal faith in her – was to secure her a return visit. He had been present at Sheila Chang's Chinese Restaurant for a three-week overdue celebration of Barbra's twentieth birthday. She was pencilled in for an appearance on the *Garry Moore Show* that was to be built on a Thirties theme. At the party Barbra tried a couple of songs from the period on for size. Rome went home convinced he had heard the voice for the record he was setting up.

It too was to be a birthday celebration. The twenty-fifth anniversary of the legendary *Pins and Needles.* That had been a revue, a WPA project born of the depressed, turbulent labor conditions of the early Roosevelt years. Cast with amateurs from – by ironic coincidence – the 'whole' garment district, it contained some of Rome's best words and music and had run for four years – five times longer than his latest show was to manage. Columbia Records were to put out the revival and Rome now put Barbra's name up. Columbia turned their thumbs imperially down. She was too way-out, too kooky, too obscurely offbeat. They counter-suggested five other singers. But Rome held out for Barbra. He got her the job. And she did it well. She came to the low-budget (and hence short on studio time) session, disciplined and well rehearsed. The actress in her as well as the vocalist was required. The combination was to earn her a particularly prophetic review from John F. Indcox in *High Fidelity:*

> . . . '*Nobody Makes a Pass at Me*', the tale of a girl who buys every product guaranteed to enhance feminine appeal but still remains unnoticed is, of course, an ageless lament. The original version of this, sung by Millie Wertz, was, until recently, available on the Decca label, but that rendition is now completely surpassed by a gorgeously funny performance by Barbra Streisand, a genuine comedy find. Here Miss Streisand sounds very much like a young Fanny Brice; again, in 'Not Cricket to Picket', she sounds surprisingly like Beatrice Lillie.

Rome had opened two vitally important doors for the singer whose talent he so admired, but in a sense they were both slammed in his face. 'After the last night of *Wholesale,*' he wryly remembers, 'she never sang a song of mine. I sent her a whole batch when she emerged as a top recording star and she didn't even acknowledge getting them. I called up and a very fake secretarial voice answered and asked 'Harold who?' I hung up. I'm too old, too talented and too long in the business to take that. We writers have a different opinion of stars. They can carry on up and down and away but they finally have to perform what we do. My wife is, shall we say, more resentful than I am. She feels Barbra is ungracious and, yes, ungrateful . . . I can understand Barbra's point of view. She runs away from the past and she was trying to put that period out of her mind.'

It can also be argued that in her search for identity as a singer, Barbra was to travel away from reviving the hidden gold of the Thirties – Rome, the Rodgers and Hart minor songbooks – for the contemporary modishness, perhaps all-time greatness of Laura Nyro, Joni Mitchell, Goffin and King. Her road, in fact, was leading not to, but away from Rome. Nevertheless, the charge of ingratitude if not ill-manners can't be lightly dismissed.

Wholesale's final curtain was rung down on 8 December 1962. Barbra Streisand found herself free. Elliott Gould found himself without an occupation. Happy Christmas, Mr Gould. For Barbra, with Marty Erlichman having beavered away on her behalf and, interestingly, Arthur Laurents now taking over as coach-cum-cornerman to her nightclub act, the path into the future was broad, obvious and glittering. The Broadway panegyrics, the latest Bon Soir triumph, the television appearances, had powerfully supercharged her career. She was not back out on the street again, but about to go into orbit. For Gould, emerging from *Wholesale* with a Pyrrhic victory, there was no obvious place to go. He was down there looking up.

Mr and Mrs Elliott Gould

For Barbra there were offers to play the best nightclubs coast to coast, the hungry i in San Francisco to Basin Street East via Mr Kelly's. Enrico Banducci, owner of the hungry i became an instant fan. 'My opinion of her,' he said, 'is her own opinion of herself. She knew her weak points and came down on 'em hard; she knew her strong points and brought 'em out to best advantage. Superstar.' As she flashed towards this rarified eminence, her financial rewards exploded into a higher octane rating too. When Liberace saw her in New York he was convinced enough of her quality – his 'people' had previously wavered – to book her as a support act for his upcoming show at the Las Vegas Riviera. The fee was $7,500 weekly. Scarcely chicken-feed. And yet Barbra playing second fiddle to Liberace's brother George even on the durable Liberace's behalf now seems bizarre casting. It is not on record what the pianist was receiving for that season but when, some six years later, Barbra returned to Las Vegas in ballyhooed triumph she had made it seem like pin-money. It wasn't just that the newly opened International Hotel were paying her the production budget of a modest movie. They gave her a piece of the real estate action. Twenty thousand shares at five dollars per, to be precise. That was the buy-in price. By opening night the stock was quoted at fifty.

Coast to coast. In person and on TV. It was now that Barbra made those guest-shot appearances on the Dinah Shore and Judy Garland shows as well as on Bob Hope's and the *Ed Sullivan Show*. The Dinah Shore stint picked her up one fan of some stature. President John Fitzgerald Kennedy who caught the show in Washington was knocked out by the way she lit up his White House screen. With typical speed he invited her to perform in person at the White House Correspondents' dinner. She accepted at the double. In those heady and, as it now seems, innocent days of the New Frontier, she was very much a Kennedy woman. The correspondents, largely from overseas press, found her a devastating dish. Barbra rose, naturally, unforcedly, to the big occasion. 'You're a doll,' she told Kennedy when they met, and when, shrewdly aware she was a rising newcomer of a star, he asked her how long she had been a singer, she cracked back, 'Just about as long as you've been President.' It'll be a moment she can boast of to her grandchildren. But the easy rapport was prelude to a sad aftermath. Dallas was only sixteen months away. When Barbra sang at the inauguration of Lyndon B. Johnson it was with a heavy and politically far less committed heart. The *élan* of that press evening seemed an age, an epoch into the past and utterly beyond recall.

There is no record of that evening, but as with television and live performances, so too was Barbra at last conquering America on disc. It was now that Marty Erlichman's single-minded, single-cliented persistence broke down the mass-market-oriented resistance of Columbia Records' Goddard Lieberson – on Barbra's terms. To his gratified amazement, that big wheel found himself with an LP chart-topper swelling dividends within weeks of its release. And Barbra had become a coast to coast, border to border, household name for the first time, and apparently for ever.

The euphoria did not spread over into the world of Elliott Gould. He sat alone in New York doing nothing. A man facing the most depressing dilemma in the world – no work to go on a Monday morning – he was discovering a truth that many corrugated years later his then ex-wife was to pin down in song – that there was no easy way down. If any way at all. Clearly there could be no going back to the chorus. He could not pack the Blue Angel to capacity on the strength of his voice. All he could do was – via his agent – go the rounds on the leading man level and wait for the phone to ring. It didn't. The silence that falls on an apartment when the phone does not ring stretches out in a lonely grievous row to hoe. For a young man of twenty-three who was up and is now down and whose girl is fêted by day and night as she out-earns a senior executive, the ground is hard on the feet, and the soul.

She had left him to his own devices in the suddenly claustrophobic, suddenly immense apartment while she flew off to L.A., Chicago, paradise perhaps.

'My mate was making it and was very happy about it,' he has since said. 'I had to deal with it and I did.' Yes. Maybe. The coping did not come easy and arguably, for both parties, has yet to stop. Elliott (two Ls two Ts – ironically he can get *his* name wrongly spelled without effort) Gould did not reach twenty-three particularly well programmed for resilience and self-reliance. Born into Brooklyn's lower middle-class Bensonhurst district, Gould (*né* Goldstein) had the classically obverse problem to the growing Barbara Joan. His mother, a penny-pinching drama coach, had set his tap-dancing feet toward show business from almost his earliest conscious days. If not a child star he had been a press-ganged child performer, a child model from nine years old. In retrospect his childhood and early adolescence seem to blur into a memory of being pushed on to a pocket-handkerchief stage to sweatily dance to 'I Got Rhythm'. His agony, embarrassment, arose from a consciousness of his own 'cute' inadequacy. The fixed, glassy-stare grin he was supposed to maintain throughout the ordeal was always beyond his willpower . . . Not the best upbringing to confirm one in a strong sense of one's own identity, or to combat a gloomy Monday, seven days a week. For a while the memory of his name in Broadway lights still glimmered in his mind. That at least gave him the right to go along every week to collect his fifty-dollar unemployment cheque. But the demeaning exercise shrivelled his soul. He reached the point where he couldn't face the depressing ritual any more. Instead he began to escalate his gambling. He made wild, foolish bets while his friends, the bookies, shook hands with themselves and egged sonny boy on. It was a futile pastime. But it did just that. It passed the time. Then, piercing the silence one day, the phone rang. They were asking him to audition for the London cast of *On the Town*.

Seventeen years later, bolstered or bemused by analysis, success and other intimate relationships, Elliott Gould's recollections are worth quoting verbatim and at length. Everything about him, the large mansion, the tactile sense of permanence, the bright smile and the Chablis, proclaimed triumph and tranquillity. But when he spoke, Gould encapsulated the psychic stumbling around, the groping for bearings that clue us in to what was then his personal battle. Whatever else it demonstrates, his account underscores what both he and Barbra were to discover – that all the reserves of love and goodwill between them were not enough to sustain a 'for life' clause on their marriage contract.

I remember [he says] thinking at one point 'when *Wholesale* is over I can't go back to the chorus from here. I can imagine myself going into other fields or finding myself in an area where I can be of use, but after this exposure I can't go back into the chorus. I don't mind being a maintenance man or where I can be doing some good for other people.' But I auditioned for *On The Town* and I remember Barbra and I having a meal and I said: 'I know I can do that show.' She said: 'What do you mean – you know you can do that show?' She's far more a realist than I. I said: 'I just know that I can do that show – I'm not being immodest, I'm not showing off – that's not going to get me anyplace. I just know I can do it.'

She looked at me with such disrespect as if I didn't know anything. They wanted us both to do the show and they wanted her to play the part that Nancy Walker played. I knew that Barbra was on a good run in her career and I felt that the best thing she had going for herself, really, was me. I was interested mainly in her life and in her career. So Marty Erlichman and she and I went to Sardi's because I didn't want her to do anything she'd be sorry for. I also knew that if she came with me that eventually we'd come back home and she'd have to – since she was programmed before we met – that she'd have to do what she had to do so that I could get on with it. Maybe there'd be some life left for us. But still, I didn't know what the answer was. She was being managed before we met and I didn't know one person from the other – there were a lot of bodies and very few people.

So Marty started to holler at me and I said: 'Marty, don't raise your voice at me. I don't *care* about your business. I just care about her welfare in relation to my soul.' I asked her:

'What d'you want to do? Do you want to go? What's more important to you? What's your decision? I'm not going to make a decision for you and you have to make the decision. And I'm not going to allow Marty to make a decision for you. You can make the wrong decision but it's got to be you who makes the decision. I'll be your friend anyway.'

She said: 'I'll go to London with you.'

I tell you, I'm very fast sometimes – too fast for my own good many times. I said: 'I'm very happy that you made the right decision to be with me. And now I'm going to let you do what you really want to do. You're right. The right decision is to come with me but what you *have* to do is pursue your career because I can't do any more for you than you can do for youself. And you're not going to be happy with me there – you're going to come back here and you're either going to be sorry or you're going to have to do something. I'm glad you made the decision.'

So this time it was Elliott who flew out. In the spring of 1963 he was in London to play Ozzie in *On the Town* at the Prince of Wales theatre. The backstage facilities, dressing rooms at this allegedly premier theatre were, he considered, like outhouses – but this was no time to *kvetch*. He was hard at dusty rehearsal work around the same time Barbra was 'playing' the White House. Their exchange of news over the transatlantic line must have required subtly different levels of tact and understatement.

The ocean did not divide them long. Loyal and supportive Barbra insisted on being in London for the opening night. The price tag on that affectionate gesture involved adding the expensive cancellation of a couple of engagements to the cost of the airfare.

Her first trip abroad was to see her best guy in the forefront of a flop.

Elliott, in fact, got tolerably good notices from the London critics. But the production overall did not. It never really had a chance. The film of *On the Town* is one of those 'in' movies whose soundtrack the British film buff can recite from end to end. The show was doomed to second place. Moreover, whatever impression this (to London) unknown was going to make, nobody was going to credit him with matching Gene Kelly's hoofer's grace, Sinatra's voice or the late Jules Munshin's adroitness.

On opening night, 26 May, Barbra Streisand was as fervent a fan as she was a lover. She spearheaded the pro-Gould 'bravos' with a frenzy the rest of the paying customers ignored at their peril. But the crucial Sunday reviews, immune to that assault, muffled the applause to extinction. But Boy was back with Girl again. They drove to the peaceful English countryside, walked hand in hand along deserted lanes. They said nothing about the future, but professional instinct told them both that Elliott would soon have to use his return ticket to America. During this dolorous period they met the artist and sculptor Jason Monet, whose wife was appearing in the show with Elliott Gould. One night, while both were performing,

Monet and Barbra went to the Criterion Theatre to see a show which Barbra loved, *The Owl and the Pussycat*. One part, she felt, she really could play. Just one of the many doors that would, in time, open for her. They seemed to be closing on Elliott. He had struck out a second time. And Barbra had to return to the States. Now everybody wanted her. He kissed her goodbye and then tried to recoup his emotional loss at London's flourishing casinos. They flourished still further as Gould, with the recklessness of the long-distance loser, pressed the wrong hunches. He was twenty-four. He remembers it well:

'The first time I went to London,' he said, 'I left owing a couple of hundred pounds on various gambling debts. I didn't have it to pay. At that time $500 seemed enormous. So I went through some of the best acting I've ever done to escape – made up great inventive tales of why I was temporarily without funds. When I went back, I paid them off.'

On the Town was off in a matter of weeks. Broke, Elliott returned to New York to a Barbra at the height of her hectic flurry of top-name television guest appearances. She now had the sass to announce that in time she'd have a royal flush of entertainment awards – Grammy, Emmy, Tony and Oscar. Well, those bold claims were beginning to sound less like loud-mouthed *chutzpah*, more like calm, studied assessment. When the *Second Barbra Streisand Album* went on sale in the autumn the immediacy with which it was snapped up confirmed that a giant step had been taken toward the Grammy.

Meanwhile Gould returned to a surprise homecoming – a penthouse on Central Park West. Once the home of Lorenz Hart, it was the kind of luxury address that Gould, and Emmanuel Streisand's daughter, had aspired to only in their fantasies. But there was real money in the kitty now. Predictably, the new pad presented Barbra with a wonderful opportunity for set-dressing. But the props came less and less now from thrift shops. The gear-change into 'luxe' must have been a shade less than smooth for a young man owing the London bookies five Cs. It wasn't of course, that he was a kept man . . .

Their itineraries had split Barbra and Elliott too often in the past months. Their 'ad hoc' improvisations to keep up appearances on their occasional location link-ups (this was still the early Sixties: they both had that Brooklyn sense of Jewish propriety peering over their shoulders) had been a drag. At least once, Barbra had put it about that she and Elliott were married – they'd eloped and 'done it' in Baltimore during the Philadelphia run of *Wholesale*! Now they 'did it' for real. Elliott joined Barbra at Lake Tahoe where she was appearing at Harrah's. It was the right state to be in. Barbra had raised the odd eyebrow in the past by announcing she was not of a mind to marry in New York State because the law there recognised only one ground for divorce – adultery. So it was Nevada. The only time in her life Barbra Streisand has, to date, entered into a contract of marriage was in Carson City on 13 September 1963. For both principals it seemed more than a formalising on paper of the status quo. Or so, at the time, it seemed.

There was one ego-salving ray of hope for Elliott Gould – an engagement to play opposite Carol Burnett in a television special of the under-rated musical *Once upon a Mattress*. This would be early in 1964. But, several times cited in photo captions as Barbra Streisand's 'companion', Elliott Gould now found himself referred to as her 'business manager'. It got to him. To an actor who had seen his name in

If you can't join 'em, beat 'em – Barbra developed a style of her own right from the start

Broadway lights, it was an uncomfortable, a demeaning relegation. It was not to be the last. Or the worst . . .

The immediate reason for their wedding had been a cabaret booking at Lake Tahoe. But Barbra's feelings towards nightclub appearances were beginning to sour. Yes, each performance was a 'one off', a challenge But it was still a tread-mill. There was the hassle of upping the caravan and moving it thousands of miles to a new gig. Of settling in to anonymously identical hotels. Of rehearsing on new stages, with unfamiliar musicians.

Fortunately, a fresh wind was blowing across the landscape. In it hung the promise of a wonderful challenge – and the sweet smell of unimagined success.

SEVEN

BEING SMART after the event we can wonder how those preparing to stage *Funny Girl* could have imagined anyone other than Barbra Streisand playing the central role of Fanny Brice. Manifestly, everyone must have recognised how much the two performers had in common. There was the same ethnic and geographical background. The same conventional ugliness, compensated for by a lively challenge not to judge the package by its profile. There was the parallel ascent from rags to Broadway riches through talent and tenacity. Moreover Barbara scarcely needed to audition for the role. Her portrayal of Miss Marmelstein, by design or osmosis, was only a chicken-liver off from being a dead ringer for Fanny Brice. Streisand as Brice ought to have been a foregone conclusion. It was not. In fact, hers was way down on the list of pencilled-in names. And for powerful reasons. The dominating influence of this schmaltzy but intimidating legend of an entertainer extended beyond the grave. Whoever played *her* was taking on more than City Hall. There was her daughter, Frances, an elegant, articulate, classy lady who saw 'The Fanny Brice Story' as a homage to a memory she cherished. And she was married to Ray Stark, the then relatively inexperienced producer who, besides a wish to please his wife and produce a hit, also felt a strong allegiance to his revered mother-in-law. With these factions breathing down the neck of the show, its gestation was more than painful. The ritual dance of pre-production interests was performed to the combined sounds of gunfire and the rasping noise of axes grinding. Its choreography was executed ankle-deep in wept blood.

To begin with, the historical life of Fanny Brice offers little more than anti-matter for a writer trying to come up with a conventional, straight-down-the-middle musical bio-pic. Married at fifteen to a barber, Fanny Brice later married Nicky Arnstein, a man who was at best feckless, occasionally crooked and, at worst, when in old age he figured he was being defamed, litigious. Her third marriage was to the showman Billy Rose of whom it is a toss-up whether his biggest claim to fame is specifically through composing 'Does Your Spearmint Lose Its Flavor on the Bed Post Overnight?', or through the universal sentiment embodied in Fanny Brice's own remark to Ruth Gordon when passing his office: 'Up there is the biggest bastard on Broadway and in my life.' With age Fanny Brice's career, despite her Baby Snooks radio show, drifted towards the anonymity that descends on those who stay too long at the fair. Barbra Streisand herself discovered a sad little fact that speaks volumes for something the two women do *not* have in common: 'You know, Fanny Brice had her nose done when she was an older woman. I found a picture of her. It said: "Fanny Brice just having had her nose fixed so that she could play more leading parts." I find that sad.'

In short, Fanny Brice's life and career do not have the ingredients of an 'everything's-coming-up-roses' happy ending. True there were fine revue possibilities in the great numbers and sketches in the Brice cannon. But her life calls out for a cynical, bitchy, knowing treatment, with a book, lyrics and tunes four times more mordant than *Wholesale*'s. This approach was hardly ever likely to happen. Not while the Starks still held the keys to the kingdom. In launching *Funny Girl*, therefore, in whatever medium, Ray Stark's position might have been comparable to a ship's captain whose wife insists on replacing his charts of a rocky harbour entrance with an air-brushed picture-postcard of the view.

But Stark, a low-key mogul on first acquaintance, is nonetheless a man capable of great single-mindedness. His average height, his pepper-and-salt-cum-sandy hair conceal the tenacity of purpose which was to take him to the top of the pile of Hollywood's powerful independent producers. A force to be reckoned with today, he was at that time one to be dealt with in his capacity as agent. He had represented Marilyn Monroe and Richard Burton. He had all the points and the muscle required for the making of a Fanny Brice stage memorial. On conventional lines, be it understood. And a film. In fact, as early in his career as the late Forties, he had commissioned that archetypal Hollywood craftsman-genius-hack, Ben Hecht, to write a screenplay. It had earned a guarded nod of approval from Fanny Brice herself ('you got some of it straight, kid') but from no one else. Certainly from no studio boss. Nor did later rewrites fare better. On the death of his mother-in-law in 1951 Stark chose to pay a publisher $50,000 not to bring out her, in part, dictated memoirs. Whether there were skeletons in the family closet considered unsuitable for dancing in the bestseller lists, we shall never know. The go-ahead for a 'Brice musical' seemed blocked for ever.

Then, in 1960 (a year after a girl named Barbara Joan Streisand graduated from Erasmus Hall) another writer, Isabel Lennart, came up with a screenplay. She called it *My Man* after the Mistinguette torch-song Fanny Brice had made her own among English-speaking audiences. Isabel Lennart was not far from being in Hecht's league. A precocious Hollywood talent, she had such happy, bland, conventional musicals as *Anchors Aweigh* and *Skirts Ahoy* among her credits. Whatever else, Isabel Lennart had come up with a screenplay that was sufficiently cosmeticised to offend neither Frances nor Ray Stark, nor, if she were still watching, the late indomitable Fanny Brice. Still Hollywood said, 'Forget it!'

What Hollywood itself could not forget was that an early (1933) film based on Fanny Brice's career *Broadway Thro' a Keyhole* had got nowhere fast. A second, in 1938, *Rose of Washington Square* had likewise foundered. Fanny Brice and Nick Arnstein had both sued over Alice Faye and Tyrone Power's portrayal of their thinly-disguised selves and obliged Fox to settle out of court for an undisclosed sum. By 1960 any would-be biographer was faced with one obvious source of potential trouble. Nick Arnstein was still alive. Yet Ray Stark did not throw in his hand. Easy surrender comes hard to Mr Stark. He decided to out-manoeuvre Hollywood by going the Broadway route. Once a theatrical smash, the staging of this rose-tinted family album would provide great pre-publicity for a film. *My Man* (or whatever) could go the same route as *West Side Story*. Fine. That is what ultimately happened. But, short-term, the plan bore one major risk. The theatre was not really Ray Stark's medium. Well he would cross that minefield when he came to it. Meanwhile the immediate need was to have Isabel Lennart re-work her screenplay into a stage 'book'. Speedily, she did. A born packager, Stark used this nucleus to create a production team. The pocket-battleship composer, Jule Styne, would compose the original music. The youngster fresh from *West Side Story* triumphs, Stephen Sondheim, would write the lyrics. Vincent J. Donahue would direct. Mary Martin, everybody's favourite Broadway musical lead, would star. The fact that casting Mary Martin as Fanny Brice was even more bizarre than casting Leslie Howard as Rhett Butler (Miss Martin had recently triumphed in *The Sound of Music*) seemed to bother no one. Except perhaps Stephen Sondheim. After a few days he announced that, while he gave second place to no one in his adoration of Mary Martin, she was so patently miscast in this project he preferred to wash the whole venture right out of his hair. He went off to do his own thing. And with tolerable success.

Stark went off to consider. After a three-month moratorium he was back with a new provisional package. Jerome Robbins, *West Side Story*'s success still glowing about his reputation, was interested in directing. The lead would go to Anne Bancroft. Anne Bancroft's star was then close to the zenith from which, in quality, it has never since declined. An actress of consummate technique and feeling she had spent several years on Broadway compensating for the criminal manner in which Hollywood had mishandled and miscast her. In works as different (though by the same hand) as *Two for the Seesaw* and *The Miracle Worker* she had won golden opinions and awards. Her skill and intelligence apart, she also possessed what Fanny Brice and Streisand did not: the flawless bone structure of a classic beauty. Frances Stark considered aloud that she was the perfect choice to portray her mother. Bancroft, for whom comedy can be a very strong suit indeed, was, then at least, keenly interested.

Meanwhile, as part of the premium involved in playing away from home, Ray Stark went into partnership on the production with the Broadway giant David Merrick. Merrick had ideas of his own on casting the lead. The irate producer who had been on the point of sacking that wayward performer named Barbra Streisand from his *I Can Get It for You Wholesale*, now urged Jule Styne and all the Starks to go down to the Bon Soir and check out a young singer he thought sensationally right for Fanny Brice. Part of Mr Merrick's acknowledged class is not bearing grudges.

The parties took his advice. As author Rene Jordan had it, the Starks were not impressed. 'I'll never let that girl play my mother!' Frances Stark announced. Somewhere along the line Marty Erlichman overheard Mrs Stark's husband mutter: 'She's terrible. Look at that chin. She'll never play my mother-in-law.' Jule Styne, by contrast, was knocked out.

As a child, the composer-producer Jule Styne had been an infant prodigy appearing at the piano with the Chicago Symphony Orchestra. He had matured into an *enfant terrible* that even equal talents tangled with at their peril. Like Stark, he possesses ferocious single-mindness, and with close to fifty stage hits to his credit he has the proven ability to translate this quality into a finished product. His ongoing involvement in *Funny Girl* was a major factor in the show's evolution. His ear and eye for talent was a prime cause of Barbra Streisand being, eventually, cast. Styne is too disciplined a creator to fly off on impulse. By his own account, before deciding on Barbra as Fanny Brice he visited the Bon Soir twenty-seven nights out of twenty-eight (thus upping his record: twenty-six visits to see Sammy Davis Jr, before choosing him for *Mr Wonderful*). On that twenty-eighth day he rested.

Convinced. Anne Bancroft was still the official Fanny Brice, but Styne, caught in a no-man's-land of musical styles (*Funny Girl* was not geared to Fanny Brice's original material), began to compose the score with Barbra's extraordinary range and musical personality fresh in his ears. She was the direct inspiration for the songs he began to note down. When, following a chance Palm Beach meeting, Bob Merrill, the composer-lyricist, offered to put words to four tunes speculatively (a verbal agreement can be worth the breath expended on it!) the Sondheim vacancy was taken care of. Fragments of those lyrics are now nurtured by just about anybody who owns a stereo system. Shortly afterwards, at a meeting in the Beverly Hills Hotel, Merrill's involvement was formally accepted. Those four songs gave the projected show its first tangible ingredient. It also gave it a problem.

Anne Bancroft attended that meeting. She has, it's generally known, a pleasant, tuneful singing voice. A brief appearance on English television with Mel Tormé proved it. But great actress though she is, as a singer she's no Streisand. She had met with Styne and sung for him while he set keys for her. But at that meeting, listening to his work, she sensibly realised she was being asked to swim out of her vocal depth. And just as sensibly she pulled out.

A policy tug-of-war now occurred. Ray Stark wanted the music simplified so as to allow a maximum choice of performers. Styne and Merrill, however, argued for the inserting of more steel into the diplomatically soft-centred book Isabel Lennart had been asked to produce. Stark, in the end, gave some ground. The musical would remain in the established (Streisand) mode. A *degree* of historical truth would be fed back into the book.

For Isabel Lennart, finding the ideal compromise between historical fact, tactful veil-drawing and theatrical impact was impossible – a treadmill of ongoing torture. Styne was pulling ideas out from under his quasi-producer's hat with a vengeance. Soon everyone else was chipping his or her ten cents in. Ray Stark had hired author John Patrick to come aboard in the role of play-doctor. Patrick had Stark's ear. It was he who had written the screenplay for Stark's (at that time) sole box-office success, *The World of Suzie Wong*. The story of a Hong Kong prostitute with a heart of gold had cleaned up in the course of giving the world's middle-class its vicarious thrill. It was this straight-down-the-middle box-office touch Stark now looked to Patrick to harness for the story of his wife's formidable mother.

Meanwhile – months were passing, Barbra Streisand was Miss Marmelstein no more – the hunt for an 'actress who could sing' continued. Eydie Gormé had the voice, the looks, but not the inclination. She did not want to break up her double act with her singer-husband, Steve Lawrence. Carol Burnett was approached. To her eternal credit she came back with a fast 'no thanks' on the grounds that 'You need a Jewish girl to play this. It's a whole different quality.' Miss Burnett, in fact, was doing herself an injustice. One has only to see her brilliant character cameos to recognise she might have made a fine Fanny Brice. The name game continued. Latest favourite was beginning to seem like Shirley MacLaine . . . but that, surely, was like returning full circle to Mary Martin.

It was then that Styne persuaded Jerome Robbins to catch Barbra Streisand's act. The professional in Robbins was even more galvanised than Styne had been. He immediately saw her potential. 'My God,' he is on record as saying, 'she's got a crop of bad habits but there's never been anybody in my time who sings like that.'

He did not require another twenty-six performances to confirm it. He invited her over to read.

Barbra, of course, had known full well that she was being clocked from time to time. But with top-notchers like Styne and Robbins doing the marching and counter-marching, it inhibited her not in the slightest. She arrived for the reading with Robbins in a determinedly 'playing hard to get' mood. Her thrift-shop Cossack uniform added the militant touch. As Stark rolled his eyes to heaven, she failed to give Robbins what he was looking for. But Robbins persisted. He arranged a second meeting. There was an open scene. 'That's not it, Miss Streisand,' Robbins protested as she interpreted an emotional scene that required her to weep. Barbra rounded on him shedding not tears from her eyes but looks that might kill. 'With words like these who can cry?' she said. Isabel Lennart stood up to applaud even as Ray Stark sighed 'You see, you see?' to anyone who would listen. But Robbins had not heard him. Privately he agreed with the actress. Her perception, allied to the talent she deployed was decisive for him. Pulling his director's rank he forced the casting issue. Barbra Streisand was cast as Fanny Brice.

In the words of a Jule Styne song it was just in time. The umpteenth set of rewrites on the book was now delivered. Aimed at resoftening an interim 'unpleasant' version, they were in no way pleasant to Robbins. He quit. Once again the project was far more 'off' than 'on'. For Styne it was not the end of existence. He had more than one iron in the fire. He offered Barbra a part in another musical in which he had an interest. Interestingly she said 'no'. Either the possibilities in the role of Fanny Brice or the determination in the soul of the son-in-law had impressed her. She wanted to be sure the venture was certified as dead before committing herself elsewhere.

And Stark was returning to the mound. He now signed a youngster fresh from the co-directing triumph of *Little Me*, Bob Fosse, to direct. Fosse worked for four months on score and book as the lurching project began to pick up pace. But Stark was far from sure he had backed a favorite. According to one account he privately asked a professional friend of Fosse's whether Fosse really had the stuff. The friend called Fosse. Fosse resigned, and went off to do his own things. With some success. The first of these was a stage musical then called *I Picked a Daisy*. Later it was to be known as *On a Clear Day You Can See Forever*. Ill winds have their virtues.

Still Ray Stark pitched. He brought in Sidney Lumet. Then Mr Lumet, for reasons best known to the principals and their advisors, withdrew from the fray.

And still Stark kept pitching. Enter Garson Kanin. As a director (as opposed to a writer or wife-chooser), Kanin could hardly be counted at the time among the favourites of the day. A Bob Fosse Garson Kanin is not – and vice versa. But, vastly experienced, he had one great virtue. He had known Fanny Brice as a friend. And he had this conviction about Streisand with which no one would have quarrelled: 'The show is going to stand or fall on Barbra. The book is not very good and will never be great. The score is fine but it's not *Guys and Dolls* or *West Side Story* or even *Gypsy*. But you have a nova, the astonishing theatrical adventure of the birth of a star. If we can explode Streisand in the Broadway sky, we have a hit.'

There was further ritual dancing required. Kanin and Styne had worked together on a previous show and had agreed to disagree. Now they had to harmonize for a while before things again became disagreeable. Director and star had to meet as well. Kanin had checked Barbra out at the Basin Street East. Now he sat down to lunch with her. Lunch was fine. Each approved the other, which was just as well. No one at this date can be certain which of the pair was up for inspection by the other, which had power of veto in the event of instant antipathy. Irrelevant now – no veto was necessary. The show was at last off and running and the Byzantine complexities could be neatly resolved in that distillation of truth – the press release. Ray Stark was able to announce officially (whatever that means) that a friend had shown his wife a picture of Barbra as Miss Marmelstein and she had immediately seen the resemblance to her mother . . .

So far, so bad. The show that was finally on was now off again. Kanin's version of the life and threatened death of the barely-born *Funny Girl* goes this way: 'Merrick and Stark had quarrelled,' he remembers, 'and David was out. Through some Actors' Equity technicality Merrick had signed Barbra's contract because he was the established producer and Ray had never had a show on Broadway. Barbra was thus not bound to Ray any longer and he was so tee'd off with all the politicking that he was ready to quit, go back to L.A. and try the movie route again. I stayed on the phone all night – literally – trying to appease both parties. I couldn't let this show fall apart. I owed that girl her big chance [*sic*]. Finally Stark had to negotiate the contract with Barbra from the beginning and by this time she had Styne and me behind her so she was able to get a much better financial deal.'

The squawking infant breathed again. Styne could at last feel safe in sitting down with Barbra to fine-tune her personal numbers – virtually most of the score. He was intrigued by her reaction. She did not care for 'People'. Her favourite song was 'I'm the Greatest Star'. The impression now was less of *chutzpah* but of a penchant for documentary truth. But it was a minor gesture of artistic concern. The bigger problem was that the wheeling-dealing, the crossfire, hadn't slackened. Maybe this kind of flak sparks up in the gestation of any theatrical enterprise worth a row of beans. *Funny Girl* was conceived as an important, maybe significant Broadway landmark. The versatile talents deployed in its creation were gifted individuals raised on the in-fighting which inevitably results from a creator jealously guarding his, or her, interests. But it is worth taking time out to point up the significance of these clashes of egos, ideas and conceptions in relation to Barbra Streisand. Her road to unquestioned stardom was littered with the debris of shattered schemes, greased with the sweat of many disappointments, signposted with misleading arrows.

But the show – at any rate the rehearsal – was on. On the morning of the third day it was nearly off again. Stark was unimpressed by what he had so far seen of his leading lady. Which was not much. He had chosen to look in on her, commuting from Puerto Vallarta, Mexico. It was there that his film of *The Night of the Iguana* was before the cameras. He returned to New York with his head full of Richard Burton and John Huston, engrossing preoccupations for any producer, any time. When he failed to see in the elementary prosaic phases of blocking out *Funny Girl* the relatively finished look of film dailies he began to get the uneasy thought that maybe he was backing a turkey. And Streisand wasn't projecting. *And* she didn't look like his mother-in-law! Once again Kanin was obliged to earn his money less as director than diplomat. Saying 'wait and see' he kept the rehearsals afloat – if largely at sea.

Isabel Lennart was mainly in the firing line. Rewrites came as swiftly as fresh coffee. It was beginning to look as though the show was to be no more a blow-by-blow account of Fanny Brice's life than, say, the Michael Curtiz–Errol Flynn swashbuckle is of Robin Hood's. Fanny Brice was a point of departure. Barbra was evoking rather than duplicating. Increasingly she was feeding lines, bits of business from her own upbringing into the creative 'pool'. The mingling of Life and Art was becoming amazingly and consciously convoluted. Two Jewish New York heroines travelling from rags to riches. Two under-fulfilled gambling husbands. On the occasion of their first wedding anniversary Elliott had given Barbra a blue marble egg. She had been touched by all the intimacies it implied. Too embarrassed to answer her mother's question, 'What did he give you?' – 'Money,' she had thrown away. Now, however, she had the incident written into the show. A reference to it would set up the final curtain. The title *Funny Girl* had been a farewell present from David Merrick when Ray Stark had been unable to secure the rights of the show's original 'little song', 'My Man'. It was becoming increasingly clear which comedienne the new title would call to mind.

Even for a cenotaph the production was proving unusually hollow. Others in the cast began to resent the degree to which Garson Kanin appeared to be allowing himself to be manipulated. Kanin's own statement, however, makes his attitude clear. As Damon Runyon would have put it in his contribution to Broadway legend, Kanin, when it came to backing favourites, was putting his shirt on a certain filly because it was nothing but a boat race and everything in it was as stiff as a plank except this certain horse.

Probably the stiffest plank in *Funny Girl* was Sydney Chaplin, the leading man. Again there had been casting re-thinks on this role. Frances Stark's viewpoint prevailed. She had objected to the talented Jerry Orbach because she did not like his posture. Sydney Chaplin could at least stand nicely. And there must be some residual goodies in the bloodstream of a Chaplin. If there are, they didn't show up in *Funny Girl*. And in any event both bloodstreams, his and hers, displayed violent rejection symptoms when the two volatile personas were presented to each other. Kanin found himself handling two leads who took a healthy dislike to each other from Day One. Chaplin, an actor who had still to achieve the distinction of which he once seemed capable, could scarcely sing. He could swear though. Profusely. Hardly a moral condemnation these days. Elliott Gould was no slouch at the game either. But perhaps surprisingly, given her early raw environment, Barbra Streisand can be highly selective in her recourse to four-lettered conversation. She finds it intellectually slack. Certainly she found what from a friend she might have tolerated, offensive from Chaplin's mouth.

Chaplin, to be just, had his problems. An actor who did not sing, he was finding himself close to being without a part. As the diminishing company (one role had already been written out completely) set off for Boston he was threatening to quit unless given more of a sympathetic crack of the Arnstein whip. The last scene in particular, he demanded, should be rewritten. He was promised it would be. The promise was honoured – forty-two times, in bloody fact, before the agony prior to the Winter Garden was over.

But agony was now what that Boston scene was all about. According to whom you talked to, Styne was at daggers drawn with Carol Haney the choreographer,

Kanin with Isabel Lennart. 'Holocaust time' was the way one onlooker described it.

Finally, on 13 January 1964, *Funny Girl* was performed for the first time before a paying audience. It over-ran by better than an hour.

'After the curtain came down,' John Patrick remembers (it had fallen at 1.45 a.m.), 'we all sat around a large table in a restaurant. For some reason I was chosen to read the reviews. They weren't good. Barbra was depressed. Isabel Lennart bowed her head on the table and cried. It was not the happiest of evenings.'

But the show – or the rewriting of it – must go on. And, with more blood, sweat, tears, sleepless nights and benzedrine, it did. Like so many plays the key problem (among hundreds) was the second act. The castrated characterisation of Arnstein offered no confrontation. It lacked credibility and conflict. The show was in danger of closing.

As Jule Styne remembers it, 'We had the dénouement with the trial, the lawyers, the whole thing, even a scene in a hospital. That way the second act came on stronger because we showed Nicky's shortcomings, but Fran Stark did not want us to present her father in that light. We lost five songs that way, including a very moving lullaby Arnstein sings to his baby daughter. After a couple of tries the second act songs for Nicky Arnstein had to be discarded. I don't regret the loss because Chaplin couldn't sing them.' In all no fewer than *twenty-two* songs were tried on for size and discarded. It's worth homing in on one 'gem'.

'They started to plug gaps with production numbers,' Patrick wryly recalls. 'Stark started to spend money lavishly on quite tasteless things. There was a number in which the chorus girls were dressed as babies and spread out in a line on their backs. Then Barbra, dressed in diapers, sang something called, I think, "How Do You Tell Little Boys from Little Girls?" The number opened and closed in one night at a cost of some $10,000 in discarded costumes, scenery and orchestrations.'

Or, if you prefer, you can take the Kanin version: 'The song was called "Something About Me Is Different". It was a charming number, but it was sabotaged by those who hated it – Bob Randolph who did the scenery and Irene Sharaff who did the costumes. They never came up with the right look for the number.'

Bubble, bubble, toil and trouble. It seems as though the entire company must have been saluting each other with quotes from the off-limits backstage tragedy.

In the midst of this farago, the still quiet voice of authority was briefly heard. Kanin's wife, Ruth Gordon, co-doyenne with Helen Hayes of the American theatre, had been watching from the sidelines. When Ruth Gordon takes a seat in the orchestra, the shades of Maude Adams, Gregory Kelly, Tyrone Guthrie, Charles Laughton are hovering near. Miss Gordon produced an observation concerning Miss Streisand that may still be the best compressed critique of the younger actress's phenomenal career. 'She's great,' she one-lined, 'but she's not yet good.'

Not yet, perhaps, but in one regard she had vastly improved. She was no longer the moody, ill-disciplined, self-preoccupied individualist of her *Wholesale* touring days. Her work-rate now was prodigious. While Marty Erlichman began to proclaim out loud that his client had turned down a million dollars worth of nightspot contracts for the privilege of appearing in a sure-fire turkey, she continued to give one-hundred-and-one per cent of herself. She almost seemed to thrive on rewrites, despite the nightmarish difficulty of having to erase previous combinations of lines and moves from her mind. Marginally tightened, the show moved from Boston to Philadelphia. There, her stamina and patience proved superior to John Patrick's. He quit. Stark immediately flew in veteran writer Norman Krasna. Isabel Lennart now had another creative input to galvanise her energies or blow the fuses in her mind. Thick, fast, contentious, the rewrites continued to rain down like leaves.

Stark by now was wishing he'd taken Chaplin up on his early offer to walk out. Instead he sent presents to the Kanins. An expert on theatrical war-games, Garson Kanin expected an early announcement that he had been fired. Accounts vary widely and wildly as to who felt what. Barbra, for instance, is quoted as saying that his un-emphatic, passive approach to directing left her feeling lost in a vacuum and that she welcomed Kanin's going. But she is also quoted as saying that after an initial disquiet at Kanin's unobtrusive approach she realised he was just giving her time to develop at her own rate and make her own discoveries. She was sorry to see him go. Styne maintains that Kanin exited as if in search of S. J. Perelman's immortal solicitors, White, Lipped and Trembling. Kanin himself claims that, owning a healthy chunk of the show, he was content to bow out. He appreciated that the time had come for a fresh, more objective eye. He would not, naturally, have stepped amiably aside for anyone but his replacement who was, he knew without doubt, an 'authentic genius' – even, perhaps, a very clever genius. The replacement was Jerome Robbins. Stark had gone back to him on bended wallet. And the general consensus seems to be that Robbins proved to be more than worth his weight in folding money. He saw the wood for the trees. He saw, for example, there was too much dross intruding upon Streisand's pure gold. Equal to equal, eyeball to eyeball, they horse-traded ideas and the show took on a leaner, tighter look. One fresh Robbins insight was in the handling of Chaplin's 'You Are Woman' number – virtually his *only* number. Originally it had been played straight; the intention to achieve a mood of romantic sex. It had come across embarrassingly coy, and had got sniggers. Barbra's instinct as the silent partner had been to guy it. That had got positive laughs. Robbins now saw that it must not be a solo but a counter-pointed duet. He had Styne and Merrill execute an instant ice-pack rewrite. A good moment had become a high spot. But the Robbins rescue operation took time. The New York opening was postponed as the company moved across Philadelphia for an additional three-week shakedown, throwing ticket arrangements for a royal loop. As the show finally came into town the essence of showbiz humour – something disastrous happening to somebody else – was perfectly expressed. The prognosis was dire. Merrick, the smart-mouths said, had gone while the going was good. The theater would be dark inside a month. Forget that the great single of 'People' was making it big. That was just PR on its desperate knees. But those same hard sellers insisted this show was going to be an all-time smash, you'd better believe . . . Most did. Perhaps even the cast. At ten-to-seven on opening night (26 March 1964, at the Winter Garden) with the curtain just forty minutes away, Robbins had them on stage rehearsing a new version of the last scene. Barbra had learned it that evening. When she and Chaplin played it to the first night audience some four hours later, it was for the first time. By then, though, they could both be certain of the tumultuous, twenty-three curtain-called ovation she was on the verge of receiving. Twenty-three curtain calls – just four short of the number of visits Styne had paid to the Bon Soir.

No need now to reprise the general reaction to Streisand's starring assault on Broadway. Overnight, the town was bulging with experts who had – didn't they tell you? – always predicted a smash. We will let one review, in the *Village Voice* synthesise the ocean of superlatives which flowed into Sardi's in the early morning hours, bearing Streisand, who had stayed up all night to find herself famous, to the crest of unequivocal 'greatest stardom'.

Yes, Barbra Streisand is all they've said she is, and fairly often in *Funny Girl* she finds opportunities to do her stuff. As a performer she represents a remarkable and rare meeting between a common touch that leads us all to identify with her and a show-business sheen that makes her our ideal. When both are going at once, the effect is thrilling. *Funny Girl* is a perfunctory musical with, *sans* Streisand anyway, not much reason for being. The story of Fanny Brice is too simple to make a real plot and its few possibilities for conflict are left wholly unexplored.

So the verdict from out of Barbra's former stomping ground.

Backstage on the opening night of *Funny Girl* with Fanny Brice's brother, Lew, (left) and her children, Frances (Mrs Ray Stark) and Bill

Looking back, it has to be said that with *Funny Girl* Barbra Streisand, as well as being multi-talented, was extraordinarily lucky. Her previous Broadway appearance had been in a mediocre show. Its general indifference had provided an ideally dull setting for her brilliant cameo of a show-stopper. Now that situation was magnified by a factor of one hundred.

Funny Girl is another mediocre musical – as the crosses born by Isabel Lennart have testified. As regards the book, neither she nor any of her helpmates was able to produce a silk purse out of a soured experience. Styne, of course, is no slouch of a tunesmith. It has been said that a fair proportion of the world's population was conceived to one or other of his more seductive compositions. But he is not in the front line of the great musical composers. *Funny Girl* is not a show that will be revived with the frequency that *Pal Joey, Kiss Me Kate, My Fair Lady* are.

Nevertheless the show was a sturdy enough peg for Streisand to hang her talents on. In its steady, inevitable progression from Brice-fest to Streisand vehicle, the show had become a stunning shop-window for a bravura display of the living performer's talents. Seizing her opportunity with every fibre in those talents, Barbra deserved every last handclap in that opening-night ovation. A merely gifted performer would never have risen above the avalanche of disasters and in-fighting which beset the staging of *Funny Girl*. A lesser performer could never have dominated them to score that triumph. Against his own hunches, Ray Stark had backed a favourite and in reaching the wire first, Streisand left the rest of the field still turning into the home stretch. With virtually no rival for the honours, Barbra left Sardi's knowing for certain that as the delicious day wore on she would have no rival as a talking-point either. Only Walter Kerr was immediately able to put this solitary triumph into perspective. Writing in the *New York Herald Tribune* he observed:

> One other reservation must be entered. Miss Streisand is pretty much alone now which means that she carries five of the six second-act numbers. The returns have got to diminish. The star's passion has many colors, her phrasing has many colors, but her voice does not have *that* many. One feels that the management is trying to cram an entire career into one show . . . inspiration wanes and craft must do in its place.

A cautionary note perhaps, but a shade niggardly to someone who had New York at her feet before her twenty-second birthday. Nothing, no one could rob Barbra of the glowing conviction that, say what they like, *she* was the show. For a while, anywhere she hung her hat, was party time.

It was not party time, of course, for everyone. As the blare of trumpets on Broadway died away one sour note intruded. It was to re-introduce Barbra to her former mentor and room-mate, Mr Barry Dennen.

Having lit out for Europe for the almost mandatory American-in-Paris stint, Bob Schulenberg (as so often before he was the 'best friend' go-between) returned to New York to discover Barbra the *Funny Girl* talk of the town. After seeing the show he fought his way to her dressing-room through a thronged backstage crowd.

'I was amazed,' he had recorded. 'The paisley walls, the black leather chairs, the plants . . . it seemed that I was back in Barry's apartment on Ninth Street. It looked exactly the same. The first thing Barbra wanted to know was whether Barry had seen her playing Fanny Brice.' And if not . . .

Schulenberg duly reported that Dennen, still struggling to make it as an actor, could not – at Broadway prices – afford the price of admission. It was not a problem he had for long. Shortly afterwards Barbra called Dennen offering him a free seat and the invitation to come and visit backstage after the show.

Dennen admired her performance. But going backstage he encountered a piece of embarrassing unpleasantness at the stage door. The doorman had not been given his name among those chosen for an audience with the 'queen'. Dennen had to insist his way through. The meeting, designed to paper over the cracks of an old love, did not, according to Dennen, pick up from this awkward prelude.

'When I got to see her,' he has recorded, 'she seemed very wary. I told her she was very good in the show and thanks for the seat. We chatted and then she asked me if she could have copies of the tapes I had. I told her I would play them for her any time she liked, but although she was now very rich and could afford to buy almost anything she liked, she did not, and could not, *own* those tapes. I felt very manipulated and we both got upset. Our meeting was not a success.'

Schulenberg, present as a kind of honest broker, could not save the evening or the relationship. He looks back in sorrow: 'I had engineered that meeting and I felt terrible hearing Barbra tell Barry that the tapes belonged to her since her voice was on them, and Barry very calmly countering they had great sentimental value for him; that they were the only thing he had left from their past.'

Tapes apart, *finita* everything. We can be sure that the number in the show which made the most lasting impression on Messrs Dennen and Schulenberg was 'Who Taught Her Everything'.

EIGHT

AFTER THE the triumph, the glittering prizes. Two weeks after the opening of *Funny Girl* Barbra Streisand was quasi-officially elevated to the American peerage. Her photograph appeared on the cover of *Time*. So, be it noted, had those of Schweitzer, Kennedy, Sinatra and Dayan. Now Streisand – prestige was riding high with the panegyrics. A *Time* cover does more than confirm the birth, or creation, of a superstar. It becomes the living source upon which show business and gossip columnists feed parasitically, reprocessing the material according to their needs, status or standards. In the world of entertainment the *Time* cover story is formal proclamation that a talent is here to stay. But in the notoriously capricious terms of that same world the stay can be brutally short. Whoever is the champion of the day, you will always find a fan, a buff, a special pleader who can produce unknown who's better. However fast the favourite is, there's always the outsider coming along faster. Barbra Streisand had no need to be warned that in her chosen trade the knives come out with the success. The star, particularly of the overnight variety, becomes licensed game for gossip writers' innuendo, and for cheap wisecracks over martinis in the 'happy hour'. The blood sport has destroyed many a vulnerable, fragile newcomer. But Streisand was to prove no easy game. She had the rare perception which told her that in this sense she would always be a victim. A curious paradox, the winning loser.

'In this business if you get along with your co-star you're having an affair; if you don't get along, you're having a feud,' she later succinctly summed up. On her guard, it contributed to Barbra's edginess immediately after *Funny Girl's* opening. She seized on the merest hint of reservation in the rave notices, the minor qualifications in the praise, and picked at them like sores. She had mentally ordered her triumph: neat. She needed it that way. None of this two-sided 'on the other hand' stuff for her. 'Am I great or am I lousy?' Her backstage muttering was Streisand, objectively, needing to *know*. Not all the combined applause on the Great White Way could make inroads into her towering insecurity. Nor could it persuade her to believe her friends' superlatives. Our own first contact with her, backstage in June 1964, revealed the measure of that insecurity. But admitting it, something of Streisand's Pulaski Street tenacity emerged too. The questions she raised in the full flush of her post-curtain ovations, sought the simple truth, not snug reassurance.

'Am I as good as they say I am? I don't know. I never know what pleases people, only what pleases me. Honestly, all this success makes me sick to my stomach. When people come over and say "are you Barbra Streisand?" I say, "no". "Funny, you look like her," they say. "Yeah, I know," I tell them, "someone else told me that." That's fear for you!'

Part of that fear stemmed, as we know, from Barbra's ambivalent assessment of her looks. Ugly? By whose standards?

'Listen – the way I look at it, if people think Shirley Jones and Sandra Dee are beautiful then they will find me a real ugly one. And if you think Sandra Dee is beautiful . . . okay, okay. Maybe to some guys my mouth is too big and my nose is too long. So what? I've had painters say they're nuts about my beauty – that my eyes belong to an Egyptian queen. They say my mouth is sensitive and sensuous and as for my nose, "don't ever change it". All I know is that with my looks I just had to be a star or nothing. I'm too whatever I am, to stay in the middle.'

Barbra Streisand, New York, June 1964, class of Shirley Jones and Sandra Dee. Less than a decade later it was the silk purse that was envying the sow's ear.

In the meantime while enjoying the heady excitement of *Funny Girl*'s stage triumph, Barbra was having to contend with the gossip writers' garbage. Usually the stuff was too wildly off the truth to satisfy even the most morbid appetites. One story, picked up by several papers around the world, was that, despite all observable fact, she was having an affair with her leading man, Sydney Chaplin. The lie affected Barbra less than the gossip peddler's lack of perception – and bad casting. Streisand's growing disenchantment with the media in general began with this sort of bilge-spilling. Her rhetorical 'Who needs it!' echoed Sinatra, and for the same reason. Talent on that scale can well afford to step over the old Hollywood maxim, 'any publicity is good publicity'.

Like many people with a streak of insecurity, Barbra overcompensated by leading with her chin. It often resulted in a kind of contrived, grating controversy.

On Broadway – in the stage version of *Funny Girl*

Occasionally, before wiser minds steered her to safety, she was guilty of a kind of cute bad taste, like her self-written entry for the *Funny Girl Playbill* biography:

> In addition to having appeared off-Broadway, on-Broadway and away from Broadway in nightclubs, on television and on the concert stage, Barbra Streisand is the recipient of *Cue Magazine*'s 'Entertainer of the Year' Award. A top recording star, a talented interior decorator, dress designer and portrait painter, she also plays field hockey. Her performance in the musical *I Can Get It For You Wholesale* stopped the show and was much admired by the critics, the public and the show's leading man, Elliot [*sic*] Gould, who married her. Barbra is a follower of Eastern philosophy and cooking, but also favors TV dinners on occasion. Her favorite day is Tuesday, since she devotes part of each Tuesday throughout the year to stringing crystal beads which are sold in a Vermont general store. She knows how to make coffee ice-cream and fix her own hair. For more personal information, write to her mother.

After that self-destructive mish-mash, the loud whisper that she was having an affair with Chaplin is pretty small beer.

The release of her *Barbra Streisand, The Third Album*, had been held up until just before the opening of *Funny Girl*. Good thinking; now over the next year it could ride all the way to the top like a surfer given the perfect wave. The number '3' is (with typical perversity) Barbra's unlucky number. She had requested the album be titled 'The Fourth'. Columbia demurred. Nevertheless, once away from the *Funny Girl* audience Barbra tended to prefer the disc to the show. Here, her judgement can be faulted. *The Third Album* has not stood the test of time. It displays the same shortcomings as the first two – a wilful insistence on taking standards and making them over in their singer's image. Nothing is presented simply. All is presented with unusual and (that word again) 'cute' emphasis, protracted melodic line, perverse tempi. This is the singer, not the song, with a vengeance. The overall impression is not of an artist faithfully interpreting the composer's intentions but of a celebrity in search of a *tour de force*. Gene Lees in *Hi Fi/Stereo Review* has it about right:

> One track on the album suggests the singer Miss Streisand might become if she would only jettison all the claptrap that now clutters her singing. This is 'Draw Me a Circle', a superb piece of fresh material. She gets directly into its mood and projects it simply. Her singing, nearly free of vibrato, evokes a strange, abstracted mood that is exquisitely apropos. One feels for an instant that Miss Streisand could be as great as the press agents say she is.

It is significant that 'Draw Me a Circle' was fresh material and not a standard. Perhaps the 'greatest star' sensed the spirits of Ella and Sarah and felt free, this once, to do the simple, direct thing. Better she had done so throughout the short-measure LP. The schmaltzy venturing into the ersatz classics, the First Bach Prelude filtering with stained-glass overtones into 'Just in Time', is possibly the low-water mark of Barbra Streisand's recording work.

Still, at the time the album pleased. And if, having to go out there and throw her best stuff night after night became a chore, there was always the roar of the grease-paint and the smell of the crowd. There was also money and being recognised by *maître d*'s. The former was pleasing all the benefactors, notably the appreciative Mrs Kind. She was now pavilioned in Manhattanesque splendour and expense was no object in the decorating of her own apartment. The recognition business was less gratifying. Shrike-voiced, sticky-fingered fans became the gauntlet she had to run, from the stage door or her apartment block to her chicly second-hand cream Bentley. There was the bore of being accosted by uncouth fans. ('Say, ain't you . . .?'). There was the discomfort of being ignored or worse ('Say, ain't you Carol Channing?') by fans vulgarly affecting to be super-cool. Too much was coming too fast. At the age of twenty-two and twenty-three she found it hard to walk the tightrope of public scrutiny that stretched between performance and persona. She hated to be recognised. Apart from the physical hassle, she didn't know how to handle the praise. Acknowledging it graciously suggested total ego. To shrug it aside was just as bad. Yet to be ignored could devastate her. 'Barbra,' Elliott Gould once said, 'is the kind of person who is hurt if her puppy walks past her.' She was in one of her better moods when, at a stoplight, a pedestrian couple moved in on her asking for an autograph 'for our daughter'. She gave it to them along with food for thought. 'Why not for *you*?' she said as she signed. There, her native spontaneity worked well for her. The reverse applied when trying to intellectualise the problem in a *Life International* interview, she came up with a rare lapse into near-pretentiousness:

> There are a lot of cold people in the theater who build walls so as not to get hurt. I don't ever want to build that kind of wall. I would rather get hurt. If my vulnerability goes in real life, it goes as a performer and an artist on stage too. I must retain the vulnerability or lose sensitivity as an artist.

At stoplights, on the sidewalk, outside, everybody owned her. Inside, if she could find out just who she was, she could be herself. It was no press agent cliché in a later *Playbill* ratatouille which referred to her as a 'talented interior decorator'. With money streaming in she could raise her thrift-shop acumen, her passion for antiques, ephemera and junk to the 21 Central Park West level. The penthouse was her decorator's oyster. She went at it with the same attack she brought to *The Third Album*. Two months after *Funny Girl*'s first night, Shana Alexander of *Life* gave a boggle-eyed account of the apartment, she being no less bemused than we had been:

> The kitchen had been half papered in patent leather but the refrigerator is still stocked with TV dinners and ice-cream. The closets are choked with mountains of thrift-shop debris, and the Goulds are in an eternal dither of interior decorating.
>
> Barbra glides down the winding stairway from the tower bedroom wrapped in a padded lemon silk robe looking as stylised and elegant as a Japanese empress, the mannered effect jarred by a kitchen spoon of tomato-dripping stew in her slender hand. She nibbles. It is a terrible visual shock, the prosthetic-looking steel spoon terminating the beautiful body line of her

upraised arm. A decorator springs forward with a lapful of swatches. 'Which flocking for the foyer?' he pants. 'Mayonnaise, garbage bags . . .' said the Japanese empress, scribbling a shopping list. She points to a swatch. 'The *oohky* brown one,' she commands. She wanders to the dining room, steps over an overturned broken antique French gilt chair. She crouches down to look at a painting on the floor, and stew drips on to one of its corners.

And there, famously, was the showpiece of the penthouse duplex – the ornately carved four-poster bed. It was the first real antique they had bought. It was understood, however, that despite its 300 years of previous existence, it had to adapt to the pair who slept in it. 'It should be like the place Desdemona got strangled in,' Elliott commanded another decorator. Barbra's ideas, though, were more specific, more dramatic. She told the bewildered designer that she wanted the entire bed draped and skirted with olive-gold damask, the top part 'draped in, folded, so that it makes a crown, with sort of tassles hanging down. There should be a red fur bedspread and damask curtains should hang from brass rods mounted between the bedposts to completely close in the bed like a train berth. But the curtains should be looped back to the bedposts, perhaps with khaki velvet ropes so as to allow the *interior*, the lace curtains . . .'

If you've got it, flaunt it.

The Goulds asked that a little refrigerator should be built into the side of the bed so that when, curtains drawn, they sat watching a horror flick on the TV at the bed's foot, they would not have to safari to the far corners of the penthouse for more coffee ice-cream. After 300 years the bed was going to wake up one morning and find itself wired for vision, sound and ice-cream.

The symbolism of the four-poster is significant (Freudian, some thought). The drawn-curtained retreat was the house of their own they had built in the trees. Whether it rained or stormed they would be warm and safe and dry. They saw themselves as Hansel and Gretel hidden from all the wicked witches, fans and journalists of the world, covered by leaves that, admittedly, had been custom-made. Neither, of course, could have privately believed it. The late-show ended. The alarm sounded. Morning. Another day, another dollar. For one. As she prospered, he did not. He was always down looking up. Inevitably they began to have less and less in common. And more to contend over. Even antique hunting – *their* thing for *their* hideaway – became an area for tacky behaviour and a quarrel. Shana Alexander was again the observer:

> . . . at the antique mart they pile out of the taxi, and Barbra plunges into the dust-covered warehouse trailed by Elliott, the decorator, the friends. 'What's this? . . . What's that? . . . How much? . . . Divine!' she shouts, dashing from lamp to chair to chest, grabbing up bits of moulding, scraps of hardware.
>
> 'Divine!' echoes the decorator. 'Great!' scream the friends. The strange procession snakes out of one warehouse and into an equally dusty shop next door. But suddenly the Goulds fancy that the proprietors of *this* shop don't like them. Maybe the owners, two sleepy-eyed Levantine types, recognise her. Maybe they *don't*! Maybe they think she isn't going to buy anything. She stalks out, upset.

Streisand at home with her poodle, Sadie, a gift from the cast of *Funny Girl*

'It's a front, Barbra. It's a bookie joint. They're gangsters,' Elliott says to soothe her. But already Barbra has dashed into the next shop and is shouting, 'What's *this*? What's *that*? Divine!' Somehow in the bargain-hunting mêlée, Elliott disappears to attend his acting classes. He says he'll rejoin the bargain-hunters in an hour. While he's gone, Barbra buys an ornate, antique piano that doesn't play ('It can be easily restored,' the shopkeeper assures her) and three enormous crystal chandeliers. As she passes the 'gangsters' ' shop next door she rushes to the window, raps on the glass, waves her sales check and shouts to the startled proprietors: 'Yah! You thought I wasn't gonna buy, huh? Well, I spent $3,000 next door!'

Suddenly Elliott returns down the street. When he hears about the piano he is furious. Now the Goulds have a screaming, four-letter fight in the street, hopping in and out of taxis, over curbs, past startled pedestrians, oblivious of decorator, friends, passers-by. Like Fanny Brice, it seems, the only thing that can embarrass Streisand is a bad performance.

How dare Barbra buy a piano, a *piano*, without consulting him, Elliott demands. 'I did it for us,' she shouts. Doesn't he want them to have a nice apartment? Doesn't he care about *their* home? Besides, she loves the piano. It is the most beautiful piano she's ever seen.

'It's hideous,' he yells. 'Elly, it has painted scenes on it,' she says grimly. What has started as a mock-fight, an actors' fight, is no longer fun. Because the fight isn't really about the piano, it's about who is In Charge and they both know it.

The world at large, well, their world, had little doubt who was boss man. The woman. It had to be she who called the shots. Like who was he? Some ex-actor – what's his name, now? – making screwball bets on ball games. A kept man. So the unjust litany ran. Each night Barbra played fictional wife to a fecklessly unfulfilled gambling man. And at the time, a man without an occupation. In an age where Troy Donahue could still get leading roles, Elliott Gould's assymmetrical face had no takers. One of the girls in the chorus, seeing him standing there waif-like recalled how she would go home night after night bemused that a star of Streisand's magnitude could see anything in a *klutz* like that.

When some eighteen months later we visited the Central Park West apartment, the demarcation line between success and Mr Elliott Gould was subtly demonstrated by his not being anywhere where we looked. It was her show. And anything Streisand does is not difficult to recall. A Sunday brunch, and she is presiding, stunningly attractive in a silken caftan and jewelled turban. The universal mother effect ('Eat, don't talk!') is Cleopatra played by Fanny Brice, directed by Vittorio de Sica. She knows that the penthouse, to some, seemed like the costly aberration of a freaked-out interior decorator. That those looking for the apogee of reckless self-indulgence could end their search right here in this caprice overlooking Central Park. But there's no denying the pride of ownership in Streisand's eyes. The dentist's cabinet stuffed with shoe buckles, the chewing gum slot machine, was Streisand refusing to let the antiques have it all their own way. Like the ice-box in the Jacobean bed. But she knew the intrinsic value, not merely the price, of her antiques, explaining them this way: 'Well, I'll tell you. When you've had no toys as a kid and been raised on strictly nothing, small things like a walnut suddenly seem like a work of art. I gotta go see about the food. Walk around. Enjoy.'

Elliott Gould, technically the host, was charming, adroit, courteous – and self-effacing. Always friendly and quick to smile there was no concealing the hint of defeat in his eyes. The past eighteen months must have been a dark night of the soul for 'Mr Streisand'.

A lifeline seemed to have been thrown to him when he was cast opposite Carol Burnett for a television version of the lightweight musical *Once upon a Mattress*. But though it augured well for his career, it did nothing to ameliorate the increasing pressure on his private life.

Today, Gould, an older wiser man, and a highly successful one as well, can reflect objectively on the stress he was under at that time. Life with the rocketing Streisand, by the husband left on the launching pad.

> Barbra's success was painful to me, because I didn't have sufficient under-standing of myself to avoid feeling weird about it – even though I knew that she was ambitious and wanted to be somebody. It was my responsibility as a man to acknowledge that. When Barbra became an enormous celebrity I tried my damnedest not to take seriously the fact that I wasn't. I could handle the fact that she was getting incredible amounts of publicity – that reporters were constantly around, asking her questions while I stayed in the background. That was no big thing. What were they going to ask me – how I did in my three-man basketball games?

Overhanging it all was how *he* saw that night of the *Funny Girl* premiere:

> People were pawing her, sticking mikes down her bosom, telling her things she couldn't believe . . . I had to realise that Barbra is *my* woman, but everybody wants her. I have to be above it because if I'm in it I'm going to get stomped to death.

The airing for *Once upon a Mattress* was to be in June. True to type Barbra loyally proclaimed it would make Elliott as famous as herself. It did no such thing. There was nothing Gould, or any other actor, could do to redress the disparity in weight between the male role and Carol Burnett's. It was she who won all the attention and the rave reviews. In desperation, Gould clutched at a passing, peculiarly soggy straw – the part of The Mute [*sic*] in a 'run-away' movie production. In the various subsequent attempts to distribute the film it was known at *The Confessor*, *Quick, Let's Get Married*, *Seven Different Ways*. But few people ever saw it under any of those titles. Many of those who have wish they had not.

The challenge to Barbra Streisand was how to give her husband some kind of ego and soul-saving support. Even without the fortuitous example of Fanny Brice's protracted underpinning of Nicky Arnstein, Barbra knew intuitively where best she could help. She started by putting her money to work. Companies were formed, Ellbar, Barbell. Overnight Elliott Gould found himself a company man, weaving dazedly through the world of deductibles, residuals, percentages and other fiscal caprices. He also found himself more overtly dubbed 'Mr Streisand', his wife's producer and financial manager. He detested with good cause, the 'Mr Streisand' label; objected, correctly, the inaccurate styling as Barbra's manager. But he could visualise himself as a producer. Television was the one territory he felt he could conquer. He tried, and lost. Some of the projects he played around with might make the blood run chill, though they might not compare too badly with the abysmal standards of American TV at the start of the 1980s. Gould lists some of them:

> There was an idea for a situation-comedy series about a married couple who spent every waking hour entering contests and never worked, while support-ing a son who ran up extraordinary sums on his credit cards. I also created a sitcom called *Y. Buy and Son* about a firm that rented anything – even people. That never did anything either. Neither did *The Bumblebee and Captain Everything*, which was about two middle-aged guys living in the same neighborhood in New Rochelle, who fantasised themselves as comic-book heroes living in the Forties. Another was *Harry Egypt* about a gangster in the employ of the Establishment. Somebody like the head of Remington, if he got into trouble, would call on Harry to get him out of it. Never sold any of these.

Rejection all around. For him. For Barbra, *Funny Girl* was off and running. And now she had signed an unprecedented $5 million contract with CBS to star in one television special a year for ten years. The unheard-of scale of the deal started all the smart-mouthing again. This was over the top. She couldn't be that good. On the evening of 28 April 1965, thirteen months into SRO performances at the Winter Garden, she proved that she was.

Bob Hope once remarked that he considered his late Thirties radio shows, with their flair and precision, the high-water mark of his career. It just may be that Barbra Streisand will, in time, feel the same way about her television specials. Her first, 'My Name Is Barbra', was certainly a landmark.

At least as important to her as that $5 million was the degree of independent control that came with the contract. She knew that in a straight contest with the pre-digested pap served up on American television she couldn't fail to come out winning. But she wanted that triumph to have an individual quality too. She flatly rejected the turgid format – 'And now an especially big hello for my first guest star . . .' – of the specials which had once featured her. The show, directed by Dwight Hemion, would be modelled around the armature of autobiography. It would be without a guest – Barbra, the whole Barbra and little else but Barbra. But it added up to four Emmys: Outstanding Programme; Outstanding Individual Achievement in Entertainment – Barbra Streisand; Best Concept; Best Choreography and Staging – Joe Layton; Best Art Design – Tom John and Bill Harp; and Best Musical Direction – Peter Matz. The basic format of the special was the growing up, the making of Barbra Streisand. As the evolution of this particular female of the species was limned, viewers saw Barbra cavorting in a hugely oversized playground as a five-year-old, rushing in a flowing gown from set to set as she frantically sang 'I'm Late'. She kidded her audience during a monologue about a weird lady by the name of Pearl – not from Pulaski Street or Rangoon or Zanzibar but 'Pearl from Istanbul'. Then in the celebrated staging/upstaging of 'Second-Hand Rose' she was waltzing through Bergdorf Goodman's in creations that said farewell for ever to her thrift-shop persona. America was convinced literally overnight. The rumours that had washed across the country from New York were visibly substantial. *Variety's* rave says it for them all:

> Destined to hit it big in all media, Barbra Streisand last week notched television to the skein that so far lists recordings and stage . . . It is by now old news that she's an electric performer, superbly gifted of voice and ingenuously charming. What counts on television is how the performer projects beyond the glass of the small home screen, and Miss Streisand burst through as though it were no more a barrier than the footlights of a Broadway stage. Her self-confidence, especially for her years and for one so recently come to stardom, is astounding, and she carries it well. Her songs, no matter who they may have 'belonged' to first, come out pure Streisand, styled as originals and somehow always appropriate for what the Egyptian visage, angular frame and off-center personality all add up to . . .

And now the spin-offs. The twenty-three numbers from 'My Name Is Barbra' provided the material for two more albums in her LP output. The first of the pair had for its cover portrait a family snapshot taken of Barbra at the age of seven by her brother Sheldon. It is a clue as to why these 'special' albums wear better than her earlier 'nightclub' derived discs. Barbra's instinct was right. Autobiography was her best element. The lack of a deep-rooted vocal tradition or lengthily-polished style is no longer a prime weakness measured against the total range of emotions through her own experience. Her rich vocal versatility is offered full opportunity as she runs the gamut from semi-inarticulate childhood to the passion of a grown woman's all-consuming love. If at moments the 'growing-up' tracks abet her besetting sin of appearing 'cute' ('Sweet Zoo', as its punning title suggests, is a favor to Jeff Harris of *Harry Stoones* fame she would better have left unpaid), there was always full compensation, like the simple, poignant beauty of 'My Pa'. The first issue from the special ends with Barbra's version's of 'My Man', Fanny Brice's borrowing from Mistinguette. Barbra's version stands comparison. The song for which Ray Stark was unable to secure a release for the Broadway *Funny Girl* ends the disc on a torch-sung climax just as, in time, it would the film.

Now Barbra was getting more control over her material and its deployment than she had ever known before. She not only captured America wholesale, she had achieved the first *rounded* success of her career in the majors. Nobody was saying now that Barbra was great in spite of a limp show or poor supporting material. The entire production had been universally praised. But it was Streisand's softly rounded shoulders that carried it all. And yet the Emmys success was not to be repeated with Tonys. We are not merely playing the numbers game with statuettes. The larger, more piquant, equation concerned Barbra Streisand and Carol Channing. That confrontation, delicately implied, occurred at a Sunday night performance Barbra gave on behalf of the Actors' Fund. Thrown into the pro's den, Barbra rose to the challenge with doubled verve, tripled brilliance. In the orchestra seats, hat-floppy, all expression masked by the familiar china-doll look, sat Carol Channing. Being Sunday, she had the night off from the bondage of *Hello*

Dolly still packing them in down the street. Whatever else had brought her to the theater, no question but she was there to check out her obvious rival for the 'Best Leading Actress in a Musical' award in the 1964 Tony race. That night Carol reigned over Barbra's parade. Her Dolly Levi won the award that really mattered to both contenders. And to clinch the supremacy *Hello Dolly* picked up no less than ten Tonys. So Carol Channing had the first laugh, but not, as events were to prove, the last.

(Barbra Streisand predicted early on that she would, in time, scoop all the major awards including an Oscar. By the age of twenty-seven she had proved it. In 1969, she was awarded the Antoinette Perry Award. It was not won in a straight performer-to-performer slug-out. It was given to her as 'Star of the Decade'. Apart from it being a short decade, the award, however merited, has all the excitement of a one-horse race. Moreover it often carries the invisible aura of backstage lobbying as much as talent.)

Triumphs or disappointments the show goes on. Barbra developed a dangerous tendency to lose interest in the grinding repetition of performances. To combat it she assumed, unofficially, the director's role, delivering 'notes' to members of the cast, the chorus, the orchestra. She called extra rehearsals to refine the already ultra-polished. This stirred up a considerable amount of resentful 'who does she think she is?' and the occasional touch of malice. At a party to celebrate her twenty-third birthday she was presented with her famous poodle Sadie (a companion subsequently nearly as faithful as Marty Erlichman). The shindig induced a well reported after-remark. 'We injected it with rabies,' members of the chorus were putting about, 'but it didn't take.' A legitimate sick joke perhaps, by the brittle standards of Broadway. But the purveyors of it, whose livelihoods were significantly improved by the three-year plus run of the show, could scarely have been proud of their grins. Barbra Streisand was not the first major talent to be concerned with the support being given the star on-stage, or on-screen. The talent that carries the show can no more ignore the rest of the package than master painters could shut their eyes to the supporting brush-strokes of their apprentices. Yul Brynner, for instance, uses video recording to scrutinise the ensemble playing in his caviare ticket *The King and I*. Barbra, quite legitimately, wanted to be sure that everyone in the show was giving it both barrels. The fact that her prefectionism was ultimately to extend to the nuts, bolts, paper clips and petty cash was nothing personal. If a talent is to be exploited, better this should be by the talent itself.

After more than a year of *Funny Girl* Sidney Chaplin had had enough. There was no way any actor could give a virtuoso performance in a second-fiddle role, particularly when the soloist was Streisand. He asked to be released from his contract. There was some minor Equity politicking but finally he had his way. The cold war that had blown around the two on-stage lovers was terminated. Conflict of a more subtle kind switched to Barbra and her stand-in, a competent performer named Lainie Kazan. The affair was virtually a parody of the familiar showbiz plot. Miss Kazan was no shrinking violet. The rumour had it that she claimed it would take a mountain of make-up, should she ever go on, to reproduce the (alleged) ugliness of the star. But for months she was spared that test. The lines outside the box office would have dispersed like a bomb alert at the news of a replacement Fanny Brice. Streisand or nothing at all, that was it as far as the cash customers were concerned. It meant going on performance after performance. Loyally, professionally, Barbra did just that. A Saturday, a two-show day, came when she was quite simply, ill. Lainie Kazan was alerted, told that she would play the matinée. By no coincidence at all, every critic, news agency, columnist in the city got to hear about it. In minutes. Sniffing the Cinderella story of a score of 'B' movies, city editors briefed their writers accordingly. The stand-in, all breathless and shining-eyed, would take her breakfast the morning after, surrounded by the glowing headlines. The brilliance of her triumph would cause the star to fade. The fairy-tale scenario did not, in the event, even get close. The news which had flashed like lightning to the media had also (Broadway being an alert-eared village) reached Barbra. She rose from her sick bed to sweep through the stage door announcing she would play the afternoon performance. She did. But as she took the curtain it was obvious to her fevered but highly professional mind, that there was no way she could go on in the evening.

Lainie Kazan did. It was a first-rate performance. It was not a triumph. By Monday, regular dosing with one part medicine to two parts will-power had cured Barbra. Coincidentally Lainie Kanzan found herself leaving the show. Her replacement, Linda Gerard, was personally selected by Barbra. Her contract reportedly forbade her notifying the media in the event of her playing Fanny Brice. Gossip time again. Barbra, it was whispered, was afraid of being over-shadowed, up-staged. Additionally the jibe was that she was paranoid – quite unable to tolerate rivals. There has to be an element of truth in this. Paranoia is second-stage boosting to driving ambition and perfection. All great stars, great champions have the flaw, however suavely the more adroit of them can disguise it. But paranoia is also Siamese-twin to insecurity. And it was insecurity as much as ego that came between Lainie Kazan and the sun.

Less excusable, in professional terms, was the way Barbra performed toward the end of her twenty-two months as Fanny Brice. Apart from drilling the cast, she reverted to her early behavior in *Wholesale*, embroidering, switching, improvising. It threw the rest of the cast. Ray Stark, returning to the Winter Garden to monitor the production, was appalled by what he saw. He went backstage and laid it on the line – either an immediate improvement or the curtain would come down, the audience returned their money. Only John Patrick's diplomacy averted a head-on producer-to-star confrontation. Part cause of Barbra's apparently capricious attitude to her performance was her chafing against carbon-copy repetition. But she enjoyed a more tranquil relationship with her new leading man, Johnny Desmond. And she made no waves when Linda Gerard went on in her place close to a score of occasions. In any event, Barbra had other preoccupations.

Toward the end of *Funny Girl*'s run Elliott Gould was in Philadelphia actually working – opening in a new show *Drat! The Cat!* Loyally, and loudly, Barbra prophesied great things for it, and him, to the world. She put her money where her mouth was only to the extent of a token $850 investment in the action. This was sound strategy, good psychology. Elliott had to make it on his own. Alone. As it was, both the Goulds were enraged at the sneering suggestions that Barbra had poured an angel's ransom into the venture merely to provide Elliott with rehabilitation therapy. Like a beaten champion rushing back to the ring too soon to disprove the 'they never come back' theory, Elliott Gould had again involved himself in a non-event. *Drat! The Cat!* was one of the myriad shows that for budget reasons – not enough dough – never had a chance. After a week of previews, nothing quite gelling, it played for all of five evenings before folding, inevitably, in defeat. It was a punch to the solar plexus to Elliott Gould. Work, to him, was an armature that supported the human day. Another failure made the comeback trail seem that much steeper. The shadows that he stood in were longer, deeper, colder . . .

Barbra observed the dilemma and felt the hurt. It took the edge off the excitement of the run up to her second television special. It was to be called 'Color Me Barbra'. Autobiography was, of course, largely played out as a string for the song pearls. Instead thoughts turned to a kind of spiritual evocation of Barbra. It was good thinking too. There was, is in Streisand, a whole palette of colour-values to work on. Production began in the Philadelphia Museum of Art with Barbra working variations on the motifs on the walls around her. It continued into the circus ring. It concluded with Barbra in concert before a live audience. More than ever she was able to exercise control. 'I'm paying the bill. It's my problem, right? I could have got Frank Sinatra and Dean Martin to clown around just like everybody else does on their specials, but who needs it?' – was the way she (though not necessarily Mr Sinatra) would have it. Ultimately it became an even greater triumph than her first special.

The show's airing brought, along with the almost audible coast-to-coast applause, the clearest cut evidence yet that in Marty Erlichman's words: 'When you're on the way up ten million people love you. When you've made it, for nine-and-a-half it turns to hate.' Simultaneous with the transmission was the appearance in the *New York Times* of the film actor *manqué* Rex Reed's coverage of the special in the making. It was an attempted hatchet piece that gave substance to the late Jacqueline Susann's observation: 'If I had an affair with Jack the Ripper, the offspring would be Rex Reed.'

Reed's article now reads like thoroughly *passé* malice. Its charges seem to be that: Miss Streisand kept him waiting; that she drove her production team and technicians into the ground; that, in philistine fashion, she ate junk food in the presence of the art museum's treasures; that she and her crew physically maltreated some of those said treasures.

The first charge is trivial. There was no reason why in the midst of producing a complex, expensive major television entertainment, her own lovely neck on the line, Barbra should revolve her schedule around Rex Reed's. His chip shows as he protests too much. Now his claim that she expected her team to work superhuman hours. True. But they were the hours she worked herself – up front where it shows. The circus sequence demanded an exhausting trampoline 'bit' from her. To give the editors scope for cutting to musical rhythms, she did nine sustained takes. Setting that kind of example she had the right to expect a rigger to haul in an extra box at 3.00 a.m. The striving for absolute perfection is sometimes branded as a clear sign of immaturity. Not so in Streisand. An addiction perhaps, but good or bad, there is no way she can ever kick the habit. So, according to Reed, she sat slumped and eating potato chips in front of a Rousseau. So what? Rex Reed's cultural snobbism as well as his chip is revealed here. Rousseau, for all his own years of breadline living, might have been the first to realise that compulsive noshing was a symptom of nervous and artistic tension. The charge that a cameraman crushed out an illicit cigarette on a 'valuable piece of a hundred-year-old Romanion oak' is valid. No doubt it happened. But though Barbra may have called the artistic shots, it didn't extend to telling cameramen where to stub their cigarettes. That a guard had to step in as she was about to lean on a Renoir you can either politely disbelieve, or assume that an official was overly nervous. Barbra Streisand, Emmanuel's daughter, friend and patron to the artist Jason Monet, is incapable of such barbarity. (Or for that matter, lend her presence, as did Mr Reed, to that queasy-making film *Myra Breckinridge*). Reed did, however, observe that Barbra indulged in virtually no smalltalk back-chat with the rest of her crew. He didn't stop to consider why. Diana Lurie, writing in *Life International* did. Covering this same taping, she produced, warts and all, a far more pertinent commentary:

Everybody knows Streisand is on top. So does she. And the more she is hailed, the more scared and insecure she feels. 'I win awards and everything but one of these days something is going to bomb. It's a scary thing. It can all suddenly fall apart.' Such massive doubt amid such success might be funny if her fears were not so very real to Barbra. When her understudy replaced her one night in *Funny Girl,* Barbra worried that the audience would prefer the substitute and she might lose her job. When she left the cast she got upset when a waiter kiddingly asked her how it felt to be out of work. Whenever she hears one of her numbers being sung on the air by a run-of-the-mill vocalist, she psyches herself into thinking the performance is better than her own. She has been known to worry eighteen hours over just such a possibility. Her audience adores Barbra – but she looks on them as her adversaries. For her taped TV show she sang five songs before a live audience. When the director, Dwight Hemion, asked her to re-do two numbers, she insisted that the audience leave. She was tired, she was not fond of the songs, and she disliked her interpretation even more. 'Tell the audience to go away,' she said to her manager, Martin Erlichman. 'I hate them. I hate them.' For half-an-hour, while the audience waited, Erlichman and the director pleaded with Barbra, pointing out that the crowd was needed for the proper sound effect. When she gave in and walked back on stage, she got a thunderous reception. She did the two numbers with dispatch, mumbled 'Thank you for staying' to the bravo-ing crowd and re-entered the control room. 'O.K.,' she said, 'let's see what we've got.'

Barbra Streisand's final curtain on the New York run of *Funny Girl* coincided with Christmas 1965. Her parting gift to the audience was the most electric heartfelt rendition of 'People' she ever delivered. More practically, she left 'notes' to the orchestra, the cast, the lighting director on how the show could be improved. (These must have made sense. With Mimi Hines taking over as Fanny Brice, the show ran another year.) Tying herself to the show for so long – she had signed for the first three months of the London run – meant Barbra walking away from all get-rich-quick offers in an assortment of nightspots. But Streisand's business acumen was as sound as her performer's instinct. *Funny Girl* had provided her with a marvellous one-woman showcase. She was as massively 'there' as Mount Rushmore. *Her* Christmas presents were some 600 requests for concerts with offers of as much as $50,000 for a one-night stand. Erlichman turned them all down, including gigs in such hideaways as Shea Stadium and the Astrodome. 'As an artist,' he said, 'it wouldn't be right for her. All she'd make is money.' But both he and Barbra had more compelling objections. Barbra was out for bigger game, to conquer the world, the old world for the opening skirmish. *Funny Girl* in London. The challenge thrilled and, of course, terrified her. She opened in London's Prince of Wales theater two weeks after the U.S. screening of her second television special on 30 March 1966. The triumph on TV was no small curtain-raiser for her debut before British audiences.

On her last night in New York, Elliott Gould presented her with a gold-plated bagel. What else could an out-of-work actor give a star who has everything?

NINE

WHEN YOU'RE convinced you have the hottest ticket in town, superstition can go walk under a ladder. The London opening of *Funny Girl* took place defiantly on 13 April. It succeeded where *On the Town* had significantly failed; it became the one show everyone wanted to see. Had to see. That spring/summer, Henley, Ascot, Lords, Epsom, Wimbledon, all found themselves royally upstaged. These fashionable institutions which drew their patrons from the pages of *Debrett's Peerage* and *Who's Who*, found fewer takers for their champagne in the VIP marquees. Everybody was in town seeing Streisand. A running flush of celebrities attended the full house first night. David Niven traded backslaps with John Huston, Peter Sellers mugged it out with Rex Harrison.

Barbra now had, of course, the toughest opponent in the world to beat – the legend of her own advance publicity. Fast and fabulous success had thrown her into the arena – the Prince of Wales theatre – and sitting there like Roman Emperors, thumbs poised, were the London critics. Not as lethal, perhaps, as those 'Butchers of Broadway', but capable nonetheless, of putting into perspective – their perspective – this singer they're all talking about. An analysis of some of the more upmarket reviews suggested that the land of Bea Lillie and Julie Andrews was not going to surrender lightly.

> Barbra Streisand in *Funny Girl* [declared the *Sunday Telegraph* critic] is a prodigious and unique creature – a kind of guardian demon of showbiz, the only three-dimensional strip-cartoon heroine in existence. Her personality is that of a ten-year-old girl show-off, teetering in her mother's high heels and camping in her old evening dress, enjoying her own pretence of fooling us that she is 'grown-up'.

Harold Hobson, doyen critic of *The Sunday Times* pushed this further, a touch of venom on his pen-nib:

> Miss Streisand has a neat, pocket-size humour, expressing itself in small, mocking gestures and alarming finger-nails that would interest a vampire. The battery of microphones enables the front rows to hear when she speaks, and the back when she sings. The rich and leisured can thus get the entire show at two visits if they arrange their seats properly. Or they could if the show were not almost entirely sold out for the fourteen weeks which Miss Streisand is contracted to appear in it.

Hobson's sour innuendo about Barbra's limited run can be fairly rebutted by a glance at the contract. So as to play London, Barbra accepted less than half her weekly Broadway salary, less than a third the figure that Mary Martin was receiving a mile away in the London version of *Hello Dolly*. Asking for more would have ruled a London production out of court. She played London as long as her commitments allowed. And as the records and the superlatives confirmed, few considered they had been short-changed.

If Barbra's financial return had been comparatively modest, a series of awards made up for it. She was voted the 'Best Foreign Actress' of that year and *Funny Girl* was named 'Best Foreign Musical'. At the U.S. Embassy she was honoured with the 'Anglo-American Award' for being the best American performer in that year's London season. Newspapers, magazines, TV, radio gave Barbra saturation coverage (with little help, note, from the lady concerned). No question but she had conquered London on a scale matched only by Danny Kaye's memorable show years earlier at the London Palladium. The after-the-curtain queues to her dressing-room were the sort of celebrity line-up to brighten the eye and colour the cheeks of Pulaski Street. Royals, stars, café society and members of the House of Lords patiently took their turn, protocol counting for nothing at this particular Prince of Wales.

Princess Margaret, an extremely competent cocktail pianist and an acknowledged pop-jazz buff, was among the first backstage with congratulations. This nailed at least one much-battered anecdote, dredged up in the wake of Barbra's transatlantic triumphs. It centred on an earlier meeting between Streisand and the Princess at a Josh Logan party in New York. There was a ripple of fun among the guests even before the two contrasting and controversial personalities arrived. Both of them had just appeared in the list of the 'world's worst-dressed women' with Her Royal Highness seeded Number One, Barbra at Number Two. But any gossip that might have been squeezed out of swift comparison between their two ensembles was dashed by Barbra arriving late. The eventual encounter is remembered for a verbal exchange. Asked why she had arrived late Barbra is alleged to have resorted to typical shy aggression with, 'I got screwed up.' The Princess is said to have 'blanched' (an unlikely reaction for the singularly un-blanchable royal.) The young man standing beside her, Tommy Steele no less, is also said to have 'blanched'. Nobody else seems to have blanched, least of all Josh Logan. An anglophile with some knowledge of royal protocol, the distinguished New York director recognised the innocence behind Barbra's remark, and the nervousness behind the question she levelled at Tommy Steele. 'You two know each other from London, huh? I mean you have worked for her sister?' (Those who regard that as blanch-making material have yet to hear Mr Ray Stark's jocular exchanges with Princess Margaret's former husband, Lord Snowdon, at the film premier in London of *Funny Girl*). Moreover, considering the life-styles of both ladies, Streisand felt no need to be socially awed – and Princess Margaret was unlikely to require it. Going backstage to add her warm congratulations to the pile, the Princess affirmed that no offence was meant, or taken, at that party in New York.

By now, of course, Barbra was all things to all journalists. Some tried to stir up a British version of the Chaplin–Streisand confrontation substituting Britain's Michael Craig for the role of the 'villain'. Craig, like Sydney Chaplin, found he had to do little more than make the right moves, noises and reactions in the limited role of the sanitised gambler. Nothing there for the gossip writers. They switched to hinting at mutual coolness between the two leads in the show and Barbra's alleged

Meeting Princess Margaret at the London opening of *Funny Girl*

indifference and aloofness to the rest of the cast. Sheilah Graham, in her book *Scratch An Actor – Confessions of a Hollywood Columnist*, wrote:

> *Funny Girl* opened in London to acclaim and stories of backstage temperament. Barbra had walked into her dressing-room at the Prince of Wales theater with her entourage and walked right out. No word of explanation until her manager telephoned to say his client would not return until she had a suite worthy of her talents. A few walls were knocked down, some fancy furniture hastily collected and the star returned. Her understudy who succeeded her when she left the show has only bitter memories. 'In the fourteen weeks she was here she never said one word to me. Her desire for perfection was driving them all crazy. Even after her last performance she was still sending notes to the musical director advising how the show could be improved. She complained about the acoustics. She complained about people casting shadows, blocking her light. She was always complaining, period. All in the name of a better show. Her leading man, Michael Craig, still cannot speak coherently about her.'

Well, as it happens Craig, an actor with a reputation for down-the-line pleasantness, is totally coherent in his rebuttal. He wrote to the London *Sunday Mirror*: 'Hollywood columnist Sheilah Graham does not tell the truth about me. She declares that my working association with Barbra Streisand on *Funny Girl* left me unable even now to "speak coherently about her". Let me say that I have never met or spoken to Miss Graham. Further, that I admired Barbra very much and got along with her very well.'

We wrote to the artist Jason Monet, seeking his permission to reproduce a strikingly perceptive wood sculpture of Barbra for this book. Weeks later, we received his handwritten reply;
'Dear Donald Zec,

I am thankful for the opportunity to pay back in any way possible the kindness and help Barbra showed me.

Please be at liberty to use the photo of the statue I made of Barbra – and yes, her son Jason was, and is, named after me.

First met her outside the theatre in Oxford 1963 where my ex-wife and Elliott Gould, Barbra's ex-husband, opened in the musical '*On The Town*'. It was a fine Spring morning and she was heavily wrapped in furs. So I have the distinction of knowing her when she only earned seven thousand dollars a week! The show moved to Manchester and ended up at the Prince of Wales Theatre, London, and during its run Elliott, Barbra and I became close friends. They became collector maniacs of my work and between them own roughly sixty paintings.

One night while our ex's were performing, Barbra and I went to see '*The Owl and the Pussycat*' at the Criterion Theatre, Piccadilly, starring a friend of mine Anton Rogers and the other part was played by a friend of Barbra's. (Diana Sands – a fellow sparring partner from the bout with '*Harry Stoones*'.) She enjoyed the show and hoped one day to play the female part.

1966. Elliott came over to London prior to Barbra's arrival to start rehearsals for '*Funny Girl*'. I was in a terrible mess financially and mentally and tried my hardest

Barbra is told to keep off the grass. Good reviews were no protection when Barbra plus camera crew got the wrong side of a park keeper in Victoria Embankment Gardens during a publicity photo session. "You can't do that kind of thing here," he said, and threatened to prosecute. Barbra apologised later at a Press conference in the Savoy Hotel.

to keep it from them. I owed seven months rent on my Bayswater flat I remember. The Goulds found out and suggested I have an Exhibition. I didn't feel ready but they talked me into it. Barbra opened the show at the then Grosvenor Gallery, Davies Street (lovely Bill and Betty Graf attended), and she got even more excited than myself whenever I sold anything. It may interest you – the London 'Times', dated June 27th, 1966, has a photo of Barbra and myself in my Bayswater Studio. Elliott and Barbra, prior to the close of my exhibition, loaned me the fare, on sales, to go on a painting trip to the West Indies.

December 1977. Barbra became my Sponsor to enter the United States and paid for a hotel apartment in New York in which my wife, son and self stayed for 6 months.

Since I'd met Barbra and Elliott they have worked tirelessly bringing and sending people over to buy my work . . .

As I've tried to convey, I owe Barbra. Yours, Jason Monet.'

The letter may not be strong on total objectivity, but it still speaks volumes. It may help in deciding whose evidence to run with – that of Barbra Streisand and Jason Monet, or the likes of Rex Reed and Sheilah Graham. And it makes stories of philistine behaviour in the presence of a Renoir that much harder to credit.

Ray Stark was once reported as saying of the Gould marriage: 'They have a tremendous communication because he's a very bright guy. They have a marvellous rapport. She has a very big respect for what Elliott thinks. On the creative level it's a very healthy fusion.' Mr Stark, on the subject of fusions, displayed greater prescience than he realised. Mr and Mrs Gould moved into the Savoy Hotel during part of their stay in London. One pivotal fact of life emerged. Barbra became pregnant. The very speedy announcement became an overnight bonanza for the gossip columnists. Those who a day before had accused Barbra of accepting only a short-term contract for London because she'd accepted offers she couldn't refuse, now virtually accused her of getting pregnant so as to have reason to quit the show. The fact that it had been a fourteen-week contract she had signed and it was a fourteen-week contract she honoured, was drowned under the cascading innuendo. So too was a more fascinating, deeper insight into the event. It was revealed some fourteen years later by Elliott Gould, nervously reminiscing at his home on Hutton Drive. He harked back to the last night of *Funny Girl* in New York.

'Barbra was singing "People" and it got to her. All of a sudden life and art came together – and she started to weep. All I wanted to do was to get her through. She started to weep because of the reality of what was going on got to her, penetrated. When the show was over, she got this standing ovation, but I was still sitting in the front row thinking about that line "People who need people are the luckiest people in the world". No one is alone. Everybody was with her. Everybody pulling for her. All of a sudden, something got through to her.' He stopped abruptly, moving into an unexpected gear-shift. 'You know, Jason was conceived at the Savoy Hotel. And I may say that was the best bit of talking I have ever done.' It begged the question. Elliott Gould obliged with an answer:

'Well, by then,' he continued, 'the star thing was really going very hard. And I really had to talk her down. I talked her all the way down through all the whole encounter, not ever dreaming we would have a child. But also knowing that it would be the best thing. Also knowing that I was being irresponsible and inconsiderate of my son, not thinking of him or myself. I was thinking of Barbra. The best thing if I could give her a child. Give her a son, my son – to be her friend so that she could understand more about where I was coming from . . . bringing her mind back down into life and, as the Lord deemed fit, we made a child that night. This was in March. He was born in December.'

An interesting notion, Elliott Gould making his wife Barbra Streisand pregnant ('as the Lord deemed fit') to give her a firmer sense of reality. Examining his fragmented account of that night at the Savoy – signs of the analysis he went into in 1965 may be visible to experts – there's no doubt Gould believes in what he says. But it takes two to tango. What the well-meaning Mr Gould intended may have been read quite differently by his compliant partner. And what about the end-product of that conjugal session in a suite overlooking the Thames? Jason Gould, his bar mitzvah celebrated, manhood confirmed, may have wished for a more conventional entry into the world than as a result of 'Dr' Gould's psychotherapy.

Analysts could probably devote an entire seminar probing possible permutations of Elliott Gould's motives. It might have been the action of an unhappy man trying,

'Mr Streisand' came too. The Goulds in London

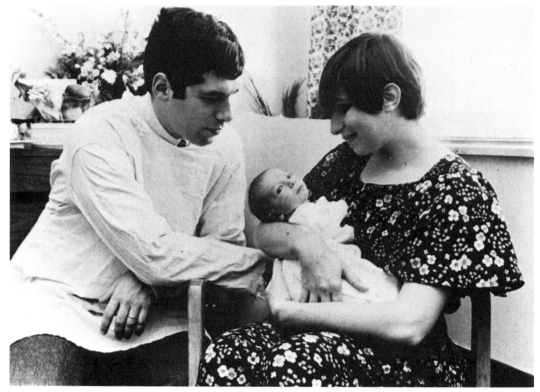

Mr and Mrs Gould with son Jason

by the mutual act of creation, to re-direct a marriage moving dangerously close to a reef. Or maybe it was Gould merely being wise after the happy event. And besides there is another viewpoint: as we have said in relation to the Streisand–Gould axis, there is the truth, the untruth, his version and hers. One can imagine her reacting to Gould's claim with a shriek of amusement and Pulaski Street candour – 'He knocked me up to bring me down! What kind of a cockamamie explanation is that?!' To Barbra, Jason was a fact of life and love and anyway she could argue persuasively that no woman need have a child she doesn't want. What Streisand is unlikely to comment on is a more subtle reading of that night at the Savoy; that she was glad to confer upon her embattled actor-husband the most tangible proof possible of his manhood and her love. It is not, finally, the concern of anyone except the two participants. We don't even know whether they ate coffee ice-cream that night.

The pregnancy was announced. The Press at once swooped, with headlines screaming of 'The Million Dollar Baby'. This was the fortune, it was calculated, that Barbra's enforced lay-off would cost her. No reporter seems to have had the acumen to consider possible tax write-offs; or the vastly richer benefits motherhood would bring to Barbra as a woman and as a performer.

Barbra left *Funny Girl* on 14 July 1966 and the curtain stayed down permanently.

The Irish Lisa Shane, her London understudy, had won golden opinions for her handful of appearances but, even more than in New York, the show was Barbra. The management were realists. There was no stay of execution at the Prince of Wales. Barbra returned to America to take on those arenas that she had turned her back on a few months before. She played Newport (the Jazz Festival), Philadelphia, Atlanta and Chicago. Finally, on doctor's orders, she had to cancel no less than sixteen other road-show appearances.

It was not, of course, her first experience of the huge open-air concert that a decade later in *A Star Is Born* she was stunningly to exploit. As early as 1963 she had given a 'one woman' show to 5000 at the Arie Crown Theater, Chicago, where she had broken the audience up by wishing aloud for the pop-corn concession. Crowds three times larger screamingly assembled in July 1964 and August 1965 to hear Barbra hold court at Forest Hills. The dinosaur proportions of these events precludes the highest art. Performer and fans tend to feed off each other, devaluing the currency of music. But Barbra gave good value for money. She could handle vast adulation as well as she could hostility. At Forest Hills she risked killing herself by responding to cries of 'Come closer' even though to do so meant trailing her microphone cable across wet grass. Let *Time* sum up this sector of her career with its snapshot of her last pre-Jason performance:

> The windup last week took place in Chicago's all-but-unplayable Soldiers Field. The stage was planted on the ten-yard line. The crowd of 14,420 people curled back and up into the end-zone stands like one big paying claque. Yet there was not a heckle of complaint about the low-fi sound and plenty of uproarious laughter at even her simplest lines. A whistle whined from the neighbouring railway yard. 'My God!' she cried, 'It's got perfect pitch!'
>
> Barbra couldn't sing a clinker either. 'Any Place I Hang My Hat Is Home' brought tumult. 'He Touched Me' touched everybody. 'Autumn Leaves', in French yet, wowed 'em, and 'People' knocked 'em out. For encores she wailed her tearful 'Happy Days Are Here Again' and, patting her bulging tummy, crooned 'Silent Night'. And that was that. With thunderous cheers chasing her, Barbra tripped backstage to her house-trailer dressing-room. There, in a symbolical act, her private hairdresser sheared her customary complicated coif into a modified Mia Farrow cut that Barbra could tend herself. Then she headed home in her chartered Aero Commander jet.

Home, temporarily, was a rented beach house at Sands Point on Long Island Sound. But it was at Mount Sinai Hospital at three in the afternoon of (as Elliott Gould has reminded us) 29 December that Jason Emmanuel Gould was born. Whatever else might leave or stay, her father's first name was secure in Barbra's reflections.

Jason had been conceived in London. He was destined to grow up in a milieu altogether different – America's West Coast. As she persevered with her post-natal exercises, Barbra Streisand was readying herself for Hollywood.

TEN

EARLY IN 1967, a few weeks after the birth of Jason Gould, an advertisement was run in the Hollywood and New York trade papers:

> WANTED: Weight Watchers Dropouts. Beefy Beauties needed for Barbra Streisand CBS-TV musical special. Must sing, dance, be under 45 (years) and over 45 (bust) and fracture the scales at 200 or more in soaking wet bikinis. Send snapshots with statistics.

The show referred to was to be Barbra's third TV special. Work-titled 'The Barbra Streisand Show' it was to be a radical departure from the first two. In fact it clearly had to be, and this was reflected in its more evocative title, 'The Belle of Fourteenth Street.' It drew alongside Barbra a number of guest stars – Jason Robards, Lee Allen (from the London *Funny Girl*) and the legendary song-and-dance man, John Bubbles. Bubbles' inclusion indicates the show's key-signature. Instead of being a triptych of unrelated segments, this show would possess a unifying theme – the Golden Age of Vaudeville. It would be a turn-of-the-century variety show using songs and sketches of that era and done straight – not as a spoof. To achieve it, the show was meticulously prepared, the great George Burns himself master-minding the research. 'The Belle of Fourteenth Street' put Barbra into period costumes. Dressed to the Gay Nineties with feathery hats and boas, parasols and high-button shoes she appeared as the eponymous heroine, a German *Lieder* singer, a boy soprano and a stripper. There were also two 'heavyweight' numbers – an eleven-minute condensed and 'cool' version of *The Tempest* in which she played both Miranda and Ariel with astonishing quick-change dexterity. She sang a number with those 200-pound-plus ladies who'd rolled in like Michelin mock-ups as a result of that ad. Going out in the autumn of 1967, the show proved to be Barbra's first clear-cut critical clinker. It was universally panned. Jack Gould in the *New York Times* said that it:

> . . . was an embarrassing outing, a concoction of deranged productions that not even the star and her major colleague of the evening, Jason Robards, could straighten out.

That was one of the kinder reviews. Barbra Streisand, conditioned by unceasing superlatives, was thrown by the critical hammering. Its timing was unfortunate too. She was about to make her assault on Hollywood. Better to have surfed in on the exhilarating creamy-white waves of a recent success than in the gloom of an overblown flop. It provided the cocktail party assassins of Beverly Hills with the raw material they thrived on, a controversial superstar on the defensive. There were going to be some useful pickings on this carcass. But that could wait. Let the

118

Barbra arrives in Hollywood. Seen here talking with Mrs Ray Stark, the daughter of Fanny Brice

'goddess' settle in first. She arrived at Los Angeles in May 1967, stepping from the plane to the best laminated smiles of a typical Hollywood reception committee. Barbra knew as well as anyone else in the trade that being a star meant being a movie star. She also sensed, after just twenty-four hours' exposure to the several faces of the town – maxim, never use a word where an innuendo will do – that there was running hostility beneath the tinsel. It was only a matter of time before the knives were out. The mordant mood which encouraged it was not merely the jealous wish to see her get her *arriviste* come-uppance. After rounds of horse-trading with Ray Stark (aspects of which she was to regret – he had her tied to a three-picture deal) she was arriving to receive a cool million dollars for appearing in her first movie. This was easily a record for any actor or actress. 'Who could be worth that?' the soured failures asked as they prayed to see her blow her chance of a show-business grand slam. Elliott Gould was with her only briefly in support. His on-off, off-on career was taking him back for another Broadway try in Feiffer's *Little Murders*. So Barbra conditioned herself to take all that flak while still trying to forget the dubiousness of 'The Belle of Fourteenth Street'.

Well – there was only one way to play it. Hers. Hollywood's envy was something both she – and they – would have to live with. They and their preconceptions were okay for short-term 'discoveries'. She had never had her nose fixed, her teeth capped. She wasn't about to now. They would have to take her as they found her. But looming darkly over all her anxiety was the shadow of the director William Wyler.

In the opening scenes of the movie *Funny Girl* Barbra Streisand–Fanny Brice stares at herself in a mirror and declaims, 'Hello, gorgeous!' It is a moment loaded with more than ordinary significance. Immediately of course, it is the celluloid apotheosis of those teenage hours, days, of stargazing into that bathroom mirror. 'Hello, gorgeous' became a 'take me as I am' declaration of intent. I say it therefore I am. With no previous screen experience, Barbra Streisand was going to dominate Hollywood, and 'gorgeously' at that.

That the director of her first (mammothly budgeted) feature film should be William Wyler has a sort of cliché exquisiteness to it. In Hollywood terms William Wyler was the Establishment producer's Establishment director. A stern character, he'd long held the reputation for running a tight studio floor. A tough disciplinarian he had no truck with the 'which way do you see the scene?' school of directing. Just the right kind of heavyweight, it might be reasoned, to impose Hollywood's rules and methods upon a feisty Broadway youngster. Part of his legend was for cutting tough ladies – Bette Davis, Margaret Sullivan – down to size. One can see how he acquired it from his frequent claim that on his sets he was the only 'prima donna'. Ray Stark's choice of director, one can assume, had not been randomly taken. But incredibly perhaps – given the scale of the enterprise – Wyler had never before directed a musical. Which leads us straight to a central factor. *Funny Girl*, in effect, had two directors. Mike Frankovich, then studio chief at Columbia, recalled the nexus of attitudes in the run-up to the production:

> When we made the deal with Ray there was a lot of discussion and argument about the director. There were several people involved and Ray was a little afraid Willie might take too long to shoot it. I had a meeting with Ray at the studio to discuss this matter and I found out Ray's biggest fear was, not how long he would take, but that he would take the picture away from Ray's control completely. He wasn't sure that Barbra would get along with Willie and there was a real problem for a couple of weeks there. Then finally I called Willie's agent and he said, 'Yes, I think Willie might be interested.' Ray finally agreed to have Willie but said, 'I'd like a condition on it. I would like to have the director who worked with her on her other shows – how about Herbie Ross doing the musical numbers and let Willie do all the drama?' I said, 'I think that's going to be easy.' He said, 'What do you mean it's going to be easy?' I said, 'I don't think Willie wants to get involved with the musical side of it.' He said, 'You're kidding.' So we had a meeting with Willie and before Ray opened his mouth Willie said, 'Look, what I'd like to do is the dramatic part of the story and you get yourself another man to do the music.'

Herb Ross was to prove himself as substantial a director as he was a choreographer. At that time Ross became to *Funny Girl* what Busby Berkeley was to countless

Thirties musicals. The film was ultimately to suffer, if not to quite the same degree, from similar schizophrenia. Yet again, Isabel Lennart picked over her umpteenth revision and was to call the chore 'a deflating, ego-crushing experience'. Meanwhile Wyler geared the production to reducing the musical content (eight stage-show numbers were struck out), strengthening the dramatic storyline. The same old political manoeuvring which had hallmarked the show now wrangled around the film. Prudently trying to buy up all sides of the street, Stark quietly approached Arthur Laurents asking for yet another rewrite. Laurents is said to have allocated short shrift to his response: 'There is a lot of my *Gypsy* in your show. I think I've already made my unsolicited contribution.'

Was Wyler right for *Funny Girl*? With the shining exception of *Roman Holiday* his films have tended towards the ponderous. There is the feel of over-made thoroughness which despite touches of brilliance, drags them down. They do not live in contemporary terms because they are not technically deft enough. The heavy staging of *The Big Country*, for instance, becomes cumbersome when compared to a flash of Hawkes' filmic shorthand. So we had Wyler's relentless 'I'll know it when I see it – let's go again' approach to directing inflicted on a movie whose flimsy plot and uncertain characters cried out for a touch of Pan, not Panzers. In the event, remove Streisand and *Funny Girl* caves in at the knees. If we remember it at all, we think only of Barbra and – as with so many of those Berkeley films – the musical numbers. Even here, Ross's talents can't make a silk purse out of a second-rate score. But that is an attempt at a final verdict. Fairness to all parties demands an action replay of the more intimate skirmishes on this happy-go-huffy movie. From the outset it was billed, that year, as Hollywood's main event. And the main contenders, whether they wanted it or not, were Streisand and Wyler. Let's take the first week of production as recalled by a publicist at the time:

It was the first week of *Funny Girl* which was on location. I don't remember exactly what time of year it was but it was awfully hot and there'd been riots over in the black sections in New Jersey, right near there. Jack Brodsky, Ray Stark's publicity man at the time, took me out there to the old abandoned Jersey Central railway station which was passing for the Baltimore–Ohio railroad – the scene in which she decides to leave the show and run back to New York. We drive out and the young guys are sitting on the stoops and Brodsky says to me, 'I hope the riot doesn't start while we're driving down the street.' We get to the place and they're doing one of the scenes where all the chorus girls are running around, bustling and hustling – 'Everybody Get on the Train!' and so on – when all of a sudden it's obvious that things have stopped and nothing's happening. So we go and gig our way through the extras to see what's going on – and there are Streisand and Wyler. He must have been doing his ninety-eighth movie with Academy Awards stretching there to here. She's in like her third or fourth day on a movie set and they're nose to nose – and her nose is bigger so she's winning. She's telling him where to put the lights. There she was, her first week in the business, telling Wyler how to light the scene!

The correct response to this anecdote is to wonder where Harry Stradling, the lighting cameraman, was during this rhubarb. The answer almost certainly is that he was quietly getting on with his job. He had, after all, achieved a higher order of artistry in his career than almost anybody else (*The Picture of Dorian Gray*, *La Kermesse Heroique*, *My Fair Lady*). So he was probably happy enough to let the 'lighting' be the nominal battleground for the clash of wills and egos. Barbra belongs to that not-so-small band of actresses – Lombard, Monroe, Lee Grant are others – with a sharp awareness of how they should be lit to look their best. Wyler had made close to a hundred films. Barbra had portrayed Fanny Brice more than a thousand times. He knew his job. She knew her face. Hollywood, naturally, was 200 per cent behind the director as the 'rich bitch, iron lady' anecdotes proliferated. Ringsiders considered she had asked for it. She had slighted the Beverly Hills conventions on her first arrival in that close-circuit village. Ray Stark had shot the works for a 'coming out' party. Everybody who thought they were anybody, plus a few genuine talents, were there. But not the million-dollar Cinderella. She was an hour-and-a-half late. And only minutes in staying. She arrived with her husband, – quaint, old-fashioned thing – sat a few moments, departed. The nerve. Well they'd certainly get her in the gossip columns the next day. They did. Go tell them that meeting the screen gods and goddesses of her adolescence, her nerves, her sense of inadequacy had all trapped her like a nervous racehorse in the stalls. Before the party the tension made her dizzy and sick to her stomach. Finally she hauled herself to her feet and put in an appearance. The encounter with the 'living legends' and the crush of celebrities and the item-chasers was too much. She rushed out to be properly sick in private. The result was that throughout *Funny Girl* Barbra got the worst press ever given to a newcomer – until, that is, she worked on *Hello Dolly* the next year.

But, strangely, though venom was the flavour of every month, she found herself being publicly defended from an unexpected source – William Wyler. He proclaimed, making sure he was heard, that the reason he'd been attracted to the movie was Barbra – 'a fascinating creature' whom he wanted to present in the best light [*sic!*]. 'I wanted,' he said, 'to see if her brilliance could be brought to the screen. The true challenge to a director is to extract every nuance of greatness from a performer. She is interesting to work with. Not so easy, not so difficult. She's got ideas on how to perform. Some are good, some are not so good.' There is a touch of 'kiss and make up' about this, confirmed by their on-going friendship. Also, who is Wyler to complain about another artist's obsessional striving for excellence?

In the meantime Barbra chose to back off from Hollywood's goldfish-bowl life in the public eye. She rented a house once lived in by Garbo, a point of ironic detail that was scarcely lost on her. Not that she was exactly alone. A companion in the unlikely form of the Egyptian actor, Omar Sharif, was able to give her some consolation during her sour honeymoon with Hollywood. He was destined not only to be in the eye of the storm raging around the early top-level negotiations on the production. He became the centre of much controversy and gossip, concerning Barbra herself, and her estranged mate Elliott Gould.

That an Arab should be cast as the Jewish-American Nick Arnstein became, with the simultaneous outbreak of the Six-Day War more than a nine-day wonder. The majority of American Jewry being pro-Israeli – a large and powerful battalion of them straddling Los Angeles and Beverly Hills – they regarded even a fictional

Barbra talks over a scene with director William Wyler on the set of *Funny Girl*

shidduch between a celebrated Jewess and Omar, the maverick Arab, as a bad case of miscasting. (Cairo was similarly to regard this movie-matchmaking as being singularly un-kosher.) If the Camp David Accord had happened much earlier both parties might have been able to enjoy chopped liver at the Stage Delicatessen, or an equivalent delicacy on the Nile, without a ripple of dissent from any quarter. In fact, despite the unpleasant irrelevancies of racist, nationalistic thinking, it was first-rate professional casting.

Barbra had arrived in Los Angeles amid talk, some generated by herself, of Sinatra, Brando or Peck being considered for the Arnstein part. All three would have been disastrous. The little matter of top billing apart, any one of those heavyweights would have broken the back of the paper-thin characterisation of Arnstein. Sinatra would have been Sinatra. Brando would have been Brando. While Peck would never have been able to shadow his nice guy charm with Arnstein's adroit footwork. Sharif on the other hand . . .

A brief account of how he came to be cast opposite Barbra appears in Sharif's autobiography:

In 1967 I was making a western in Hollywood and I used to have lunch in the studio canteen every day. And, every day, producer Ray Stark and director William Wyler used to sit down at the next table. They were looking for a co-star for Barbra Streisand. That started people joking: 'Why not Omar Sharif?' One day, William Wyler reacted. 'Well *why not* Omar Sharif anyway?' The question had its impact. Dumbfounded, they all looked at him. So he repeated: 'Why not? Think about it.'

Some years later in the darkened bar of the Beverly Wilshire Hotel, Sharif expanded on the theme to us with an engaging absence of ego (a difficult exercise since unattached but not unattractive females close by eyed him covetously – and he them).

In *Funny Girl* I was doing feed lines really. I was something for Barbra to play off. It's the story of the Ugly Duckling and Prince Charming, really. The way Willie Wyler saw it, it was a fairytale. It just needed someone who would know how to wear white tie and tails, quite honestly, and not speak with an American accent. That's all he really wanted. Barbra wanted me too, and we signed and everything. Then, lo and behold! the Six-Day War. We hadn't started the film. Then there were troubles. A lot of people wrote letters saying – you're going to give all this money to this Egyptian and for all you know he's going to give it to Nasser. And Barbra's mother got a bit worried about her daughter. The studio wanted to cancel my contract. If Willie Wyler hadn't said, 'I'm not making this film without Omar,' they actually would have changed me. Barbra had no misgivings about it whatsoever. There was a big meeting of all the top brass and I sent in Abe Lastfogel to represent me. He was sort of the head of the Jewish community here and they had this enormous meeting. Finally, because of Willie Wyler, they stuck with me. And also because I was making two films that year for Columbia – the other one was *McKenna's Gold* with Carl Foreman and we hadn't started that yet and they wanted to cancel both contracts. Carl also stood up and said he might cancel the film as well.

The story sheds an admirable light on the moral courage of two directors. Foreman, as the witch-hunt era confirms, has an honourable record in the area of standing up to be counted as an opponent of political prejudice. And Wyler would have no truck either with political interference on his show. He was brilliantly supported in public by his two leading performers. When a still of their first (film) kiss was released and the Arab press had one of its periodic fits of bigotry, Sharif tartly commented: 'I don't make a point of asking a girl her nationality, her occupation or her religion before kissing her – either on the screen or off!' Predictably, perhaps, Cairo had taken a far harder line over the on-screen, off-screen relationship than Israel and its supporters. For kissing a Jewish girl who had given a gala to raise funds for Israel, Sharif was formally declared a traitor to his country. Barbra scathingly cut this contemptible chauvinism down to Brooklyn size and style: 'You think Cairo was upset? You should see the letter I got from my Aunt Rose,' she rasped.

Wyler showed acumen as well as courage. Sharif, who is in the world class more as a bridge player than as an actor, can nevertheless produce creditable performances on the screen. Carved in what *Variety* calls the 'sleek sheik' mould, he contrives to bring a quality of rakish insouciance to his roles. Wyler felt he could draw on it, and succeeded. At the end of it all, Sharif was brutally short-changed in the verdicts on the picture. The lumpen qualities in *Funny Girl* were attributed by many (with dubious qualifications) to Sharif's performance. The charge is crass. Forced to play second fiddle to Streisand's virtuoso performance, Sharif works wonders with the non-material, the ersatz character. And there is evidence that Barbra shared the view.

At that time she had virtually refused to be interviewed by the media. However, *Funny Girl* was about to be released in England. Several reputations other than her own hung on its success. She was interviewed for BBC television by Michael Dean. She was charming, witty, relaxed, unfussed and unfussing. After the hour or so of questioning the cameraman for the interview, John Bailey (later to rise to be Director of Photography on *American Gigolo*) congratulated her on her Fanny Brice performance. But . . . 'I wasn't so impressed by Omar Sharif,' he added. 'Well, I thought he was pretty good,' Barbra shot back at once. She was not unpleasant. She offered the judgement not as a verdict but as an opinion. Maybe with Streisand they're one and the same. She then smiled at the cameraman and presented him with a cinnamon stick.

A cynic, of course, might have suggested that she has a personal interest in that opinion. Sharif has stated that Barbra 'wanted him' to play Arnstein. He does not quite say when. Whether it was before or after they met. The question is not entirely academic. Speedily, as *Funny Girl* progressed, it was assumed that since the two stars were not fighting they must be having an affair. Sharif confirms it to us with his own special brand of sleek innuendo:

> Barbra Streisand, who struck me as being ugly at first, gradually cast her spell over me. I fell madly in love with her talent and her personality. The feeling was mutual for four months – the time it took for shooting the picture. How many of my affairs seemed to last till the end of a shooting!
>
> Barbra's villa served as our trysting-place. At the time, my own villa housed my family. We spent our evenings, our weekends at her place. Our contracts ruled out any travel.

There is a quality of sexual opportunism – 'sure, I can fit you in, my schedule's perfect for the moment' – that flaws this 'true confession'. On the other hand to have the Valentino of the decade eating out of her hand must have been sweet indeed to the erstwhile skinny, 'crazy Barbara' of Flatbush. By day, a million dollars for working with this suavely-handsome international sophisticate. By night, the pleasure of his company. Other nuances added piquancy to the saga of Streisand and Sharif. For the crucial finale of the film, Barbra, singing 'My Man', insisted that Sharif be present on the set. The legend is that while she sang, Omar, out of camera, held her hand, presumably transfusing with his warm touch, the subtle overtones the number demanded. Since she was later to demand the reverse in a later movie, *On a Clear Day* – namely that Yves Montand be decidedly absent during an equivalent scene – the contrast has been markedly noted. Sharif expands on the legend, indicating that personal feelings aside, his presence on the set was a sensible, professional requirement:

It was the last scene of the film and I was at home packing. We had already said 'goodbye' to each other and everything. The studio called and said, 'She wants you on the set.' So I went over to the studio and there'd been a big row between Barbra and production and everybody because she wanted to do the song live which is not done in big musicals – it's pre-recorded and they sing to playback. But she said, 'No. The only way I want to do this song is I want to be behind the curtain, like in the scene. I come out – it's all black. You put the spot on me and I sing it live and you record it live.' And she finally had her way. And then she said she wanted Omar. So I left my suitcases half packed and went into the studio. What she wanted was this: the previous scene was a scene where I go into her dresssing-room. I'd just come out of jail. And I tell her we're not going to be together any more – it just doesn't work out. There were lines in that scene which moved her tremendously. She wanted me to go behind the curtain and play that scene over again so that she would come out very much moved, and sing. The scene had the line 'I never gave you anything.' She says, 'Yes, you gave me a lot. You gave me a blue marble egg – and you also made me feel beautiful.' And I say, 'You *are* beautiful.' And that line moved her enormously when I said it because I really believed it. I loved her and I used to tell her that she was beautiful. And when I said that line she used to be tremendously moved. Because she had a thing about her looks. I don't know about now. So we went behind the curtain and said these lines and she came out and did the song absolutely brilliantly. She came out in tears. She did this by herself and she did thirteen takes. Because she wanted to. The director, from the first take, said it was wonderful. She kept saying, 'I can do it better, I want to do another one.' And after those thirteen takes, I left.

Omar may have rolled up his tent and departed but the 'My Man' anecdote did not end there. Isabel Lennart considered that in giving the song its first Hollywood reprise since a jokey snatch in *Fashions of 1934* Ray Stark was plunging the film's finale into the suds of soap opera. Jule Styne too was shocked that the film should end with such a Sixties Piaf-cabaret-torch-song belting. 'Nobody sang like that in the Twenties,' he objected. 'She violated every code by doing "My Man" the way Fanny Brice would never have dreamed of doing it!' Wyler could not agree. Barbra Streisand had never been Fanny Brice. A brilliant one-for-one characterisation would never have played. He was serving Barbra straight. It was his idea to shoot the finale against the limbo of black drapes. The old hand in him warmed to the magic of a 'live' performance.

But another, more intriguing aspect of the story relates to the lines Sharif recalls. Above Oscar's fish restaurant, Elliott had given Barbra a blue marble egg. Many times told her she was beautiful. It was she who had had those lines written into the dialogue. Much of her emotion when she came through that black curtain must have arisen from a growing sense of the break-up of her marriage. The end of the affair with 'her man'.

Some people may still, just, have kept an open mind on the Streisand–Sharif pact. Elliott Gould was less tentative. He was furious. He was also marooned in New York. Ironically his ill-fated, clumsy career was at last taking a turn for the better. *Little Murders* had not lasted long on Broadway but it had led him to *Luv* –

in summer stock but opposite the redoubtable Shelley Winters. That had led in turn to his being signed for the movie which, the turning point in his career, he officially acknowledges as his first – *The Night They Raided Minsky's*. In it he gives what is still arguably his deftest screen performance. But it was while making it, chained to New York, that dozens of willing friends poured poison in his ear to the effect that 'Garbo' was not entirely alone in her secluded habitat. Sheilah Graham, displaying the salivating reactions of Pavlov's dogs, yelped in the *Citizen News*:

Elliott Gould's boiling mad that his wife Barbra Streisand has dated Omar Sharif. He telephoned her in Hollywood and told her he was 'furious'. Talk of possible trouble between the Goulds began when Sharif escorted Barbra to an exclusive fashion party two weeks ago at a discotheque in Hollywood.

'I'm furious with Barbra, and told her that,' Gould told me. 'Barbra should have known that she is in a very difficult position out there where the press doesn't like her because she has been unco-operative. I'm a very secure person but as a man I have certain reactions,' Gould went on.

Gould, an actor, said he asked his wife, 'Why in hell did you go to the fashion show with Omar?' and that she replied, 'Because the ticket would have cost me $250.'

Miss Streisand, 25, born and raised in Brooklyn, has earned millions of dollars from her singing and acting career.

Throwing in that innuendo Miss Graham chose to ignore the disarming wit of Barbra Streisand. But for Gould it was bad news. The item, widely syndicated, was now translated into the writing on the wall . . .

The film *Funny Girl* was released to a clamour of mixed reactions which underline two major factors: the first, that whatever anybody may have thought about the film, Streisand stood triumphantly apart from the general considerations; second, that given the strictures of family loyalty, it is mighty hard to produce a historical movie about your mother-in-law.

Renata Adler wrote in the *New York Times*:

The movie is an elaborate, painstaking launching-pad with important talents of Hollywood . . . treating Barbra Streisand rather fondly, improbably, even patronisingly as though she were firing off a gilded broccoli. Miss Streisand's talent is very poignant and strong but the movie almost does her in.

Donald J. Mayerson of *The Villager* wrote:

We are presented with an overblown, irritatingly fake Hollywood production . . .

But many critics loved the film, gearing their praise to Streisand's scintillating command of the screen. Pauline Kael was outstandingly generous in the scale of her comparisons:

Offset, sharing a joke with Omar Sharif during the filming of *Funny Girl*

Streisand [she wrote in the *New Yorker*] has the gift of making old written dialogue sound like inspired improvisation . . . she can probably do more for a line than any screen comedienne since Jean Arthur in the Thirties . . . It's Streisand's peculiar triumph that in the second half when the routine heartbreak comes, as it apparently must in all musical biographies, she shows an aptitude for suffering that those [other] actresses didn't. Where they became sanctimonious and noble, thereby violating everything we had loved them for, she simply drips as unselfconsciously and impulsively as a true magic muse. And the tears belong to her face; they seem to complete it as Garbo's suffering in *Camille* seemed to complete her beauty.

Some critics, going beyond the performance, made significant observations on the *appearance* of the star. Rex Reed, happily paying off an old debt, declared:

> No more cracks about Barbra Streisand's nose. It took the combined efforts of God knows how many people to do it, but I'll be damned if they haven't made her beautiful. In the most remarkable screen debut I will probably see in my lifetime, the toadstool from Erasmus High School has been turned into a truffle, and I, for one, couldn't be happier about the transformation.

There can be no question that Harry Stradling worked countless miracles of lighting and cosmetic tact. But even without it, Barbra Streisand, in film as in life, becomes beautiful by the sheer force of inner personality. Her will drives the transformation. She possesses the great star's ability to have a love affair with the lens. And she knows how to present her best side to that cold, impersonal hunk of glass. In tossing the conventional screen image into the trashcan Barbra was striking a blow for all the other 'uglies' – Donald Sutherland, Glenda Jackson, Dustin Hoffman . . . Elliott Gould.

Her best or, more properly, better side is her left. She keeps a very low profile indeed on her right. The entire visual orientation of *Funny Girl* is structured around this consideration. The helicopter-bit boat shot, the position of the sun over New York; the direction of the tug; the position of the liner it pursues – all are choreographed around the preferred profile. Barbra Streisand is not a screen actress who in close shot can be made to come and go every which way. But what does it matter? When *Funny Girl* was premiered in New York at the Criterion Theater, Broadway traffic halted for Barbra as amid the cheering of thousands of fans she crossed the Great White Way on a Crawford-, Davis-, Garbo-vintage red carpet. Six months before the opening, the advance sales exceeded those of any road-show in the history of the theater, including *The Ten Commandments*, *South Pacific*, *Lawrence of Arabia* and *My Fair Lady*. After one movie Streisand's position as a star in the great Hollywood tradition was not in question. At a million dollars she was cheap. Indeed, compared with the Monopoly money paid to Redford-class performers – the bidding opening at three million – Barbra's salary for *Funny Girl* seems almost like a down-payment.

London's reaction to the movie matched the fireworks of New York – just a question of lighting the touch-paper and standing back. Critics teetered towards the ecstatic over Barbra's bravura performance, were lukewarm about the film. The Royal Premiere in the West End was dominated by Streisand, the word 'charisma' sprinkled liberally in the news and feature columns of the papers. Princess Margaret and her then husband, the extremely gifted photographer Lord Snowdon, were the royal guests. In the line-up for the presentations, a major event to Hollywood contingents, Snowdon asked Ray Stark about the film. The producer, introducing the attractive Mrs Stark, explained that *Funny Girl* was the life story of his mother-in-law, adding the tension-relieving quip, 'and any time you'd like me to make a film about your in-laws, my lord, just give me a ring.' (Collectors of similar gems will know of the occasion when Her Majesty the Queen, meeting Lord Grade's mother, Mrs Winogradsky, said, 'You must be proud of your son,' to which the grey-haired lady from Odessa beamed in response, 'You too!')

At the party at Claridges which followed the premiere, the guests waited for Princess Margaret and Barbra to lead them from the private ante-room to the main ballroom. At the theater earlier, the playing of the National Anthem signalled Princess Margaret's arrival in the Royal Circle. For the entry into the ballroom, the orchestra played 'People'. Streisand made no move, continuing to chatter with guests. Finally, the Princess, smiling, said, 'I think you ought to go in, dear, they're playing *your* tune.' It was at this party that Barbra Streisand was introduced to the Canadian Premier, Pierre Trudeau. The moment appeared to have little significance at the time, except, of course, for the two individuals concerned. The impact of each upon the other was powerful enough, that night at Claridges, for both to seek ways to renew contacts. The Streisand–Trudeau 'happening' was to do more than dominate the headlines. It was to provoke a priceless challenge across the floor of the Canadian Parliament.

But Barbra's 'Canadian experience' was some distance ahead. She returned from her blockbusting success in London to renew her 'marriage' to Hollywood, for better or worse.

The worse was an unwelcome carry-over from a TV show transmitted before she arrived in Hollywood. It was her 'Belle of Fourteenth Street' special. The knives that were out had a carcass to carve. Underdog Hollywood was gleeful. The bitch-goddess had got her come-uppance. For Barbra, the panning had practical significance beyond the psychic wounds that were long in healing. She chose not to do another television special again for some six years. But already in the pipeline (eventually to be aired a year later, in 1968) was a special spin-off from an earlier enterprise, correctly entitled a 'Happening'.

It happened in New York – Sheep Meadow, Central Park to be precise. Barbra had flown there in mid-June 1967, virtually direct from the *Funny Girl* set. She went straight to the park. The 'Happening' was a concert sponsored by Rheingold Beer as a gift to New York. It was literally a gift. There was no admission. First come, first served. The first came at 6.00 a.m. for a concert that would begin fourteen hours later when New York's summer temperature would have dipped all the way down from pushing a hundred to the mere low nineties. By 8.00 in the evening there were an estimated 135,000 people awaiting the entrance on stage of the evening's sole entertainer.

A fair number walked out before she completed her marathon ordeal. When eventually the two-and-a-half hours of performance had been edited down to an hour, it was well-received on television. But the live performance left a good deal to be desired. Barbra's stage technique was rusty. Her commitment to the lyrics was half-hearted. Her volume was suspect. René Jordan, however, points out that, in a sense, with a 'Happening' on such a scale it is less a case of minding the quality than feeling the width.

'Her performance,' he wrote, 'had the precarious equilibrium of a surfer riding a tidal wave. Forget about doing it gracefully; the main thing was to manoeuvre the crest . . . The throngs had not come to listen to her but to congratulate themselves on their own stamina. They had sweated for endless hours to be able to tell everyone that they'd *been* there. Each was on his or her private trip to the stars; she was just the spaceship.'

In retrospect, three aspects of the 'Happening in Central Park' seem quite phenomenal. One: that a performer so young and relatively new could command such crowds. Two: that a performer so subject to attacks of stage-fright before a live audience could fight off her terror and confront so massive an audience. Three: that it took the New York sanitation department four days to square away the garbage revealed by the next dawn's early light.

The annual 'Oscar' ceremony of the American Academy of Motion Picture Arts and Sciences is, itself, a less than pure happening. It is all things to all participants. It is Hollywood preening itself, unabashed, before a TV audience of zillions. It is as much a self-congratulatory flag-waving trade show as it is a manifestation of scrupulous critical judgement. Nevertheless, despite the saturation 'puffing' for her in the trade papers, few people in Hollywood begrudged Barbra's Fanny Brice earning her a nomination for the best performance by an actress in 1968. Even fewer, though, would have given her more than an outsider's chance of winning the Award, at her first shot. In the year that another musical, *Oliver* was to win the best picture award, competition for 'Best Actress' was as fierce as the category had ever known. As Ingrid Bergman was to read out, the nominees had been Joanne Woodward for *Rachel, Rachel* (for which she had already received the New York Film Critics Award), Katharine Hepburn (the previous year's winner) for *The Lion In Winter*, Patricia Neal (winner in 1963 for *Hud*) for *The Subject was Roses*, Vanessa Redgrave for *Isadora*.

Barbra had no great expectations of winning. By now into her third production (*On a Clear Day*), she felt herself more ostracised than ever by Hollywood's 'palace guard'. With typical directness she announced: 'I want to win more than anything else in the world, but I can't believe I'm going to get it. It's the Jewishness in me, I guess, the pessimism. I can't win. Not me. It's the agony and the ecstasy.'

That night Elliott Gould apparently endured similar emotions. He was now in Hollywood making the film that would take him out of the wilderness into a land flowing with milk and money. And his name above the title, *Bob and Carol and Ted and Alice*. He was staying with Barbra. Only he wasn't. They were now formally estranged. He was only camping at her place. But there are occasions, an Oscar night being one of them, when the rule book says you close ranks, enter arm in arm, 'business as usual' during altercations. Gould, who hated the strait-jacketing of tuxedo events, loyally played out his role. The husband there to lend moral support for the crushing moment when she would not hear her name called, or for playing cheer-leader when, the unbelievable happening, the star takes that flying leap down the aisle and raises a lump in the throat of tele-America.

The role of husband, companion, moral support and, if the worst happened, a shoulder to cry on, daunted Mr Gould. He decided that a little pot is no dangerous thing. When, as seen on coast-to-coast hookup, he scratched his ear, it was a signal to a friend that he was flying a little. A private signal. His demeanour was suave enough to win him a last minute nomination for best supporting husband. From Barbra, on the other hand, the evening elicited close to both the very worst and the very best in her.

The worst was embodied in the Scaasi original she chose to arrive in. A dire compromise between Thrift Shop and high fashion it was a see-through pants suit in clear sequin-covered tulle. Patch pockets covered the breasts to a fully frontal view. But with an apparent failure of nerve she chose to wear a conventional bra as well. Panties in nude-coloured silk lent her a retreating persona of 'bare-buttocked embarrassment' to quote one rag trade paper. As an act of splendid non-conformist defiance the wearing of the suit failed dismally. Overawed perhaps by the big occasion, Barbra had lost her flair for 'look at me' outrageousness. The suit was neither high style nor high anti-style. It failed. But then . . .

'And the winner is . . .' When Ingrid Bergman had opened the key envelope she paused a moment in surprise. She was only the first to catch her breath. The 'Best Actress' result that year was the one nobody had put money on – a tie. Barbra's forecast was at fault. She had won. But so had Katharine Hepburn. The absent party. The star of *Lion in Winter*, in less than perfect health, and perhaps a little underawed by the prospect of her third Oscar, had not attended the ceremony. Barbra tripped towards the stage and Ingrid Bergman, alone, almost literally. Her high heel had caught in the too-low-slung bell bottom of the pants suit. For a micro-second that lasted a year, she teetered on the brink of a prat-fall in front of not merely a nation-wide television audience but worse, the snickers of the entire Hollywood Establishment. The moment passed. She recovered her balance and, thanks to her keen intelligence, her poise.

Her short speech of acceptance ranks among the most clearly spontaneous and most genuinely graceful of the scores of mumbled 'I'd like to thank the members of the Academy' responses. She began with an inspired one-liner. Smiling down at the gilded statuette she murmured, 'Hello, Gorgeous' – her opening line in *Funny Girl*. Then she said quite simply that she was honoured to be associated in the winning of such an award with Miss Hepburn. Saying this she contrived to make the securing of half-a-loaf seem rather more precious than winning the whole. More than one veteran of scores of such ceremonies conceded they'd been given a sagacious lesson that night in diplomacy and good manners.

Elliott Gould was applauding frenetically as she returned to her seat. It may well have crossed that sharp brain of hers that it could be the last ovation in their marriage. But if so, it could only have been a fleeting thought. She had already overdrawn on her emotions. Quite apart from the cliff-hanging torment of the Awards, she had just expanded a normal person's lifetime of dog-fight emotions in the making of her second movie. Off screen.

Barbra wins an Oscar

ELEVEN

THERE ARE certain situations in which Barbra Streisand and Walter Matthau could almost be guaranteed to get along well together. Bar mitzvahs, weddings, race tracks, Carnegie Hall or New York's Russian Tea Room – all the elements there for the Catskills humour and culture on which both these volatile characters were raised. What is debatable, however, is whether they should ever work together again on the same movie. They did so, once, on *Hello Dolly*, that $24 million aberration by 20th Century Fox, clashing royally one unhappy, venomously hot June day in 1968. It was 5 June and the fact is significant. It was the day that Bobby Kennedy was shot. That appalling event, his brother's assassination still an unhealed wound in America, induced such shock and disgust that nothing else that day occupied the minds of the citizens. No time, for sure, for intelligent adults, touched by the universal grief, to be embroiled in the hassle and the comparative trivia and superficialities of movie-making. Worse still, a movie like *Hello Dolly* with its flat-footed ideas, paper-thin characters and totally ersatz exhilaration. Whatever Streisand thought of her role as the husband-hunting Dolly, Matthau had come to loathe his role as the idiot, egocentric Horace Vandergelder, the posturing object of Dolly's marriage plans. Long before the major flare-up between them on 5 June, Matthau had become increasingly disenchanted with his co-star and her special brand of film-making. A series of minor irritations blew up into the stormy confrontation on 5 June when the man raised in the ghetto of New York's Lower East Side gave it with both barrels to the girl from Pulaski Street, Brooklyn. His mood soured at finding himself the wrong man in the wrong movie, and darkened further by the news of the Kennedy killing, his tolerance threshold was virtually at nil. Streisand, being Streisand, was intent upon doing the best she could, which meant making suggestions, asking questions. It was more than Matthau, the World War II Air Force sergeant with six battle stars, could take. Versions vary as to precisely what followed. But the thrust of Matthau's mordant attack seems to have included (with a gesture towards Gene Kelly): 'Why don't you let *him* direct the picture?' And the tart, 'You don't have to be great *all* the time!'

Later, Matthau was to flesh out the incident in an interview with writer Clive Hirschorn for his admirable book on Gene Kelly.

> Barbra kept asking Gene whether he didn't think it would be better if I did this on this line, and that on the other, etc., etc. – and I told her to stop directing the fucking picture, which she took exception to, and there was a blow-up in which I also told her she was a pip-squeak who didn't have the talent of a butterfly's fart. To which she replied that I was jealous because I wasn't as good as she was. I'm not the most diplomatic man in the world, and we began a slanging match like a couple of kids from the ghetto. I think Gene thought one of us was going to die of apoplexy or something, or that I'd belt

her, or that maybe she'd scratch my eyes out – or worse, that we'd just walk off leaving twenty million dollars' worth of movie to go down the drain.

At one time during the tetchy proceedings, Matthau dubbed his co-star 'Madame Petomane'. Vaudeville buffs at least will be familiar with the legendary skill of a certain music-hall star named 'Monsieur Petomane'; *peter* being the French verb 'to fart' will give the clue to Monsieur's celebrated act which concluded, so it is said, with a flatulent rendering of 'La Marseillaise'. We may assume that Matthau's description of Barbra as 'Madame Petomane' was not out of deference to the French national anthem.

More than a decade later, the row on *Dolly* still touches a nerve with both contenders, though for different reasons. Barbra Streisand reflects on it more in sorrow now than in anger. And Matthau? Hindsight, evident contrition, plus a need to watch his blood pressure have combined to make him drastically review the battle. And yet . . .

Early in 1980 we sat opposite him in the private executive dining room at Universal Studios in California. It was a press lunch to launch his current release, *Little Miss Marker*, the Chablis flowing as freely as Matthau's caustic reminiscences. The versatile genius whom Neil Simon rates as 'the greatest instinctive actor ever' was in fine form. Scrunching his pliant face and charcoal brows in a variety of expressions, he fired a series of poison-tipped one-liners in which analysts, actors and other screwballs got their come-uppance from the master. We had a recital of how he lost his virginity in Lille, France, with all the pertinent details from groin to gratitude. The amiable monologue was abruptly interrupted by someone asking, 'Tell us, Mr Matthau, why did you so dislike making *Hello Dolly*?' Matthau's mortician's smile glove-puppeted into crumpled irritation.

'Why ask me that?' he growled. 'It's like an old boil. It's like asking, "How did you like that cancer?" '

For once, Matthau's renowned footwork was a shade uncertain. But the inscrutable comment revealed that the trauma was still there. The taunting memories were all jostling back into his mind.

Fox bought the film rights to *Hello Dolly* in 1964. The show had opened on 16 January of that year at Broadway's St James Theater with Carol Channing in the title role and David Burns as Horace Vandergelder. It was an immediate sell-out and ran a total of 2844 performances, making it the second longest-running musical in Broadway history. (*Fiddler on the Roof* was later to have the edge over it by 398 performances.)

At Fox, the accountants with noughts before their eyes in the euphoria of *The Sound of Music* shelled out the $2.5 million plus a percentage of the gross for *Dolly*, convinced that this was the time to press their bets. Richard Zanuck, now the chief decision-maker, asked Gene Kelly to direct the picture. With *The Sound of Music* money flooding in, Zanuck intimated to Kelly he wan't going to count paper clips. The movie would cost around $20 million plus, which would make it the most expensive musical ever made. The gnarled old tale of which *Hello Dolly* is a gossamer-light offspring goes back to 1835 when an Englishman, John Oxenford, gave the first version of the story in a play called *A Day Well Spent*. Others toyed around with it with mixed success. In 1938, Thornton Wilder, America's distin-

The scene in the draper's shop from *Hello Dolly!*

guished dramatist and Pulitzer Prize winner, adapted the basic tale for his play *The Merchant of Yonkers*. It was no hit, but fifteen years later he tried again with *The Matchmaker*. This time, with the benefit of Ruth Gordon as Dolly Levi, the play took off. Paramount Pictures produced their film version of it with Shirley Booth in the title role. In the familiar cross-fertilisation of the trade, David Merrick later refashioned it as the stage musical. Now Fox had it. And Gene Kelly. And who . . .? As Julie Andrews ruefully discovered after *My Fair Lady*, being the star of a Broadway smash gives one no special dispensation when the film role is discussed. Her stage version of Eliza Doolittle was no less masterly than Rex Harrison's Professor Higgins. But in accordance with Hollywood's crass and blinkered logic, the film role was given to Audrey Hepburn. The logic, like the film, was seriously flawed. The decision as to who would play Dolly was similarly fraught.

Carol Channing had played the part superbly on Broadway. After eighteen months of record grosses, she finally left the cast, handing over the glittering prize to a succession of stars which included Ginger Rogers, Martha Raye, Phyllis Diller and Betty Grable.

Would Channing be given the film? The reasoning, in her favour, was: why buck a winning streak? She's big, she's great in the part, hell, she *is* Dolly! But then Fox, the money men, the head counters and the cinema circuit veterans, took a cooler view of the situation. Would Channing, with those clockwork eyelashes, throaty-like Muppet squeals and 20,000-volt persona, be right for the gutsy but schmaltzy Mrs Levi? The smart money argued that she would not. When that decision was communicated to Miss Channing, she made all the brave, magnanimous noises, though clearly the news was painful to her. Richard L. Coe of the *Washington Post* stated the case for choosing Carol Channing:

Would you believe Barbra Streisand for the screen's *Hello Dolly!* Well, that's the knuckle-headed fact, a glorious throwback to the dear old Hollywood that put Gertrude Lawrence in *The Glass Menagerie* and, how ironically, Shirley Booth into *The Matchmaker*, the source of *Dolly*.

The perversity of not choosing to get Carol Channing's musical comedy classic on film is hard to fathom. While others have played 'Dolly' on stage, hers is the only one which, in four years, never has played to an empty seat. Like Miss Gordon's non-musical 'Dolly' Miss Channing's is sheer bravura, larger than life, gloriously electric and genuinely touching.

Barbra had visited Carol Channing during the stage run of *Hello Dolly!*

137

Miss Channing's own comment, when it was clear that the dice were loaded in Barbra Streisand's favor, had style: 'I'm glad that, if I don't get it, so young and decided a talent as Miss Streisand would.' She told of a phone call she had from Julie Andrews (who had the film version of *My Fair Lady* filched from her by Audrey Hepburn): 'Never mind, Carol,' Miss Andrews reportedly consoled her. 'You'll get your *Mary Poppins*.'

Producer Ernest Lehmann, who had written the screenplays for *The Sound of Music* and *West Side Story*, had been assigned to produce *Dolly*. He had automatically considered Channing for the lead in the film but decided, after seeing her in *Thoroughly Modern Millie*, that her personality was just 'too strong for the cameras to contain.' Julie Andrews was considered, then rejected (wisely) on the simple notion that she was totally wrong for it. The same argument removed Elizabeth Taylor from serious consideration though she was known to be keen to play it. So then there was Barbra Streisand. What is surprising, when one surveys the front runners at the time, is why it took so long to get around to her. The argument that she was manifestly too young for Dolly Levi was an irrelevancy that could easily be buried under the mountain of flim-flam upon which the story is poised. Streisand had all the vocal attack, dramatic punch and man-devouring style that this interfering matchmaker demanded. She also had talent by the shipload which made Matthau's (later manfully recanted) analogy to 'a butterfly's fart' a gigantic mis-hit. Paulene Kael encapsulates the general view by saying that 'Streisand uses song as an intensification of emotion . . . she totally dominates the screen whenever she's on. And when she's given a chance to let her energy out, she's great.'

So Lehmann invited Barbra to play the role. The offer surprised her. Preoccupied with the filming of *Funny Girl* at the time, she shrugged it off with 'Yeah, okay, swell.' Later when the contract and the script arrived and the whole pre-production ritual dance began, she confessed to being 'kinda surprised' that the favored role of the year was hers. She was genuinely thrilled at having Walter Matthau in the Vandergelder role. If anyone could give this smaller-than-life character substance, it was this veteran of a score of triumphant characterisations. Technically, Matthau's problem was to save this 'idiot character' (his words) from being totally emasculated by this praying mantis named Dolly. And lurking behind were the nagging rumours that Miss Streisand was a 'problem star', given, it was said, to 'directing her directors.' The basis for that assertion was the feedback from William Wyler's experience directing her in *Funny Girl*. (When asked, long after, what he thought of Barbra Streisand in that film, Matthau is quoted as saying with deadly charm, 'Not bad considering it's the first film she ever directed.')

Gene Kelly also had no illusions about directing this highly motivated, perfection-seeking performer. He had no prejudices either. Nevertheless he confessed to coming on to the production 'with my dukes up', only to discover that there was more myth than matter in the tales of Streisand. Having signed to direct the picture (the choreography being separately handled by the brilliant Michael Kidd), Gene Kelly focused his mind on what he saw as the key challenge – directing Streisand. He'd heard, he said, that 'she was a difficult lady'. He decided to grasp that nettle immediately. He flew from Hollywood to New York for a meeting with Barbra, at the Oak Room in New York's Plaza Hotel. In this leather-backed emporium for hustling, haggling and decision-making, Gene, not one to fool around, came straight out with 'Barbra, is there any truth to all these stories that you don't want to rehearse and that you're difficult?' Barbra, with barely a hint of irritation, replied, 'No.' All she needed, she told Gene Kelly was a director to guide her, that she was dying to do the role, and that he, Gene, could count on her. 'I told her she would have to work damn hard because the part called for a matron and she was still a young and blooming woman. She agreed with me and said she would.' Nothing dramatic there. Other stars with 'reputations' – names like Lee Marvin, Marlon Brando, John Travolta suggest themselves – have no doubt been similarly challenged and given an earnest of their best intentions at all times. Barbra Streisand certainly intended to give Gene Kelly, Walter Matthau, *Dolly* and 20th Century Fox everything her dynamic talents could generate. But the nature of the animal, compounded of fear, insecurity and a kind of siege neurosis, stalked the production almost from Day One. In fact even earlier than that. The rumours from Wyler's *Funny Girl* were a rag-bag of innuendo, gossip and less than half-truths.

Fox's nervousness at the time was compounded of apprehension about Streisand's alleged weight-pulling on the set and an uneasiness at the anti-Streisand lobby in Arab-speaking countries. Major studios do not like it when their product is threatened abroad. In the fiscal holiness of Hollywood all currencies are equal in the sight of Mammon. Even Egyptian piastres. The same front-office tremors followed the banning of Elizabeth Taylor's films in Egypt, more for her close support for Israel, less for the fact of her becoming a Jewess on her marriage to the late Mike Todd. The studio was less bothered by the personal, leered-over gossip items which feed the dubious maxim of the trade – 'all publicity is good publicity.' What cannot be refuted is that the Sharif–Streisand affair – that part of it keyhole-gazers could get a glimpse of – sold tickets. If, obliquely, it contributed some way to the eventual destruction of Barbra's marriage to Elliott Gould, tough luck. Gossip items in the 'trades', on the powerful Rhona Barrett TV spot on *Good Morning America*, in magazine layouts and on the radio outlets, all bore the flavor of money. As the Garbo saga proved, and Marilyn Monroe, Elizabeth Taylor and Marlon Brando confirmed – the more contentious the star, the better the public like it. Only when the bones of the carcass have been picked clean and dry, will it turn to some other celebrated victim.

Streisand's reputation, falsely founded or not, offered a portrait of an unrelenting perfectionist, whose obsession with how she looked, sounded, and performed would make strong men weak, and top directors wonder how the hell they got into this. Matthau had heard the stories long before they had met, notably from Sydney Chaplin who emerged from *Funny Girl* with no residual affection for his co-star. We may make allowances here. To be the son of the great Chaplin, who was disliked and long-ostracised by the powerful studio chiefs in Hollywood, is a tough inheritance for a striving actor. A maverick with a short fuse, Sydney Chaplin was unlikely to strike harmonious chords with Barbra. He was one of those who marked Matthau's card about working with Streisand. Fed with this 'ammunition', Matthau could scarcely judge which were the 'blanks' and which the real McCoy – he arrived for his first meeting with Barbra with more than a few preconceived notions. He felt that she was 'prejudiced against him from the beginning'. Not true, she says, tacitly ascribing the charge to something close to paranoia. As one ring-sider had it,

'Both got the Indian sign on each other early on . . .'

They met, then, Barbra and Matthau in Millburn, New Jersey, where Walter had gone to see his old friend Maureen Stapleton in a revival of *The Glass Menagerie*. His daughter, Lucy Saroyan, spotted Barbra seated in the audience. Walter said he didn't know her but, with the tales of Chaplin lingering in his mind, felt a tug of mischief in the making. According to Barbra, he said, 'Oh, you're Barbara Harris. I see you've had your nose done.' (An obscure joke, unworthy of the champion needler at his best.) 'I was so shocked,' Barbra said, 'I couldn't even answer him.' For Streisand to be rendered speechless by a short, verbal right hook is an indication of her deep sensibilities about her features. It did not bode well for the screen partnership.

Filmed in Todd A-O, the major production set-up was a $3 million replica of New York's Fifth Avenue of the 1890s. It occupied a giant share of the then unlimited acreage of 20th Century Fox's Roman-sized empire. The scene is the mighty backdrop for Streisand's number 'Before the Parade Passes By'. Four thousand extras, eleven marching bands, six floats, twenty-eight horse-drawn vehicles, a whirr of penny-farthing bicycles, twenty assistant directors, seven cameras . . . no one could fault *Hello Dolly* for size. The sheer scale of it, tethered to a story as limpidly unconvincing as the one confected for the movie, was guaranteed to heighten the misgivings of the two leading performers. And Barbra was not only apprehensive about the vacuity of the material. She was developing strong second thoughts about the basic casting, about a girl in her twenties playing the mature Dolly Levi. With millions already riding on it, it is a bad time to wonder whether the thoroughbred should ever have been entered in the race. The professional in her kept Barbra Streisand on parade and ready to work. The soul-searching artist, however, was having sleepless nights. As the producer Ernest Lehmann recalled, she telephoned him on several occasions in the middle of the night to ask him what the hell she was doing in the picture, insisting that she shouldn't be anywhere near it. How, she wanted to know, do you get Barbra Streisand to play Dolly Levi in a way that made sense of the woman? How indeed. (Some years later Lehmann could have exchanged notes with Sydney Pollack who also had the interminable, agonizedly questioning late night calls from Barbra during the filming of *The Way We Were*. Directors, it seems, turn in early at their peril when making movies with Barbra Streisand.)

When an actress is unsure about the validity of the role she is playing, look out for bizarre variations on the character. Gene Kelly, whose consummate artistry has a built-in bonus of a shrewd and compassionate understanding of the insecurity behind great talent, detected Barbra's confusion but could do little to remove it. 'If only there had been more time,' he told Clive Hirschorn. 'I'd have tried to help her work out a clear-cut characterisation. But we had a tight schedule and I left it up to her. The result was she was being Mae West one minute, Fanny Brice the other, and Barbra Streisand the next. Her accent varied as much as her mannerisms. She kept experimenting with new things out of sheer desperation, none of which really worked to her satisfaction. And as she's such a perfectionist, she became neurotic and insecure.' But, he recognised, 'as the picture progressed, she tried very very hard to make her characterisation work, and I have some fond memories of her constructive attitude, a side which is often ignored by other people. A couple of

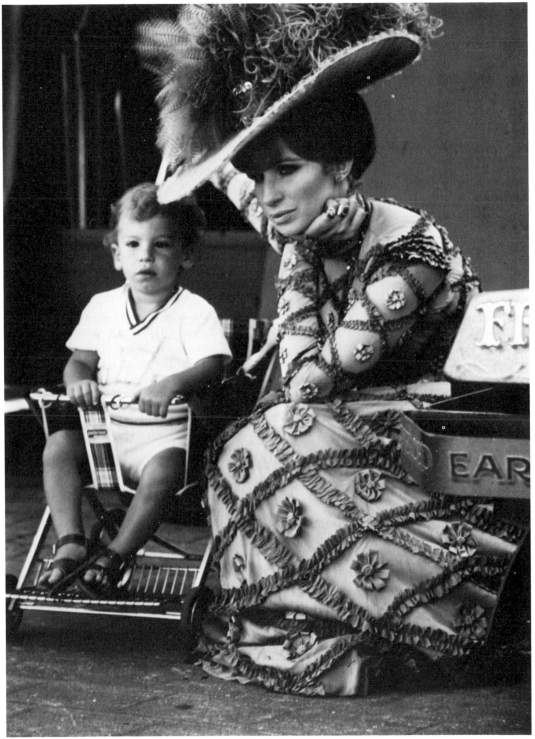

With her small son Jason on the set of *Hello Dolly!*

times, to try to get on the right track, Barbra would work weekends with me.' On the cavernous, deserted studio lot, Barbra, her then 18-month-old Jason playing with Gene's daughter Bridget, would flog the tired horse that was *Dolly*.

Meanwhile Walter Matthau was having his own problems with the limply-drawn Horace Vandergelder. Given a role to which he could triumphantly harness his powerful talents, Matthau coos like a babe. A stubbornly resilient survivor of heavy gambling losses and a heart attack, he was more likely to feel at home inside a Neil Simon character than inside, say, the Ruritanian, black-serge parade gear, four-foot sabre and all, in the ninety-degree heat on the studio backlot. He claimed that Barbra was often late on the set, though it's doubtful whether there could have been any scheduled time limit for the marathon task of preparing her, costumed, feathered and made-up, for the scene. As he growled to an interviewer on the set one day, 'tomorrow I'll go in to the studio at 7.30 in the morning and be ready to work at 8.30. Streisand will be a half-hour late – she's *never* there – and then there'll be twenty minutes of conversation, so we'll probably go to work at 9.20.' Matthau's sardonic comments, which may have carried more irony than truth, reflected his mood that day. Even his (then) fee of $750,000 plus a percentage, seemed an insufficient sweetener for stumbling around playing Vandergelder to Streisand's dominating Dolly Levi. But it was not the imbalance between the roles that riled him. His irritation with Streisand herself was beginning to show. As he groused to the interviewer: 'She steps on your head and your tail. She's gotta wave her goddarn feathers across your balls and in your eyes, otherwise she's not happy.' The notion that Barbra, who needed all the help she could get on the movie, would intentionally up-stage or otherwise disconcert Matthau – a major pit-prop to the movie – is unworthy even by the actor's familiar needling standards. As for keeping everybody waiting, it is fair to interpose this from the British actor on the movie, Michael Crawford:

Any woman arrives late and so does Barbra. At least she has the civility to apologise. If she's late it's probably not her fault. It's the Star-plus-Entourage system, the team which is necesary to project a costly investment – that star. Those people work hard. They need around three hours to earn their money by getting her ready for her nine hours' work. Sometimes she needs three hours more than anybody else. Barbra's hairdresser had the worst job because that coiffure was very elaborate. She would arrive at about eight and get on the set about half ten or eleven. There was always something wrong with the hair or the costume zip jammed, and then there would be a bunch of hysterical women blaming each other. Gene Kelly . . . just smiled that little friendly tight smile that is his danger signal with a gentle nodding of the head. It indicated a sort of internal prayer: 'Jesus, give me strength to deal with this situation!' Then after dancing, sweating and lunch it takes the team a half-an-hour to put Barbra's mouth back . . .

If Barbra Streisand was aware of Walter Matthau's growing testiness – she probably wasn't – it would have been less significant than the more pervasive hostility she sensed from the press and the public at the time. There is no little poignancy in the way she described it to a colleague who visited her in the Art Nouveau-style bungalow she used on the lot. 'When I first came here to sing in a nightclub a while back everybody had heard about me and I could feel the excitement. I was kinda keyed up, you know, and famous stars and celebrities arrived every night to watch me work. But when I came back with three movie offers and everything, I could feel the hatred as I got off the plane. It was like a whole other thing. I could feel my unwelcomeness.' But doesn't success breed fast friendship and love in this town, the visitor asked her. Barbra Streisand's swift, almost reflexed response reveals the intensity of her emotions, what a few might argue is paranoia: 'Oh yes, sure. But with hostility and hatred underneath. Chocolate-covered hatred is what it is. They love you and hate your guts.'

'They', one might conclude, is an other-side-of-the-fence collective of the press, jealous movie stars, envious producers and downright ill-wishers. It recalls her considered judgement: 'people who don't have success hate success.' Applied to Hollywood, at least, the Streisand view would carry any jury. Add to this resentment the massive insecurity she felt over *Dolly* and we can imagine the normally unruffled Gene Kelly feeling as though he were under siege. Maybe a lesser genius, a lesser human being, might have thrown in the towel with a miffed comment to his replacement – 'You can have the two of them, and good luck!' Instead he kept the ship afloat, placating Matthau, reassuring Barbra. During key rehearsals and at the end of 'takes', he had worked out a sign that told her she was getting it right. It was the old British 'thumbs up' gesture. The rehearsal or the 'take' over, she glanced instantly towards Gene. If he gave her the thumbs up sign, she knew she'd got it right. Thumb down, and it was back to the drawing board. Christian martyrs in the Colosseum faced the same sort of discretionary justice. But they had a little more riding on it than *Hello Dolly*!

As the production progressed so did the storm clouds. As Lehmann remembers it, 'It was not a happy film. There were things going on that were terrible. The intrigues, the bitterness, the back-biting, the deceits, the misery, the gloom. Most unpleasant. It's quite amazing what people go through,' he said, 'to make something entertaining for others. I'm always shocked by it.'

On one occasion on the set Barbra asked Walter, 'How's your ulcer?'

'I don't have an ulcer,' replied Matthau.

'My maid said she heard on the radio that I was giving you an ulcer.'

'You may be giving me another heart attack, darling, but not an ulcer.'

In a turbulence of that magnitude, Matthau and Barbra were like two doomed space objects hurtling towards each other on a collision course. An intense heatwave at the time made its own burnishing contribution to the eventual verbal fireball. The unit had moved to a new location at Garrison, Yonkers, north of New York. A railway station, circa 1880, and some streets were reconstructed. It was on this location where the feud between the two stars finally blew its top. It was a mercilessly hot and humid day. Swarms of mosquitoes took off from a nearby lake and *Blitzkrieg*ed the whole unit. Barbra was being Streisand, which is merely to record that, faithful as ever to her work, she questioned, made suggestions, enquired of the cool but courteous Gene Kelly whether a scene might conceivably come out better shot this way or that. The set-ups between shots stretched out longer and longer. Then suddenly almost everything became darkly eclipsed with the ghastly news that Robert Kennedy had been assassinated. Matthau's fervent commitment to America was typical of many immigrant-descended families who had pulled themselves up and out of the cold-water flats of the Lower East Side. The assassination appalled him. Strutting up and down as the vapid Vandergelder, waiting upon, by his lights at least, Barbra Streisand's whims, ignited the fuse. As he told the writer C. Robert Jennings:

> I took it hard. I wasn't going to vote for Bobby Kennedy. Still, I was knocked out and Gene was too. I couldn't work that day – and it was a 100 degrees in Garrison. Giant brutes [high wattage lights] surrounded us in a complicated outdoor scene. With the Kennedy thing and the heat and all this electrical power my head felt it was being smashed, plus the talk about where the bullet hit, the brain operation and all. Suddenly Barbra sneezed and I took that as a personal insult. I went into a wild, furious incoherent tirade about her. Kelly put his hand on my arm and tried to pull me away – that's all I remember except that I had to get my lines out, and I did *not* use any profane language . . .

So there it was. 'Suddenly Barbra sneezed' – here Matthau clearly confesses to a mighty display of over-reaction. But then as he himself has admitted. 'I am not a humble man. I am occasionally lovable and always totally impossible. I like people, even schmucks. When they become too terrible or boring, I make up stories which amuse me.' So that sultry, ill-fated day he gave Barbra the 'why don't you let *him* direct?' treatment; and the sour 'you don't have to be great *all* the time.!'

Three hours of shooting were lost in the final melée. A truce was called with both stars giving undertakings to Gene that from then on they would be civil to each other. It was a bizarre situation rich with possibilities. The sardonic Mr Matthau, his contrition wrapped in a coating of tangy garment-district humour; the hurt Barbra Streisand wondering, as though this damned awkward movie wasn't enough, why she should be the victim of Walter's guillotine jokes. Given that deployment of forces, with both parties solemnly pledged to display civility, Neil Simon could work it up into a hit. 'We tried to be civil – that's why things got worse,' was the way Matthau benevolently judged the aftermath. 'I'd come to work and say to myself I'm going to be nice to Barbra even if it kills me. In the end the strain was too much. We just had to face the fact that the chemistry between us was wrong.'

Ringsiders agree that on the set the day after the storm, someone said to Barbra and Walter, 'You two should say hello.' Walter ('I am not a humble man') Matthau agreed while reverting instinctively, though jokingly, to tribal custom: 'I think she should say hello to me first because I'm older.' Another voice entered the arena. Walter's mother, Rose, having come up from Manhattan, instantly endeared herself to Barbra with her no-nonsense, Jewish mother directness. 'You look lovely, so how come you're fighting my son?' Barbra's response, bearing more than a touch of Hasidic wisdom, would have made the late Emmanuel Streisand proud: 'He told me he fights with *you* a lot,' she said, 'so I guess he only fights with the people he loves.'

Characteristically, Barbra Streisand allowed Matthau to make most of the running in the statements made after the event. Yet she is saddened whenever the episode is recalled. She has said, 'He never did apologise to me and that's what hurt even more. I think the saddest part of what happened was that a man of Walter's stature and ability seemed to feel threatened by *me*.'

Whether Matthau, in fact, felt threatened by Barbra is arguable. The fact that, demonstrably, a kindly human being resides inside the needling persona, and his undoubted superstar power – all have combined to make Matthau revise his verdict on the fracas. It was evident, when we raised the *Dolly* incident that day in the Universal dining-room, that Matthau was eager to throw rose petals where once rapiers had gleamed. To him, Barbra Streisand was an 'enormously talented woman. Brilliant. Scintillating. Absolutely marvellous. And giving,' his hosanna continued,

so very giving. Believe me the whole thing was so blown up. Anyway it was probably my fault. I snapped at everybody that day, and probably did so for the next two weeks. You get days like that. It could have been anything. It's like the story of a man, an anti-Semite, who passes a synagogue and there's an old Jew who's bent over tying his shoelaces, and he kicks the old man in the backside, saying, 'Damned Jews are always tying their shoelaces!' It was just a boring little fight. A momentary clash of personalities. I've clashed with many actors. But it was exaggerated. You have those yellow magazines who have a headline every day, every week. 'Robert Redford throws children into oven' or 'Steve McQueen chops up mother and father and eats them in soup'. Barbra and I are friendly. We don't hate each other . . . that's the truth, and it's so boring! . . .

And to prove it, Mr Matthau affected slumber, and emitted a snore. If quotes like 'a pip-squeak who didn't have the talent of a butterfly's fart', 'Madame Petomane' or similar one-liners briefly entered his mind, they didn't show in his face.

To him, no less than to Barbra Streisand, *Hello Dolly* was a nightmare unredeemed by its huge grosses at the box-office. When the last shot was in the can the producer Ernest Lehmann, director Gene Kelly, Walter and Barbra hauled themselves away with a relief that was almost tangible. Barbra, following a pattern common to all her movies, presented gifts to both Gene Kelly and Walter Matthau. The gesture was spontaneous and sincere, not lip service to an accepted Hollywood routine. To Gene Kelly she gave a copy of the famous World War I poster, a three-sheet size picture of Uncle Sam pointing his finger over the words I WANT YOU! On it, Barbra wrote: 'To Gene, thumbs up, and thanks for everything. Love, Barbra.'

On Walter Matthau's last night of shooting Barbra presented him with a beautifuly crafted antique inkwell reflecting his passion for the racetrack. The head of it was fashioned into a jockey's cap. The base was a horseshoe inscribe: 'Walter, I wish you wealth, health, and a little bit of luck, Barbra.' With it was a card bearing the inscription, 'May your horses always come in first.' She had unearthed the gift months before. What had happened between them would not rob her of the pleasure of giving it to him. Matthau was surprised, and touched. He concealed it behind the familiar churlish pose. 'Why are you giving me a gift?' he asked her.

'I always give gifts to the people I work with,' Barbra said in her candid, 'it's no

As Dolly Levi in *Hello Dolly!*

big deal' manner. 'It's something I thought you might like.'

It was not enough for the little boy inside the towering but vulnerable Mr Matthau. 'Why didn't she say "I'm giving you a gift because I love you"? ' he muttered to someone on the set. Magnanimity on that scale would be hard to find in saints. Expecting it of Barbra Streisand, at that time, was *chutzpah*. In spades.

The Streisand-Matthau fracas poses this question: would it have happened on a more professionally rewarding motion picture? Even with the tragic intervention of the Bobby Kennedy assassination, would Walter have blown his cool with Barbra if both had been involved in a movie worthy of their zesty talents? We know that Barbra had reservations about the role of Dolly as constructed in the screenplay and therefore about her capacity to play this older woman with any degree of conviction. Matthau had developed an even stronger dislike – for the whole package. 'I never liked *Hello Dolly* no matter who did it,' he said to us. 'I never thought it was a very interesting musical. As a matter of fact there are very few musical comedies that I have liked in my lifetime. I think I liked two – *My Fair Lady* and *Guys and Dolls*. In fact I don't like the device of musical comedy. They asked me to do it and said, "Here's the script." They said they'd pay me a lot of money to do it. I said, "Fine." ' Had he known that the experience would, as he said later, produce all kinds of symptoms – 'pains in the lower abdomen, severe headaches, palpitations, I was in agony most of the time' – he might have said, 'Hello Dolly – and goodbye!' Maybe the other leading characters in the drama might have backed off too given the prescience to detect the fatal flaws in the whole project. It was producer Ernest Lehmann's view that if anybody could pull it off, it was Gene Kelly. 'He had exactly the qualities we needed on the picture – tremendous energy, vitality, and a maddening cheerfulness.' In the event, they were not enough.

The problems of translating the musical to the screen emerged almost from the start. One weakness, as Lehmann saw it was that Thornton Wilder's play *The Matchmaker* on which *Dolly* is based is not all that much about Dolly Levi. A great deal of activity centres on the two subsidiary characters, the clerk Cornelius and his assistant Barnaby, the whole spun-sugar nonsense taking place on the famous Fourteenth Street parade day in New York. 'In fact,' Lehmann says, '*Hello Dolly* is a pretty infantile story, and very early on in adapting it to the screen I realised my biggest problem would be how to make it less silly.' On the basis, if you can't fool them, stun them, Fox elected to inflate the over-blown subject into a full-scale multi-million dollar road-show. The device rarely works if the nucleus is flawed. It could not work with Barbra Streisand. Turning up in the Harmonia Gardens after fourteen years' absence implied that she was ten years old when last she was there. No amount of revolving sets, Busby Berkeley (in this case, Michael Kidd) routines, sound and fury, can camouflage that sort of myopic film-making. And yet . . . and here we come to that special quality of Streisand's, the ability to make sense out of nonsense; to force audiences and critics alike to suspend belief. She seems not merely to dominate the screen – no small achievement when we're talking about Todd A-O – she compels total involvement from the audience. Photographed with extraordinary subtlety by that genius of the motion picture camera, the late Harry

Stradling, costumed by the designer Irene Sharaff, Streisand's almost defiant, feather-hatted bravura signals 'Okay so it's not *My Fair Lady.*– but enjoy!'

The critical responses to this recklessly expensive movie were mixed. Barbra was held, correctly, to have been miscast (because of the manifestly absurd age question) and to have overcompensated like crazy by mugging in the manner of an over-energised Mae West. Her supporters countered with a shrugging 'So what?', arguing that 'Dolly' *became* a vastly more fascinating creature because of the life that Streisand breathed into her. If she redeems this movie – and a fair judgement must decide that she did – it is in spite of, rather than because of, the other forces harnessed in the project. If Michael Kidd's choreography reveals less of the verve and style expected of this gifted dance creator, one should acknowledge the difficulties inherent in one expert working for another. As Ernest Lehmann remembered it, 'It was difficult for Gene to work with Michael Kidd. Being a choreographer himself, Gene was naturally concerned with the way the dance routines looked and, although he tried to be as diplomatic as possible, the presence of another choreographer and dancer wasn't exactly the best set-up in the world.' As he told Clive Hirschorn, 'I'd often find Gene muttering away in the background about something he felt was wrong in the dance direction. He admired and respected Michael . . . but the relationship between them became "egg-shell" time.' The musical score itself revealed weaknesses which even the combined skills of Matthau and Streisand could not overcome. Some of the numbers were heavy-handed and obvious, as in Matthau's one song, 'It Takes a Woman'. The score, like the film itself, just strains too hard – 'busts a gut' was one reviewer's verdict. As for the casting in the movie, there are all the signs of committee-thinking with cerebral atrophy at high level. We can forgive them the choice of Streisand over Channing on the theory that, when gambling for high stakes, you press the hottest number. Even Matthau as Horace Vandergelder carried the collateral of a talent that could overcome with sleight of hand the plodding uncertainties of the script. But casting Britain's Michael Crawford in the role of Cornelius was close to unintended farce. An amiable and versatile performer, Crawford in *Dolly* stretches his theater-bred talents beyond their limits. When, in a voice that is neither, he sings 'My arms were sure and strong', a glance at his thin arms and meagre frame brings you dangerously close to a belly-laugh. Few serious critics, taking *Hello Dolly* in total, found any real substance or merit to it. *Newsweek*'s Joseph Morgenstern was particularly scathing, speaking of 'this plodding dinosaur of a film.'

> It's there because it's there, an impressive industrial exercise in which everyone came dutifully to work in the morning and picked up where they'd left off the day before. Kelly stages his turn-of-the-century comedy in late 1940 style, as if movie musicals stopped growing when he stopped dancing in them. Like Michael Kidd's choreography, Kelly's technique is antique at best, incompetent at worst. The 'Hello Dolly' number comes in fits and starts because no one knew how to make it build, visually or dramatically. The 400 million extras in the big parade scene look like a routine rabble because no one knew where to put the cameras.

No everyone – us included – share in this withering criticism of Gene Kelly. He directed the material he had. Given the rag-bag of bogus characterisations, and the brief to make a gut-busting road-show out of it, like Runyan's Harry the Horse, he did the best he could. His camera is usually in the right place at the right time, moving in the right direction at the right tempo. Yet even Joseph Morgenstern had to exclude Barbra from the general indictment. 'She has an uphill fight with the foolish material and the flatfooted style. She needs help and doesn't get it, and it hurts. She dies utterly when she's off the screen and comes obediently back to life when she's on. She may be in trouble from time to time but she bails herself out, and the movie as well, with great resourcefulness.' This theme – Streisand rising triumphantly above the mediocrity of the movie she's in – was repeated in later years, underscoring the truism that talent can gleam through the murkiest skylines. Few could express that more eloquently than that most perceptive of movie-watchers, Paulene Kael. Noting that this 'staggeringly unimaginative effort . . . is full of that fake, mechanical exhilaration of big Broadway shows, the gut-busting, muscle-straining dance that is meant to wow you,' Kael declares, 'at the centre of the . . . noisy mediocrity, there is Streisand, an actress who uses song as an intensification of emotion.' (Streisand – 'I'm an actress who sings . . .' – probably lit a celebratory candle to Kael for making that fine distinction.) 'Streisand totally dominates the screen whenever she's on. She doesn't seem to have any limitations,

'Her scenes with Louis Armstrong are joyously performed twosomes.'

but,' Kael adds sagely, 'this dominance could become one. Even in terms of their own dumb material, the scriptwriter, the producer Ernest Lehmann, and the director fell asleep at the controls. Couldn't Streisand have been allowed more songs? One feels that she's in a straitjacket through most of the dialogue, trying to hold herself down. When she's given a chance to let her energy out, she's great. She's a very sexy lady, which is what keeps this show from withering away on the screen.'

There are some choice moments in the musical which tend to be lost in the shuffle of recriminations: Barbra's 'Hello Dolly' solo is a blazing piece of musical gusto; her scenes with Louis Armstrong are joyously performed twosomes. She gives the great Satchmo as good as she gets and the movie one of its more inspired moments.

But not even Streisand, at full throttle, her sexuality flung across the vastness of Todd A-O can escape comparison with that other piece of turn-of-the-century nostalgia, *Meet Me in St Louis*, an early Judy Garland triumph. Moreover, 'Put on Your Sunday Clothes' emerges as a poor man's 'Trolley Song' while 'Elegance', if you are tempted to make the comparison, doesn't stand well against the 'Couple of Swells' number from the Garland–Astaire *Easter Parade*.

Still, as the bankers at Fox could legitimately argue, 'If *Dolly* was a flop, lets have more of 'em!' Despite the (then) enormity of the cost, $24 million, the film is substantially into profit. The notices – the good and the bad were evenly matched – seemed almost irrelevant. In general, people went to see it because of Streisand. There are always audiences prepared to settle for great performers in bad roles and indifferent films. If both performer *and* the film are great, it is a bonus. But often, those who seek that rare moment of individual magic on the screen must be prepared to take the whole package. The rough with the smooth. Producers, directors and Mr Walter Matthau might assert that *working* with Barbra Streisand carried the same stipulation. But then the reverse applies too. Barbra, in her confrontations with directors, actors and writers, was also obliged to take the rough with the smooth. It is to her credit that, provoked or not, she has remained remarkably tight-lipped in the face of the verbal assaults made upon her.

The pressures upon her during the shooting of *Dolly* were not merely professional. Her relationship with Gould, made icier because of the gossip 'linking' (to quote the favourite Hollywood euphemism) her with Omar Sharif, troubled her deeply. It hardly helped when a London newspaper, reporting that Gould had been fined £331 in New York for sixty-three parking offences, headlined the item, 'Mr Streisand Pays'. She did not offer in mitigation that Eddie Fisher was dubbed 'Mr Elizabeth Taylor', Gary Merrill 'Mr Bette Davis', while a succession of Zsa Zsa's husbands dutifully signed on as 'Mr Gabor'. She knew there was no consolation for that kind of put-down. Instead she rarely referred to their estrangement. If she said anything at all about Gould it was to say what she genuinely believed – that 'one day he'll be a big star.' She described him once as 'the American equivalent of Jean-Paul Belmondo', adding, 'I think he's representative of the thirty-year-old-man, the postgraduate, which is a terrific symbol of our times.' Asked then (1968) whether she thought they would ever get together again, she produced the jaunty, Streisand-style response, 'We're not dead yet.'

But the words had a terminal ring to them.

TWELVE

No IMMEDIATE success for *Hello Dolly* was expected for the most obvious reasons. It was not immediately released. With 'Standing Room Only' notices regularly posted outside the stage production, David Merrick saw no point in offering the public a box-office choice. To clinch it, he had the contractual right to withhold his permission for the release of the film indefinitely. Indefinitely going on eternity was the way it must have seemed to the fuming Fox board. Merrick was shrewdly edging his Broadway production toward all-time records by calculated and tactically timed tranfusions of new blood. New Dollys. A backup of former stars, all with their respective cluster of still faithful fans, stretched out longer than the line of Horace Vandergelder's parade. Great stars generating the nostalgia that sold tickets. Ginger Rogers, Betty Grable, Dorothy Lamour, Ethel Merman and, a subtle variation, Pearl Bailey. With their massive capital investment piling up interest day by day, the studio began to wonder whether its stymied road-show may have to go out as released by 21st Century Fox.

Merrick, however, was being squeezed by an exquisite, gold-plated nutcracker. Not only did he own the Broadway show, he owned stock in Fox. The point was emphasised for him by the red carpet showing of a roughcut of the picture. He emerged from the viewing convinced there was small fiscal future in allowing Broadway to hold Hollywood, his bigger grossing brother, to further ransom. Merrick gave his gracious permission for *Dolly* to be 'pre-released' (*sic)* as a seasonal gift for Christmas 1969.

Barbra, no less than the Fox pack, had chafed at the hold-up on the musical's release. But, unlike the accountants, she could enjoy – in spades – distinctly positive compensations. To begin with, she had now formally become what many on *Funny Girl* had alleged she always had been anyway, her own producer. She formed her own production company, the modestly entitled First Artists, Inc. Well, it was not *quite* her own company – it was a triumvirate. The two other founding partners were a couple of other *arriviste* youngsters – Sidney Poitier (first film: nineteen years earlier) and Paul Newman (first film: fifteen years earlier). These 'first artists' were joined a year later by Steve McQueen and subsequently by Dustin Hoffman who, still later, was to involve the company in internecine litigation.

The working mechanics of the association were as follows: First Artists was a subsidiary of Warner Brothers. In return for making three pictures without the million-dollar (plus) front money that any other studio would have to pay them, the stars could generate whatever project they wanted, provided the budget was under three million dollars for a 'dramatic' film and under five for a musical (this, remember, was 1969). Warners would receive the distribution rights, reimbursing First Artists for two-thirds of the films' cost of negatives upon delivery of a finished film. The artists perhaps described themselves as first because they were to get

First Artists, Paul Newman, Sidney Poitier and Barbra Streisand

twenty-five per cent of the gross – a quarter for every dollar the cinema owners returned to Warners – right off the top. The immediate name of the game, however, was, as always, control. Barbra was totally up-front about this. 'I have always,' she said, 'had to be free to play the roles and sing the songs I felt strongly and instinctively were right for me. I know that my new associates have the same desire for artistic individuality and total commitment. This company will fill that need for each individual and at the same time we'll have a teamwork situation based on mutual respect and understanding.'

It all sounded like the pious, self-convincing hopes for a happy marriage. Barbra's actual marriage was convincing no one. There had been her dalliance with Sharif, with the affable Egyptian doing little or nothing to diminish the rumours. Meanwhile Elliott Gould had demonstrated somewhat literally his re-acquisition of clout by swapping punches with a *papparazzo* outside a Hollywood theater. A law suit ensued. The tabloid coverage polarised Hollywood opinion according to those who were for Barbra and those who sided with Gould. The few – those with an affection for, or vested interest in, Barbra Streisand – felt it was time for him to go. He was spoiling the act. The many – rooting for the underdog – felt he could only preserve his individuality by walking away to do his own thing. They took pleasure in seeing the erstwhile 'Mr Streisand', if not exactly living high off the hog, at least proving that he was no candidate for the role of over-shadowed husband in the earlier scenarios of *A Star Is Born*.

Nevertheless, apparently by mutual consent, Barbra and Elliott continued to make all the right noises about each other. They scrupulously avoided falling into the game Hollywood relishes, a public slanging match. But their final acknowledgement of the inevitable, a joint statement issued 13 February 1969, struck a farcical note of dignity, like a decorous prat-fall by Charlie Chaplin. 'We are separating,' they said, 'not to destroy but to save our marriage.' It reminded us of Lee Marvin's famous mistress, Michelle Triola's 'Lee is probably the most pure man I have ever known in my entire life. That's why I have to suc him.' Trial separations, in Hollywood at least, have usually meant, in marital terms, a kind of Ellis Island stopover, while more permanent arrangements can be made. For Barbra and Elliott there was a genuine need to cease hostilities, clear the battlefield and assess the damage. If it was all over, one unseverable bond remained. Jason, then three years old. On that proud co-production both names get equal star-billing in the credit titles.

But nothing, certainly not the occupational hazard of a broken Hollywood marriage, prevents the show from going on. Four days after receiving her shared Academy Award, Barbra flew to New York, then to London for location scenes on her third film, *On a Clear Day You Can See Forever*. Another musical, and another cool million. We can infer from this that the movie was ahead of her First Artists commitment. The film marked a switch to another studio, Paramount, the production in the hands of the skilled producer, Howard Koch. Vincent Minnelli (at Barbra's request: she had admired *Gigi)* was the wise and distinguished talent selected to direct the picture. It was good casting all round, particularly in terms of the personalities charged with handling Streisand's special brand of well-intentioned turbulence. As a result, there was a monumental improvement in working relationships and professional co-existence.

A great deal of the credit for this must go to Koch who does not object to the suggestion that he is a quiet and canny realist who shoots trouble halfway. He had, in fact, cut his teeth on Sinatra, having happily stayed the course with the actor for more than five years. 'I'd heard stories about Barbra,' Koch told us, 'but I always had confidence in myself that I'd find some way to work around whatever problem might arise. If I could make it with Frank, I thought I could get along well with Barbra. With Frank you never know which way he's going to go. He's a great talent but he also has tremendous moods. And so has Barbra. Not that she was my first choice. I couldn't get her – she didn't want to do it. After Barbra's success in the play *Funny Girl* I knew she was right for *Clear Day* and went after her.' Audrey Hepburn had been considered but decided not to accept the role. Raised on musicals, she certainly had the ability. Her Eliza Doolittle in the film version of *My Fair Lady* suffered from the vision of Julie Andrews hovering in the minds of the critics. Also the largely period style of *On a Clear Day* might have seemed like the same mixture as before. Moreover the story, as conceived by Alan Jay Lerner – a series of wham-bam reincarnations from an over-the-top Brooklyn character, Daisy Gamble, to an English Regency temptress – required a physical attack more suited to Barbra's Flatbush than Hepburn's finishing-school accents. However hard Barbra's advisers may have played hard-to-get on her behalf, Streisand was determined to play the part. Who else could play the whacky, grimacing, co-ed from Brooklyn? Barbra could lead you on a tour of the area blindfold. As for the high-blooded, low-necklined Regency beauty – Streisand could scarcely wait to get inside that skin. In both incarnations she would get to sing better songs than many of those that had previously come her way on film. The Brooklyn end of the story has Daisy Gamble gate-crashing a medical school class in hypnotism which puts her into an involuntary trance. The professor (Yves Montand) discovers she has extrasensory perception and, one trance leading to another, falls in love with her. For her Regency persona (the scenes were shot in the famed Regency Brighton Pavilion), Streisand had the late Cecil Beaton to design her costumes, and Deborah Kerr to help her with the precise 'butter would be better' inflections of upper-class England. For Barbra, four-poster bed and all, Regency Brighton with its chinoiserie and eclectic decor, English tea – and Deborah Kerr yet! – was Pulaski Street's equivalent of Eliza at Ascot. Barbra became so adept at the aristrocratic accents that one joker quipped that Princess Margaret would curtsey to *her* at the next Royal Premiere.

By contrast, the language barrier was never more than half dismantled by Yves Montand. His finesse and world-weary Gallic charm seem not to travel well. Certainly not to Hollywood. Cukor's uncharacteristically tired *Let's Make Love* had given the French actor no scope other than off-screen with his leading lady, Marilyn Monroe. The ravaged authority he brought to the French productions of, say, *The Witches of Salem* or *Z* couldn't be exploited in *On a Clear Day*. The producer Koch's comment upon this flat spot in Montand's film career is unconsciously ironic: 'I love him as a person. He's a lovely guy. But I think he was wrong in the final thing. The chemistry didn't work. They didn't rub together. I think she and Richard Harris would have rubbed together . . .' Only ten years later it seems incredible that anyone should have suggested Richard Harris – he turned down the role – as first choice for a part that once, incontestably, would have been Cary Grant's. But Koch was right about the failure in the chemistry. Streisand and Montand were not as potent as Streisand and Sharif or as volatile as the off-screen Montand and Monroe. It was to become the story of the week – that, whereas Barbra had commanded Sharif's presence on the sound-stage to set her up for her climactic number, for the equivalent moment in *On a Clear Day* she positively did not want Montand.

'We had an interesting thing there,' Koch said.

She was playing it off-stage. She had to look at a certain area off-camera, otherwise her nose gets too long. There's a position, just off-camera left, that you have to concentrate on in the way you light her so that her nose doesn't look extremely long. Now, when you're doing a close-up off-stage you usually play it to the actor off-camera and he plays back to you and you see the reaction. She came to me and said, 'I don't know how to say this to Vincent but I want to *imagine* who I'm singing the song to. I don't want any face there.'

I said, 'I'll tell him this – we'll just put a blank up.' She said, 'Great!' With a blank off-camera she sang this whole sexy song – with a fantasy to whom she was singing the song. I don't know who she was fantasising about. I've asked her every time I've seen her. She won't tell me. Probably fantasising somebody intimate in her life.

Well, just who that 'fantastic somebody' might have been is no easy matter to pin down. The men in Streisand's life are too diverse, as we shall see, to sort into categories. But the significant aspect of the episode is that Montand seemed hardly to have cared. Furthermore he seemed even less concerned to induce chemistry off-screen than on. One can see his point. He had had his moments already as Piaf's protégé (with all that that implied) and, on his Monroe film, had by all accounts suited his action to the title *Let's Make Love;* above, all, as the husband of the monumental Simone Signoret, he might well have found Barbra Streisand a comparative lightweight. It's probably safe to assume he was taking the money and running, content with a Gallic shrug or two to keep this twenty-six-year-old in her place. One thing is certain: Montand had no intention of playing the same sort of suit as Omar Sharif's. Streisand, alert and imaginative, could not have observed Yves Montand without thinking of Piaf. Their styles and backgrounds had often been compared. Piaf's rise from the gutter had been paralleled, in less deprived terms, by Barbra's rise in America. Barbra's intelligence must have told her that against any yardstick, she had, to date, failed to out-punch the little sparrow's lived-in intensity. And if, subconsciously, she was playing the comparison game, Barbra would have been aware of an equally great talent hovering close by: Montand's wife, Simone Signoret. A glance at this fine actress had to evoke thoughts of Françoise Rosay and, further back, of Sarah Bernhardt.

Barbra was soon to back out of returning to Broadway in a musical written round the divine Sarah because of her reluctance to sign a run-of-the-play contract. But if the notion of Streisand playing Bernhardt seemed too fanciful by half, Vincent Minnelli, for one, hadn't the slightest doubt that Streisand was one of the few world-class talents equal to the role. At the end of the movie he presented her with a portrait of the great actress to emphasise his conviction. (Here the director displayed considerable prescience. Ten years later it was to be announced in Hollywood that Barbra Streisand was planning to film Bernhardt's life.)

Minnelli had been, of course, married to the singer Judy Garland. In this respect he witnessed an American tragedy version of Piaf's French scenario. Even down to the similarity of the final, well-meaning boy husband, Judy Garland's career seemed markedly similar to Piaf's doomed, drug-strewn life. Not that Minnelli, the kindly veteran of several famous movies *(Meet Me in St Louis, An American in Paris, Lust for Life, Gigi, etc.)*, would have made such comparisons. If life with the tragic Judy Garland had taught him anything, it was the extreme fragility of a unique talent, sustained largely by overspent emotions. With his card thus marked, he had a tactical advantage over most of Streisand's other directors. His reflections on working with Streisand tend to confirm this. So does the antique silver coffee service, minus the sugar bowl, Minnelli has in his Beverly Hills home. Barbra presented it to him at the end of shooting. The coffee pot was inscribed: 'To Vincent whom I adore . . Love, Barbra.' On the creamer were the words, 'You're the cream in my coffee.' (Streisand, ever practical, had omitted the sugar bowl in the gift because Minnelli was forbidden to take sugar.) 'I may tell you,' he said, 'that this gift remains one of my great treasures.'

> Barbra received some bad press during the filming of *Funny Girl* and had been accused of taking over as director. But it was recognised she had an infallible instinct about what was seemly for her and occasionally it conflicted with what Wyler wanted. Wyler is one director actors don't fool around with. He doesn't like being told what to do. But I have no ego about such things. The important thing is to make the picture. Consequently, I listened to what Barbra suggested and implemented some of her suggestions. I found her creative, bright. We got along beautifully.

Minnelli has a more charitable view of his picture than the majority of critics:

> The movie was not my greatest musical success but neither was it Paramount's greatest musical failure. We got the same cameraman [the late Harry Stradling] who photographed her in her first films – he was marvellous. Judy and I worked with him on *The Pirate* and all the cinematographers were busy at that time and we brought him on the lot. He was a rough and ready fellow. He said, 'You ready for me? It's dark down here,' and I thought, 'Oh Christ!' When I saw the first day's rushes – fantastic! *Fantastic!* [He] got the beauty of Streisand without tampering with it. I thought she was just stunning.

Perhaps Streisand's caper from Brooklyn to *Burke's Peerage,* heaving bosoms and all, stumbles over into high camp, but with Scaasi dresses, Beaton gowns, Barbra in her best zinging style, there's enough fun around to force suspension of normal critical judgements. What Barbra proved yet again was that the evaluation of her performance is a separate entity in the assessment of the film. This is the point the *Daily Variety* critic made about *Clear Day,* adding in that context: 'Miss Streisand would upstage Mount Rushmore.'

But in spite of that trick, or because of it, the film's weaknesses are plain to see. On a shot-to-shot basis it is always attractive and stylish. The art director in Minnelli is incapable of devising an inelegant set-up. Also the score is rich and subtle. But the movie's visual beauty, Streisand's drive and vaunting sexuality, are merely polishing a flawed gem. Yet when the film was released, Barbra herself received some of the most glowing notices of her career. *Newsweek,* for example, spoke of the manner in which 'she flashes lightning-like between Melinda's airs and Daisy's earthiness.' In the opinion of the *Hollywood Reporter:* 'Forced to do a British accent, Miss Streisand does it with the nature of a mimic-born (maybe the whole Brooklyn bit is made up too). She is with the technique and conviction beyond many more experienced actresses.' The writer, James Powers, adds this sage thought: 'If Miss Streisand will just get *Funny Girl* out of her system, there might be no limits to her growth and diversification.'

In the event, the film did not emerge as the gold-plated money-spinner everyone, specifically the Koch–Lerner–Paramount triumvirate, had hoped for. It had cost between nine and ten million dollars to produce, rather more than chicken-feed for that era. But given the fail-safe elements of film financing, television sales and foreign pick-ups, the film, Koch says, 'got close to its investment.' He added a significant afterthought which was to be echoed later as leading players began demanding Mickey Mouse money (four and five million and more) before they would trundle their less-than-youthful bodies into a movie:

I think the salvation of the motion picture business is not paying those tremendous salaries and giving away all the control of your picture to an employee, whether it be an actor or director. I think we have to get back to the basics – a good screenplay and a good production and not give all the money up front so that it's a fight to get out. If you pay, say, five million to a Bergman or three million to some star or two million to Brando for two days – to recoup that two million you've got to take six million, probably eight million – four to one – today.

How much control a star should have on a picture drew this from this former studio boss: 'I think Barbra, like many great performers,' he said, 'need producers. They need somebody to pick their material. And they need direction. They can't look at themselves objectively. They just can't. I don't care who it is – once they get the call on what they're saying and who's writing it and who's directing it and who's producing it – they start to wane.'

In spite of Minnelli's velvet glove directing and Streisand's benign responses, *On a Clear Day* had its backstage dramas, during and after the shooting. On 22 June 1969, while in London, Minnelli received a phone call from his daughter Liza. 'Mummy died today.' she said. Though Judy Garland had long remarried, the news and the manner of her death were clearly painful to Minnelli. Hard on that blow was the terse message that his current marriage had broken up and that his wife was seeking a divorce. 'How did I feel at the time?' Minnelli smiled wanly. 'When I'm on a picture I'm on a picture.' This was Minnelli displaying the tough-mindedness of the professional who, in Bogart's definition, knows he is one because he can produce his best effort when he is not feeling his best. The same built-in resilience enabled him to shrug off Montand's acrimonious complaints about his role in the picture.

Montand might have charged that, thanks to indiscriminate butchery in the cutting room, his part had been reduced to that of a supporting player's. It was the same complaint Anne Francis had made after *Funny Girl*. In fact, in the case of Anne Francis' Georgia James role, it *was* a case of history largely repeating itself. It had been a 'fringe', an optional role, excluded altogether from the stage version at a very early pre-Broadway stage. In Montand's case, since one critic has written 'His performance does not kill the film single-handedly – but nearly,' 'the scissor-work on his role may be regarded as an act of merciful amputation. In any case, *he* should worry. It now seems inconceivable that Jack Nicholson, then determined to raise himself into the Big League, should have had his talent so under-used as Ted Pringle, a minor role. If Montand was a supporting character actor, Nicholson, playing Streisand's stepbrother, was an extra. In a remake today he would have the lead role.

It would be foolish to deny that Barbra had influence. But that she could, or would as a comparative newcomer, have over-ridden Koch and Minnelli in the cutting room is as insulting to them as it is to the film's editor David Bretherton.

A final postscript from Koch throws further light on how Streisand's thrift-shop thinking dominated her, now, seven-figure calculations:

> When we went overtime and had to pay her more money, she asked for certain things that were not in the contract – like items on the set that she wanted to become her possessions. We didn't want to pay her more money, so we made a deal with her. Strange. One of the things she wanted was a trailer that we owned here. All the furniture. All the wardrobe she wore. Some stained-glass windows we used on the set. I think she probably took seventy to eighty thousand dollars worth of stuff to her home. It was good for us because those things are expendable anyway. I went to her house. It was fun to go there and see all the items from the sets.

Howard Koch, a family man and distinguished figure in the Hollywood establishment, was more to Barbra than just the boss man who, with Minnelli, called the shots. 'She seemed to take me as, like, her father image,' he said,

> and she'd ask me a lot of things quite away from the movies. She was going to rent a house – the George Axelrod house on Carolwood and she told me the rent was some $1800 a month. It would apply against the purchase price of, I think, $280,000. When the time came for the purchase or to let it go, it was down to, like, $240,000. So she asked me what she should do and I told her the land, four-and-a-half acres, and a great house, she'd never regret it. It's got to be worth four or five million dollars today.

But even without the shrewd advice of her producer, Barbra kept her eye on the small change, and the fringe benefits. When the studio wanted to use her Thunderbird car for a scene in the film she charged a minimum rental of fifty dollars. She levied a further fifty dollars for the use of her poodle, Sadie, for a scene in which she walks the dog down Fifth Avenue. Even with a million dollar pay cheque, old anxieties die hard.

Time heals. Howard Koch's current thoughts of Streisand bring a smile to his face where once a frown was the expression of the day. When Arnold Scaasi, the famous dress designer, came to the studio for wardrobe fittings with Barbra, Koch had enthused, 'You Italians are marvellous!' Streisand pole-axed the compliment with the shriek, 'He's about as Italian as Moshe Dayan. Arnold's real name is Isaacs which is Scaasi spelled backwards.'

Most stars these days have the right to approve all photographs of themselves before these are sent out to the media. Retouched stills are resubmitted for approval, rejected prints are destroyed and shredded along with the negatives. Marilyn Monroe, the most photographed body in the world, meticulously examined every still, searching out every line or flesh wrinkle like a bomber pilot pin-pointing a target. Publicity men felt themselves growing old as Marilyn, magnifying glass in her hand, scrutinised every miniature contact, uttering a steely 'No' to the majority of them. And just in case the minions didn't get the message, she had a pair of nail scissors on hand, to shred all the stills she hated. Sophia Loren, whose own collection of stills – from Sofia Scicolone, through Sofia Lazaro, to the *Millionairess* and Madame Ponti – occupies an entire gallery in her Italian villa, operated the same screening process, and for similar reasons.

Barbra Streisand, with maybe more at risk (at the time) than Marilyn or Sophia, ran up a historic retouching bill of $25,000. And then she 'killed' most of those too. Streisand's ritual for viewing the colour slides of herself, enlarged on a screen, was like an average day at the Bastille. Squatting on the floor eating Indian nuts, she sorted the photos into three categories: O.K., Hold for Second Look, and Kill. She cried 'KILL' so often someone once asked her whether she wore a hawk on her wrist. But Barbra's stubborn insistence that she knew best was probably true. 'I haven't made a mistake with my public yet,' she claimed after a particularly heavy shredding session on *Clear Day*. The same concern extended to her costumes. The late Cecil Beaton, designer and photographer, used to handling royalty, at Buckingham Palace or a Hollywood film studio, admired Barbra's relentlessness. 'Barbra will be producing and directing soon,' he said with shrewd foresight. 'In designing gowns for her you never have to be afraid to ask her, 'Is this going too far?' So many actresses are afraid, they don't dare. But with her you can go the whole hog. She'll never accept anything until she's convinced in her own mind it's 100 per cent right for her. It's a constant battle of attrition with her and her taste – which is very exhausting.' So Beaton was exhausted, Signor Scaasi (or Isaacs) under pressure; Minnelli listened to 'suggestions' and Koch counted up the bills. Streisand at work. In this respect she was scarcely different from other screen goddesses who with steely resolve knew how best to exploit their own strengths and conceal weaknesses.

Streisand's plus, as a human being, was in her determination to be the best kind of mother young Jason could have. Unused to physical exertion she nevertheless learned to swim, play tennis and exercise as much as an example to Jason as for herself. Her attitude then, shared by Elliott Gould, has made a fine healthy specimen of their son. 'I grew up in these Jewish homes where the mother always thought if you swam, you drowned – or if you take dancing lessons, you break all your bones, are handicapped. I don't want my son Jason to see fear in Mama's eyes when she's out there on the diving board and he says "Jump!"' Overcoming the deep-rooted physical fears endemic in a Flatbush upbringing, for Jason's sake, was one of Barbra's gestures towards wise motherhood. She had kept to her pledge to give Jason a broad-based education for life. Perhaps, instinctively aware of how her late father, Emmanuel Streisand, Ph.D,, would have advised her, Barbra sensed that the more rich and successful she became, the greater the risk of emotional imbalance and bogus value-judgements in her son. When Jason was barely three years old, she told one interviewer: 'I want him to go to school where there are children from all types of financial and integrated color backgrounds. I want him to play on the streets. I want to get a house where he can sit out on the sidewalk like I used to do. I can never understand the mentality of these people in Hollywood who ask me, "Do you have your baby with you?" Where else would he be?'

Nowhere else, of course. He was usually on the set for a mandatory kiss and cuddle between takes. The need for this physical contact, and the sense of security it gave, was mutual. Jason was the one powerful reality in her life. The more the

A scene from *On A Clear Day*

accolades, the cover stories, the blandishments avalanched down, the more frightened, paradoxically, Barbra became. She drew a parallel between the two parts she played in *On a Clear Day* and her own 'schizophrenic personality' – 'The frightened girl as compared to the strong woman in me.'

The split persona presented problems. Returning to New York in mid-May from her location work in England, Barbra was the guest of honour at the Friars Club, the famous all-male showbusiness club. The occasion, in the grand ballroom of the Waldorf Astoria (1200 guests, a record for the room), was to celebrate Barbra having been chosen as 'Entertainer of the Year'. Only one other woman, Dinah Shore, had previously received this honour. It was a discordant evening, partly because of the Don Rickles-style savagery which gave a lethal touch to the jokes that shot across the crowded room; but mostly because Barbra couldn't tune in to the brash, buddy-buddy chauvinism of it all. She was no more than coolly polite. To the back-slapping gentry all around her, that mood was close to being the crime of the century.

Las Vegas, which is Friars Club audiences with sacks of quarters and sun-burned knees, was hardly an improvement. It had been six years since Barbra's last professional gig there, backing up Liberace. The stakes she now sang for were more than a nought or two higher. She was to open the new International Hotel there. As a stockholder, she no doubt felt that, if she were to transfer money from account to account, she might as well do it on a scale large enough to make the effort worthwhile.

For the first year she received in excess of $100,000 for every week she appeared, together with a significant share of stock in the hotel. Each subsequent year she was to be paid a sum approaching a quarter of a million dollars. By Vegas standards these figures, even *circa* 1970, were monumental.

'I thought the Streisand deal was perfect for her and good for the hotel,' the International's entertainments booker said. 'She was permitted to buy stock in the hotel at the market price which was very cheap then. We charged fifteen dollars a person to see her. You put 4000 in that room with two shows a night, and you've got $60,000 a day without whisky. So how much are we losing . . .?' Barbra's own patter struck a more vital nerve. Pointing toward the casino, she told the crowd, 'They want you high-rollers in there!' and they loved it.

But she herself did not roll too well. Repeating the error of that fly-by-night punctuation of *Funny Girl's* schedule in Central Park, she arrived in Vegas with her act, by her standards, underprepared. She was also 'underpsyched' for Vegas's uniquely uncompromising challenge. Part of the problem was that *Clear Day* had over-run its schedule. She hadn't had the time to forget Beaton and orientate to Barnum. Also, barely completed, the International was approaching its deadline for opening like a collapsed marathon runner arriving at the tape on all fours. All openings of restaurants, nightclubs and hotels are frenetic cliff-hangers. There are a thousand and one bugs between kitchen and credit card signing that have to be ironed out. The International was off the terrestrial scale in opening-night problems. Two thousand and one and rising. As Barbra rehearsed, curtains were being draped, fixtures hammered into walls, paint fumes wafted into her throat. Never mind the sound balance, could the extractor-fans be wired by sundown? Centerpiece to this chaos she part-owned, Barbra could scarcely have had her gut-fear of live performance eased by the knowledge of who would be out front when the spotlight came on – if it came on – for real. Her return to cabaret would be viewed by (in no particular order of merit): Cary Grant, George Raft, Nureyev, Tom Jones, Tony Bennett, Natalie Wood, Robert Culp, Andy Williams and Claudine Longet, Sammy Cahn, Peggy Lee, Norman Jewison, Danny Thomas, Ed Ames, Phil Harris and Alice Faye. Also hovering out there would be a series of ghosts from her past. Phyllis Diller who had offered her the pick of her Bon Soir wardrobe, the Smothers Brothers (co-stars from the Judy Garland show) and Jule Styne. Most poignantly of all, linking the International, Las Vegas, to Loew's Kings, Flatbush Avenue, would be the woman who had epitomised the American and Barbara Joan's dream – Rita Hayworth. The debut at The Lion had nothing on this.

In the event, Barbra was lucky to escape from the flirtation with disaster that opening night, her bankability still intact.

To begin with her repertoire was becoming embarrassingly threadbare. A second-hand rose has only so much perfume. Material from her latest LP was not really sufficient enough a change of tune. Worse, by far, was her patter between songs. Stand-up comic lines had been written for her – possibly by Dostoevsky. It would scarcely have mattered if Molière, Carl Reiner, Joseph Heller, Mel Brooks, Bill Cosby and Woody Allen had pooled resources on her behalf. Ad-libbing, Barbra can be genuinely, perceptively witty. In character she is a great comic actress sustained by that priceless ability to suggest she has only just thought of the line that second. A stand-up comic, a Fanny Brice, she is not. Exposed in her own persona at the International, before that star-spangled audience, she died the death of a thousand yawning silences. On the strength of the reviews, running the gamut from poor to panning, the hotel would have been justified in asking for its stock back. Columnist Joyce Haber, who had termed her a 'girl monster' after her first film, now wrote that her delivery was cold, her patter dreary, her repertoire inappropriate.

A less than 'greatest' star might have been cowed. Many a fighter has thrown in the towel in Las Vegas. Barbra was not, did not. She accepted that her delivery was 'cold'. The morning after she admitted, 'I was aloof on stage, but that was because I was scared and in a state of shock. I don't enjoy working in front of a bunch of strangers.' She wasted no further time. She set about righting her act. She pruned the linking material with Draconian ruthlessness. The improvement was dramatic. What followed redounds to the credit of two ladies. Joyce Haber felt professionally obliged to return, and had the fibre to modify her original hostility:

> The press has never been over-friendly to Barbra personally, but it had never been so unkind professionally. I had to see for myself. What I discovered was a very improved show. Barbra made it all worthwhile. The old magic was there. That night, La Streisand got a standing ovation after an hour of superb singing and very little chatter.

There was a mystery, never explained, to that 2 July to 30 July stint in Las Vegas. During its run, the show was laboriously and expensively taped as another television special. It was to be the Central Park concert writ small and hopefully

With Liza Minnelli at the 1970 Academy Awards where Barbra presented the Best Actor award to John Wayne for his performance in *True Grit*

better. It was never screened. Portions of the tapes were transmitted on the *Ed Sullivan Show*. But, as a whole, the performance was shelved. Someone, perhaps Barbra herself, must have considered it belonged more to Vegas than to the United States and the world.

The latest album that Barbra had, in part, incorporated into her act marked a significant change from her last straight album. Taking as heard, *What About Today?* brought Barbra out of the tuneful Thirties and Forties into the all but swung out Sixties. *What About Today?*, the sound of better things to come, was Barbra's best album to date. 'Alfie' is not a song with subtlety enough to last and even Barbra could not disguise that fact. In general, though, she deserved this handsome review in *Cash Box:* 'Barbra Streisand, whose sound is always distinctive, has moved into the contemporary bag with a vegeance on her new set. The songstress vocalising is dramatic and sizzling, and, with this album, she's in a brand new bag, the color of which looks gold.'

Thank you kindly. Well worth the dressing up for the Richard Avedon portrait whereby Barbra could wear her Bernhardt heart on her sleeve.

163

Away from any kind of studio – sound, movie or television – 1969 ended on a sour note for Barbra. She discovered that anywhere she chose to hang her hat was not, after all, home.

Buying the Axelrod house on Carolwood was an amicable, civilised transaction. But when Barbra attempted to stake out a similar claim in New York she walked headlong into a rare kind of nastiness. On 2 December 1969 the *New York Times* ran a story stating that Barbra was considering a complaint to the New York City Human Rights Commission for her being rejected by a Park Avenue co-operative apartment building. Barbra had wished to buy a twenty-roomed apartment valued at close to a quarter of a million dollars – a week's potential salary at the International. She was rejected. The reason, she maintained, was because of her race. The residents she claimed had a provable history of systematically discriminating against Jews and, indeed, an investigation into such a charge was currently under way. In denying the truth of this, however, the wife of the building's manager stated that Barbra's application had been vetoed because she was a 'flamboyant type'. Barbra riposted in a written statement: 'I have been criticised in Hollywood for not attending premieres or giving parties . . . I had thought that the mid-Victorian notion of actors as undesirables or second-class citizens was a prejudice which had gone the way of the bustle. I am an actress by choice; I am proud of my profession and I am not prepared to accept an infringement of my civil rights because of it.'

Proud, fighting words. The well-heeled, pseudo-gentry of New York having one of their periodic fits of self-suiting prejudice is a bad joke. (Ironically, Omar Sharif, in November 1980, was banned from working in countries in the Arab League because he appeared in *Ashanti* which was shot partly in Israel). The objection to Barbra Streisand was more than absurd. It was vulgar. New York's Attorney General Louis Lefkowitz ordered a special inquiry into the affair. That achieved, Barbra decided she didn't want to live in the building anyway. Instead, she bought (at around twice the sum) a five-storey brownstone on East 80th Street.

She'd made her point in a manner that only the rich, the powerful and the genuinely indignant can make. But the dust blown up by the affair having settled, honest appraisers are entitled to a nagging thought that Barbra might have protested too much. The words, if not the spirit, of the complaint against her was that she was a 'flamboyant type'. Set against some of the episodes and personalities Barbra was shortly to be concerned with, 'flamboyant' must have been the most innocent adjective of the decade.

THIRTEEN

IN JANUARY of 1970 Mr George Hees, a member of Canada's Loyal Opposition, rose to his feet in Parliament to address a question to his country's Prime Minister. The premier's attention apparently elsewhere, he nailed him with a decidedly un-Parliamentary taunt: '. . . if the Prime Minister can take his eyes and mind off the visitors' gallery long enough to answer!' The national leader was Pierre Trudeau. The visiting distraction in the gallery was Barbra Streisand. The Prime Minister, having produced her as his guest at the Manitoba Centennial Gala in Ottawa's National Arts Centre, had now brought her along to see him putting in a few hours looking after the store. Trudeau had long enjoyed – if that is the right term – the reputation of being a gay dog of a swinging bachelor, escorting a string of long-legged beauties whose high IQs matched his own. Nevertheless, accosted by that question in the House, he was, by all contemporary accounts, embarrassed, blushing, smiling self-consciously with less than his customary composure.

Yet he should have seen it coming. He and Barbra were hardly new acquaintances. They had met several times previously; first in London when both were there for respective flag-waving chores – the film premiere of *Funny Girl* and a Commonwealth Prime Ministers' Conference. Later, in November 1969, they had linked together again in New York to take in some movies, theater, the Fifth Avenue Raffles Club and a little Greenwich Village-style fun. The Canadian capers merely shifted their good friendship to Trudeau's home territory.

The publicity at the time was, of course, enormous. Here was one of the few politicians in the world able to aspire to the description 'statesman' in tandem with possibly the best-known female in the world this side of Golda Meir. Forget Burton and Taylor. Invoke Anthony and Cleopatra.

The Canadian public were understandably concerned. A CTV interviewer came to the point with commendable directness in the course of a cross-country television hook-up. The exchange went as follows:

PHILLIPS: The other question concerns your private affairs and I know you have quite a different concept of your rights as a private citizen than I do. I think everybody is interested in the fact you have seen Miss Streisand not just once as a casual encounter but three or four times while she has been in the city. I think the public is entitled to know whether you are developing a serious relationship with her.
TRUDEAU: Well, (a) I'd say your facts are not quite right, and (b) it's none of your business or the public's business.

Whatever the facts, Trudeau was being disingenuous. The coming together of two such talents offered daunting possibilities. In a collision of two highly-motivated personalities with strong, individual power-bases, who would give way? A *prima*

165

Canada's Prime Minister, Pierre Trudeau, escorts Barbra to Winnipeg's Royal Ballet
amidst rumours of a romance

facie case existed, perhaps, for believing that a Trudeau–Streisand household might be located in Hollywood where the partner with the greater personal ambition, the greater immediate drive would need to be. Trudeau's discernment would not have been faulted if he considered Barbra Streisand worth a mass rejection of his ministerial cares. This conjecture was not merely shared by the media; political circles viewed this zappy republican equivalent of the 'Prince and the Showgirl' tale less benignly than the Canadian public. A politician of ferocious energy and resource, he could afford to shrug off innuendo or any disquiet about time spent on private preoccupations. No one has ever been able to accuse him of playing harder than he worked. It is just that Barbra seemed of such matching stature that it was impossible to conceive of her in an occasional, a part-time role. And the relationship did go beyond the gossamer thinness of the 'in' social whirl. In her

Playboy interview she lifts a curtain on a startling potential scenario. Here the exchange, while still probing, was a little less than eyeball-to-eyeball.

PLAYBOY: What about your relationship with Canada's Prime Minister Pierre Trudeau before his marriage? He escorted you to the Arts Center in Ottawa once and jumped from the limousine to open the door. Did you ever think a prime minister would be opening doors for you?
STREISAND: No. It happened to be overwhelming.
PLAYBOY: Did he ask you to marry him?
STREISAND: I don't want to answer that. But he's an extraordinary man. He's a wonderful leader and a very young-minded, spirited, hip figure who goes to Parliament in sandals.
PLAYBOY: Did you ever reflect on what it would be like to be first lady of Canada?
STREISAND: Oh, yeah, I thought it would be fantastic. I'd have to learn how to speak French. I would do only movies made in Canada. I had it all figured out. I would campaign for him and become totally politically involved in all the causes, abortion and whatever.
PLAYBOY: What made you change your mind?
STREISAND: Certain realities.
PLAYBOY: Would you ever have considered getting him to change his career?
STREISAND: No, I would never have wanted him to. His life was too important to a whole country, to a world. I don't feel mine is that significant. It's significant in that it gives people a fantasy life or some pleasure, but it's not like being a prime minister of a country.
PLAYBOY: Do you still have any contact with him?
STREISAND: No, not any more.

A little over a year later, all speculation along that axis was off. Trudeau dissociated himself from the form-book odds being placed on the eligible thinking-premier's beauties. All but one. The world learned the lucky candidate was Margaret Sinclair. Give or take a few years, the world saw the jet-setting Jagger fan ruefully back at square one.

It is not hard to see why Barbra should have been attracted to so athletic and intellectual a practitioner of high-style as Trudeau. Separated from Elliott Gould (their Dominican Republic divorce was effected in July 1971) she had been drawn to a type no casting director with any conscience could have proposed Gould for.

Not that Trudeau was the first. Splitting from Elliott Gould had emancipated Barbra in a way that, at the most publicised level, exactly paralleled the experience of tens of thousands of middle-class American women. Closer now to thirty than twenty, she was far more self-possessed, vitally uninhibited. She could enjoy the fantasy fulfillment of being briefly linked with Warren Beatty – take that, Erasmus Hall High! – in the gossip columns, without losing any sleep. One would hardly cast Beatty as Trudeau either, nor even as Elliott Gould. But one of Barbra's key and most consistently repeated statements about herself – 'My taste is eclectic' – holds true for the men who entered that indeterminate space between her public and private self. Superseded by that kind of manpower, it was fortunate that Elliott

Gould was now flexing his own muscles professionally.

The 'trades' were proclaiming that Elliott Gould was out of the eternal doldrums. *Bob and Carol and Ted and Alice* had won him a nomination for the 1970 'Best Supporting Actor' Award. Barbra, despite the hugely flacked *Dolly* being in with seven chances, was not even a starter that year. The possibility that roles might be reversed and she might become the 'one-time Mrs Elliott Gould' was good, brief, wishful-thinking for Elliott and his supporters. The clear, pre-match favorite, he was robbed of a leap down the aisle by the consistently excellent, doom-laden Gig Young for his performance in Sydney Pollack's *They Shoot Horses, Don't They?*

Meanwhile, the potential 'one-time Mrs Elliott Gould' was the current co-party-hopper and Love Story sparring partner of Ryan O'Neal, the logical end result in looks and screen persona of a decade of aftershave commercials. Trudeau, Beatty, O'Neal – who now could say that she was an ugly duckling when she had swanned around in *that* company? Much later Richard Avedon was to declare that Barbra had made herself beautiful by willing that she be so; I will it, therefore I am. No woman could feel a 'plain Jane' who has had a Beatty light her cigarette, a Trudeau run round to open her car door, an O'Neal to appraise over the candle-light.

For a short period, she and Ryan lamely attempted the difficult trick of *not* being seen together. O'Neal had an additional reason for caution. His recent estrangement from his soap-opera soulmate Leigh Taylor-Young, coupled with stories of his living it up with Barbra, would inevitably prejudice *his* chances of an Oscar, for *Love Story*, Hollywood's most strenuous attempt ever to have a novelette taken seriously. But Ryan's and Barbra's efforts to keep their friendship to themselves ended in a spirited incident in a Santa Monica parking lot. Barbra and O'Neal and his younger brother (Kevin was the 'date', Ryan the chaperone, get it?) had driven to the Civic Stadium to take in a rock concert. They had gone on from a party where Via Veneto-style candid cameraman, Peter Borsari, had asked for and, in spades, been refused a shot of the two stars together. He tracked them to the concert and caught them in his flash as they left. Kevin tried for a camera interception. 'I can sue,' Borsari shouted. 'Sure,' Kevin cracked back, 'I'm broke.' Words came to shove, to punch, to blows. Barbra and O'Neal were vindicated. But they were no longer a tucked-away gossip tit-bit. They were front page news. The old moral had again issued a reminder: they who live by the lens must sometimes die by it a little. And sometimes a lot.

Barbra must have wondered whether the Ryan connection was worth the glossy paper it was written on. To anticipate titles by some years, this conjunction of the stars was scarcely to be billed as the 'main event'. For Barbra, surely, it must have represented a kind of dalliance holding pattern. Ryan O'Neal, whatever his charm, good looks and skills, hardly added up to that sum of father-figure authority – force, intellect, power, even threat – that to differing degrees Trudeau in the past, others in the future, were to offer. The patent place O'Neal occupied in her life was the old Ronald Reagan part – the personable guy who ends up, probably by mutual consent, not getting the girl.

When Ray Stark had signed Barbra for the film lead in *Funny Girl* he had driven a hard, if not finally unreasonable, bargain; he had built into the contract an option

Coming clean with George Segal in *The Owl and the Pussycat*

on her services for three more pictures. For a while, wearing her Ellbar Company hard-hat, Barbra and her need for control, a sense of personal independence, had tried kicking against the contractual straightjacket. But to no end. When you hold options on an Oscar winner, that you will exercise them is a formality. In late 1969 she came on to the set for the first day's shooting on *The Owl and the Pussycat*.

In the event, she was delighted. Any rancour had evaporated. The film was under the (solo) direction of her trusted friend Herb Ross, who had put so much into *Wholesale* and *Funny Girl*, and she was playing opposite George Segal, an actor deft, technically controlled, personally assured enough to give as good as he got on screen but always in a spirit of harmony rather than rivalry. (Originally the idea had been to do the movie with Elizabeth Taylor – Barbra's one female rival in the top box-office ten – and Richard Burton. The notion has the same light-footed felicity as casting Ernest Borgnine to play the lead in a bio-pic of Fred Astaire.) Biggest bonus of all, however, was that in her fourth picture she would be playing a contemporary character who did not sing. She was playing comedy again but, so to speak, with a straight part. It was as good as a vacation. 'Now I can make a movie in ten weeks,' she rejoiced. 'No songs. Like a normal person. You do a movie in the daytime and then you go home at night.' It was a part she knew well. Repeating her acclaimed Broadway performance (opposite Alan Alda) in London, Barbra's old *Harry Stoones* colleague Diana Sands had collected an award at the American

Embassy on the same occasion as the *Funny Girl* star. Way back then Barbra had seen *The Owl* and had digested the part of Doris, the pragmatic and happy-ending hooker. In a sense, of course, she had grasped it earlier by keeping her young eyes open along the Manhattan backstreets.

As Doris, Barbra plays the ultimately soft-centered core of a contemporary fantasy – the friendly neighbourhood whore. Unschooled, unloved, unconnected to life by the television's drip-feed, she still totally captivates. She's there, gorgeous, toughly vulnerable, for every fantasising male to redeem. The male who is lucky enough to have the on-screen job is the Segal character, Felix, the owl of a minimal-talent writer who works in a book-store, and who is, of course, as much in need of salvation as Doris. They meet through the geography of co-existing in the same apartment building. The hooker's work schedule clashes with the writer's. When he complains, the stage is set for a classic (largely inverted) battle of the sexes. It may not be *Pride and Prejudice* but Bill Manhoff's highly successful play is in the classic *It Happened One Night* cum *The Awful Truth* tradition. Boy meets girl and they strike sparks until enough heat is generated for them to fuse.

The movie is also of course in another tradition – the confined Broadway play 'opened up' for the screen. As such it fares a lot better than most. The adaptation was by Buck Henry, an equally adept piece of casting on the part of Rastar Productions. Henry is, of course, the man who scripted *The Graduate* to prodigious instant box-office records. Richard Corliss, in an incisive assessment of the writer in *Talking Pictures*, succinctly reveals the brilliance, and the flaws:

> Buck Henry came out of cabaret and television comedy and most of his work has never escaped the aura of his origins. If some of *The Graduate* sounds sophomoric today, if *Candy* fails to transcend its blackout format, if *The Owl and the Pussycat* plays like nothing so much as a horny sit-com and if *What's Up, Doc?* seems in desperate need of a laugh track, the reasons may be traced back to Henry's formative days in *The Premise* and on *Get Smart*. These are the training grounds – the minor leagues – of comedy; when so much material has to be manufactured so quickly, one solid laugh in four times at bat is a pretty good average. Unlike Paul Mazursky and Larry Tucker, Henry (so far) hasn't created characters; instead he's written lines for a character someone else has created. And unlike David Newman and Robert Benton, he rarely has been able to inhabit his characters. He just seems to be passing through on the way to another gag-writing assignment.

The Owl and the Pussycat is horny sit-com. What makes it so enjoyably successful is the aplomb with which the two players embrace that fact and then, occasionally, manage to infiltrate a subtler, more haunting performance between the interstices of the surface plot. They are helped in this by the skill of the 'opening up' process. *Newsweek* was quick to associate both factors:

> The surprising merit of the film is how much mileage it gets out of its vulgarity, as humor and as good juicy sentimentality. Henry and Herbert Ross give us a New York that sneaks up on us in its quick funny black facsimile of how it really is. Apartments are equipped with tape recordings of barking watchdogs

and police locks cantilevered against the horrors outside. The streets are lined with street-walkers and the movie houses are bordellos with popcorn stands. A fellow stops at the corner news-stand and the newslady holds a paper up to his nose and asks '*Screw*?'

With so much quasi-reality to get her teeth into, Barbra revelled in shedding the period costumes of musicals bordering on the epic. This was travelling light and she was 'up', relaxed, nowhere near the psyche-tearing need for confrontation with a Matthau or a Wyler. She was visibly content and 'coming through' for Ross. But she could still do little right in the jaundiced eyes of the smaller fry about the sound stage. She was accused of skulking in her dressing room. She was accused of giving Buck Henry a hard time. She was accused of being hollow, a 'vacuum', alive only when working, a cipher the moment the word 'cut' brought her out of a scene. She was accused of favoritism towards sycophants palpably telling her what she wanted to hear. And so on. It became tedious. The whine of complaint is the sour sound that surrounds success. The downright envy of mid-talent cannot endure proximity to high ability. All this *kvetching* tells us more about the would-be 'prosecutors' than the accused. An entirely different viewpoint came from one of Barbara's peers. From George Segal. Contrition rather than vindictiveness was the key-signature to his remembrance.

> I loved making *The Owl and the Pussycat* but I gave them a lot of problems. I was probably more of a prima donna than I had any right to be. I was concerned with the hours and other people working and things like that – being a star before I really was one. It's irresistible. I've never known anybody able to side-step it. You are just overcome by the fantasy. It's such a rush and you're treated in such a deferential way. In yourself you're still the guy who couldn't get arrested for ten years and suddenly here you are, you've finally arrived and you look around and you start to believe it. It results in aberrant behavior. I try to be forgiving with myself but I must have been terrible to be around. Barbra was impeccable. I remember her as being an absolute professional. And I learned from her a little bit how to do it. What you really do when you're floundering yourself is you look up and see how somebody else is handling it.

Ten years on, with Segal himself established as a kind of eccentrically mature star with a quietly amazing range, it is his assessment that emerges as the safest bet.

He and Barbra had to embrace more than just the sitcom vitality/vulgarity of their roles. They had to embrace each other – nude. For Barbra it was a watershed requirement. Still implanted in part of her being were the 'nice Jewish girl' injunctions she had known as a girl. The relatively uninhibited social-sexual liaisons she had known latterly may have come in handy in helping her 'get down' the part of Doris. But flat-out nudity – what would her mother think! And say! Diane Streisand-Kind had already seen her daughter in Doris's famous hand-on-heart-and-heart-in-the-right-place working clothes and announced to the world's press: 'She had on a skimpy costume and was very embarrassed when she saw me. I'm really shocked at all those things actresses have to do today, but I guess it's part of the job.' Now Barbra was no longer 'very embarrassed', she was 'very, very embarrassed'. She was about to relinquish her skimpy costume in favour of no costume at all. Herb Ross takes up the story:

> She only calls me 'Herbie' when she's uptight. Otherwise I'm Herbert. The whole picture forced a kind of intimacy on all of us and we all ended up loving Barbra most of all. But for that scene, as soon as I heard, 'Herbie, I gotta talk to you,' I knew she had big reservations even though I'd thought we'd worked them all out. She got me into a corner and said, 'Herbie, I can't. I've got goosebumps and they'll show. Herbie, I just can't. What will my mother think?'

It was time for Ross to earn his money. Building on his longstanding and affectionate relationship with this sudden reincarnation of Miss Marmelstein, he patiently explained how crucial the scene was to the film – how good Barbra would look. He talked, talked again, talked some more. More time passed. In the safe modesty of being actually between the sheets, Segal found an answer to this unforeseen hiatus. He slept.

Barbra's first nude love scene

'George, who had overcome his inhibitions,' Ross remembers,

> took a nap and I kept working on her. Finally she said, 'Oh, what the hell, I'll do it once.' The set was hushed, the cameras rolled and Barbra (one . . . two . . . three . . . go!) threw off her robe and did her first nude scene. It was perfect. I yelled, 'Cut and print! Beautiful!' But you know Barbra – the perfectionist. She wanted a retake. I think we were all shocked because everybody burst into laughter, including Barbra. We did the retake.

In the event, the film ended up with a deliberately tame American 'A' rating, the moment of nudity lasting no longer than five seconds of heavily shadowed screen time. But whichever 'take' was used, Ross had not exaggerated as to how Barbra would appear – not, in the least, in the eyes of the *Newsweek* critic. He or she wrote of 'a funky love scene from which one will never be able to forget Streisand's lovely spinal furrow and her frenetically healthy urgency as she scrambles in the sheets, coaxing the non-professional Segal breathlessly with "Attaboy, attaboy, attaboy!" '

'Segal,' the same reviewer justly declared, 'gives a remarkable performance – he is a foil without being a foil, his Geiger counter matches Streisand's at all times and yet, somehow, he creates the absolute quiet of tenderness.' Which is saying a lot in that reviewer's book. For of Barbra herself, the praise is utterly unstinted.

> Streisand [*Newsweek* of 16 November 1970 said] displays the most amazing comic energy seen on the screen in a very long time. In *Hello Dolly* and *On a Clear Day* she was forced to manipulate her personality and talent like some inspired Silly Putty in order to outface the exigencies of those big deals.
>
> But now all the circus junk and the mastodon droppings have been cleared away and we have Streisand plain. There she comes right where she belongs, in a real New York street, ducking through the sleazy rain in a fake-fur minicoat, white boots scrambling, tote-bag swinging, cursing out a departing bus in her interborough voice and, with a shrug and a chomp on her Juicy Fruit, flopping into a passing car. That's the way girls used to come into our movies, and our fantasies, and it's about time we remembered that Streisand is the latest of our girls – our Lombards, Harlows, Blondells, Monroes.

High praise indeed. But not unmerited. In *The Owl and the Pussycat* Barbra married being 'the greatest star' to being an utterly on-target actress. The end product was exactly that split-focused pinpointing of a role *and* that mysterious surround of personal charisma.

There was one sour, finally irrelevant, postscript to the, in the event, run-of-the-mill nude scene. Towards the end of the Seventies *High Society*, a 'man's magazine', came out with an issue featuring several colour blow-ups of Barbra bare-breasted. The magazine managed to create an entire layout and cover story around the photos. Barbra did not 'lie down' and think of the publicity. Fastidiously, she filed a $5 million invasion-of-privacy suit, demanding that the article be pulled and all negatives confiscated. The issue was recalled immediately – but not quite immediately enough. The recall count was 3000 copies adrift. They had disappeared from New York City news-stands to become an overnight collector's item.

By comparison with her first three epic-musicals, *The Owl and the Pussycat* was a low-budget production in the Barbra Streisand canon. It therefore opened with a refreshing absence of ballyhoo. Yet first time around in 1970-71 in the United States alone, it grossed almost $12 million. It was the 'sleeper' of the year, if a Streisand picture could ever be so termed. It was also timely. After the resounding-ly neutral thud of *On a Clear Day*, following it up with a turkey might have severely restricted – perhaps even cut short – Barbra's subsequent movie career. She might, at best, have been pigeon-holed in the 'musicals only' slot. As it was, one week after the premiere of her fourth film, hard-headed *Variety* was calling her 'a sizzling hot property'. She had proved she did not need a vast infrastructure of a production to keep her before the public. In *The Owl and the Pussycat* she gave her earliest, clearest indication that she was the complete reason for seeing a movie, whatever its scale.

The lesson was not lost on her. The pleasantness of shooting *The Owl and the Pussycat* and its subsequent box-office success had reminded her of what she had known way back when in Brooklyn – that there was infinitely more to Hollywood than Broadway with or without Cecil Beaton. She proceeded to draw breath. Before, she had danced to a piper, from role to role. Now, since each new movie had to be her best shot, she would take her time and set herself just right. In the meantime there was Jason, perhaps her complete reason for being Barbra Streisand. Then there was her talent for decor to rediscover; and learning the art of living. As she told *Life*:

> I look forward to working less and simplifying my life, to fulfilling some of my potential as an individual and as a woman. My little-girl fantasy of being a recording star, a theater star, a concert star, and a movie star is impossible to maintain; each of them suffers. There is so much else to learn, so much more to do. What I'd like is more time – time not only to read the stacks of political journals that have been piling up, but almost time to read *Good Housekeeping* to find out different ways to decorate my son's sandwiches.

There is, of course, relaxing and relaxing. Barbra's version was of the kind to daunt your average workaholic. She relaxed non-stop, finding, in the political field for instance, that her own actions spoke more satisfyingly to her than all the political journalists' words. A former active campaigner for Eugene McCarthy and John Lindsay she spent much of her time and energy going to bat for Bella Abzug, with whom she formed a close friendship. In November, not only did she appear at two fund-raising parties on behalf of the Congresswoman and perform at a 'Broadway for Bella' benefit at Madison Square Garden but, more surprisingly (and given her inhibitions about being 'recognised'), commendably went street campaigning too. It was a time when America was deeply divided on the issue of its involvement in Vietnam. As the first formal defeat in the nation's military history drew inexorably closer, Barbra stood up to be counted well to the left of centre. She performed again at a rally designed to raise funds to be put to use by Congressmen prominent in their opposition to the war. A little later, in 1972, she put her mouth where other peoples' money was by singing requests over the phone on behalf of the Pentagon

Papers relief fund.

In all of these activities, clearly, Barbra was being liberally partisan. But alongside them ran a whole raft of charitable calls on her time – for, among others, the National Association for Retarded Children and the U.N. Children's Fund. In the meantime projects, schemes, properties (bricks and mortar as well as typed) competed to catch either Barbra's eye or the eye of one of her team. Despite the welter of public activity, Hollywood refused to accept that the Streisand 'people' behind the scenes weren't moving their client on to the launch-pad for another major shot. Hearing nothing to confirm it, 'announcements' were leaked or less subtly planted. One report seemed to have more optimism than substance to it. Anthony Newley proclaimed to the media that a formality was all that stood between Barbra returning to Broadway to star as the Josephine to his Napoleon. The British *Sunday Mirror* was full of the exciting 'news'. Jack Bentley wrote: 'Gavin Lambert's script is already under way. So arc the words and music by Tony and his old co-writer Leslie Bricusse. Said Tony during a call I made to his Los Angeles home: "Barbra is sold on the idea. She just wants to okay the final script." '

Ah well, in the world of showbiz each day brings a Waterloo to someone. The okay never got through to the front. Nor, indeed, did it to what might have seemed a likelier prospect given Barbra's enthusiasm for the subject matter. Early in 1971 it was announced that she would be playing Sarah Bernhardt in a film directed by Ken Russell. Once again a fatal thumb was turned downward during the initial pre-production period. Advisedly, one would say, in both cases.

Barbra Streisand is not a theatre person. A period musical on Broadway, however witty (and revealing) its Empire lines, would have constituted a reversion to the cul-de-sac of typecasting. Then there's the point that no known theater sound system can accommodate Newley's choked-up vibrato in duet with Barbra's resonance. While not denying Newley's and Leslie Bricusse's reputations as gung-ho British imports, Streisand would have been on the lookout for more scintillating satellites.

Equally, Russell, once a film-maker of impressively mandarin flair (his studies of Delius and Isadora Duncan were first-rate), is fine when under the constraints of BBC producers and budgets. But given his head, he has gone on to lose it. Newley's and Russell's ideas being conceived and then aborted, Barbra Streisand was well out of them. But with a performer of her calibre and bankability, projects, deals, 'packages' and propositions arrive every hour on the hour. Her signature, for the established producer, means added prestige. For the born hustler, the Cadillac, the house on Malibu, the ultimate meal ticket.

For the moment – Christmas/New Year 1971/72 – Barbra's most positive professional act was to return to the International, Las Vegas (now renamed the Las Vegas Hilton) for another cabaret engagement. This time she prepared her act with a vengeance. After her former hard-fought, Pyrrhic victory, it is good to record that her MacArthur-like tenacity in going back was rewarded by some of her best reviews ever. There was a unanimous deployment of superlatives. The *Las Vegas Visitor* set the tone: 'The performances have never been more superb, her range more astounding, her personality warmer or more captivating . . .'

Barbra, temporarily stepping off the Hollywood whirligig, was visibly, audibly a more mature performer. But the triumph perversely reinforced her determination to score as a major screen actress. She needed new stimulus, the framework and occupational therapy of a new production. It came at last.

She had gone to a special screening of Peter Bogdanovich's *The Last Picture Show* with the head of Warner Brothers, John Calley. Legend has it that she turned to him and said: 'I want him.' Bogdanovich, that is. Calley, friendship and box-office going nicely together, had consequently approached Bogdanovich in the context of *A Glimpse of Tiger*, yet another project that Barbra and her 'people' were dickering with.

There was an irony here. *A Glimpse of Tiger* had been an Elliott Gould co-produced vehicle that had ground to a melodramatic halt some two weeks of shooting down the track. It had done so in such a manner as to call in question once again Gould's future as an actor, even (if you believed his most embittered enemies) his sanity.

After *Bob and Carol and Ted and Alice* Elliott Gould had found himself the hottest thing in town – no longer 'Mr Streisand' but – 'Now who's the greatest star?' – the estranged husband of a Mrs Gould who was also in pictures. Understandably after the spirit-crushing years in the wilderness he had turned into an actor who could not say 'no', appearing as lead (and just at the time Barbra was easing up) in five pictures in eighteen months. A decade later it seems fair to say that none of these pictures seem 'major' – not even Altman's *MASH*. But they were certainly 'major' in the making. Gould, by the time of *A Glimpse of Tiger* was like a club fighter being sent into the ring with too little respite between bouts. He was also nearer some personal breaking point.

The cast had gone into pre-shooting rehearsals. These were gruesome. Gould, after years of soaking it up, now seemed intent on dishing it out. Any emphasis in delivery, any interpretation differing from his own conception evoked tantrums going beyond nine on the Richter scale. Then, on the first day of shooting on location there was an edgy, out-of-left-field accident. The setting was a Manhattan subway station. An incoming train went briefly out of control. No one was hurt but exposed nerve-ends were pincered. When two of Gould's friends, David Carradine and Barbara Hershey stopped by to visit, Anthony Harvey, the director, quite correctly (as 'professionals' they should have known their presence was a distraction) ordered them off the set. Gould was incensed. Harvey was fired. Reports say that the next morning co-producer Jack Brodsky countermanded this decision, and Gould was so close to going berserk that Kim Darby, his co-star, became terrified. Bodyguards were called in. After two weeks of raw larynxes, bloodshot eyes and less than a reel of usable film, Warner Brothers aborted what was already stillborn.

Kim Darby took to her bed, a bulletin describing her as being 'emotionally shattered'. Gould's behavior received Hollywood's staccato verdict, variously termed a 'freakout', a 'bomb-out' or 'wig-out'. Shortly afterwards, in the deep purple light of a discotheque, he looked hollow-eyed, unshaven; wearing an old Army greatcoat, he seemed costumed, programmed for disaster. Later, much later, Gould gave his version of the drama:

I got burned. The project was full of turmoil from the start and to make it work I had to stick my neck out as an artist. I accepted financial responsibility for the collapse of the film and I have only now finished off paying the costs. They got a psychiatrist's report on me and concluded from it that I must have been crazy at the time. That entitled them to collect half a million dollars insurance. Apart from the four hundred and twenty-five grand they were getting from me. The second surprise for me was that they took the basis of my film and turned it into *What's Up, Doc?* which was terribly successful. They turned my part into a woman's and who played it? – yes, Barbra Streisand.

Well . . . yes and no. Mainly no. Peter Bogdanovich has set the record a little straighter:

> I read the script and I didn't want to do it. It was kind of a comedy-drama with a lot of social overtones and I didn't like it at all. But I told John Calley I'd love to do a picture with Barbra. 'Let's do a screwball comedy,' I said. I saw Barbra as sort of a Carole Lombard and I thought she'd be fine for that. I sketched an idea. Barbra will play a wacky girl and Ryan will be a musicologist who gets involved with her. It will be a farce. Based on three sentences and enthusiasm we started work. I hired David Newman and Robert Benton to write it. For four days we sat and talked out the plot, then they went away and in two weeks completed the first draft. It wasn't right. They did another. It still wasn't right. Calley suggested we hire Buck Henry. He joined us and we tossed around more ideas trying to find the right direction. Then Buck wrote a draft in two weeks. It was good but we kept working on it to improve it.

The involvement of Buck Henry laid low the bad-mouth allegations of Barbra's indifference, animosity, hostility towards him on *The Owl and the Pussycat*. The involvement of Ryan O'Neal – he had stepped in as a replacement for Gould during Warner's initial attempts at a salvage operation – may well, of course, have had a tiny influence on the agreed involvement of one Barbra Streisand.

Leaping ahead, the records show that in the short and medium run, *What's Up, Doc?* occupies an amazingly high place in the table of box-office returns notched by Barbra Streisand films. In a list published by *Variety* in the spring of 1978 it is second, having grossed $28 million, above *Funny Girl* and *The Way We Were*. Only *A Star Is Born* ($9 million better off) stands above it. Not bad for a salvage operation. Part of the film's success has to be attributed to the relative dearth of screen comedies in the late Sixties, early Seventies; part to snappily opportunistic merchandising along the (true-life supported) lines of: 'The boy from *Love Story* meets the girl from *Funny Girl* in a screwball comedy from the director of *The Last Picture Show*.' The truth is that, pleasant enough, funny in places, very funny in some, *What's Up, Doc?* is not such a good picture. It is not a *Bringing Up Baby*. Yet it was Howard Hawks's brilliant Grant–Hepburn comedy that was Bogdanovich's flash-point of inspiration. It was homage. But he did a double heist job. On the verbal comedy of the Thirties (that era when Hollywood realised the leading man could do gags and didn't need a comical side-kick) he superimposed the sight-gags of the Twenties and Thirties.

Given that *What's Up, Doc?* is essentially an oblique compilation film, Barbra was back to the dilemma which faced her on *Hello Dolly*. How to play a series of 'bits' bolted together end to end. In fact she struts her jaunty stuff very stylishly, living for the moment and justified by the knowledge that the picture's parts are greater than the sum. This, in part, explains (again) the wide spectrum covered by the personal reviews. John Broeck in *The Villager* was evidently captivated: 'Streisand, minus her Flatbush twang, is wacky, campy, and endearing – her best performance to date.' Bruce Bahrenburg, by contrast, in the *Newark Evening News* mounted a considerably in-depth attack:

> Miss Streisand knows no subtleties in her comedy craft. She is an outrageous mugger. Nothing is done in low key. The opening scene in which she pursues O'Neal in a hotel drugstore is painfully bad. Sometimes she attempts softness in her love scenes but the brassiness of the preceding moment drowns it out. Miss Streisand's competition in the comedienne fields are Lucille Ball and Carol Burnett. She could learn a great deal from them. In *Doc*, her competition is Madeleine Kahn, who plays O'Neal's fiancée. She is extremely funny in being exaggerated without losing the shape of a real character. This is what Miss Streisand can't do because she is basically a variety peformer, not a movie star. The qualities that make a Marilyn Monroe a movie star, from looks to timing, are not evident in Miss Streisand's film roles.

The point about Madeleine Kahn is well made. Otherwise the critique probably overstates. Madeleine Kahn had a precisely defined minor role. Barbra carrying the film was carrying the ball in a contest where, too often, the coaches had sent her on to the field without a game-plan.

Ryan O'Neal has chivalrously rationalised the 'bittiness' imposed on Barbra's characterisation this way: 'She felt that Judy was sort of a fantasy, and if you're playing a fantasy you can go many different ways because a fantasy can do anything.' Yeah . . . well. Another of O'Neal's observations seems more pertinent:

> Now sometimes she did not agree that a scene was right when Peter thought it was. I must say I always sided with Barbra. I would listen to both arguments, then I would make my choice. Most of the time mentally I stayed out of it. But I usually thought she was correct. But Peter made her go the other way and she, being a professional, always went with what he said, in the end.

O'Neal himself drew much of the critics' fire. He bumbles through the film not as a character (which would have been fine) but as an actor (which was not). The performance is that of a Seventies sophomore miscast in the Thirties play that requires a flurry of actor's 'business'. Lacking such techniques the sophomore falls back on reminding the audience he's sexy and next afternoon will be out there quarter-backing the team once again. Again, he's unconsciously revealing:

> I was afraid of Howard Bannister. I'd never known anyone like him. Peter was a guiding light for me in terms of how to play the part. I was not that character. I was hardly close to him actually, and Peter had to show me how to do it, then I would do it the way he showed me. It came out as a kind of

compromise – something really in the middle – which was what he wanted.

Bogdanovich had the last laugh. Shrewdly he bypassed any special screening for the critics. He didn't want the gags falling on the cold, arid landscape of a sparsely attended professional audience. They had to take their chance in a public showing, and risk the contagion of a packed house laughing each other into more laughs. Initially, the strategy may have misfired. Denied a caviare or the red carpet treatment, some critics, it is alleged, deliberately filed jaundiced reviews. (It is possible, of course, they were not overly struck by the film). Long-term, however, Bogdanovich was vindicated. People did laugh. Word did go around. There were not so many other laughs in '72 and by next year the loudest was Warner's on the way to the bank.

The laugh must have had a long echo. Barbra had now appeared in two contemporary, relatively modest-priced movies and both had been enjoyable. Both had made money. With her participation in First Artists potentially going for her, maybe it was about time The Actress and The Producer started working both sides of the camera.

With Peter Bogdanovich relaxing in the wings during the filming of *What's Up Doc?*

FOURTEEN

IT WAS not the most devastating message ever to have been drummed out of the African bush but, early in 1972, one hundred Hebrew National hot dogs lay quietly wilting at Nairobi airport. They had been despatched there in a crassly misconceived spirit of kosher cultural exchange by a New York delicatessen. It is a well-known fact that in the heart of darkest Africa, Tarzan, Jungle Jim, Alan Quartermain and Ayesha all subsist on weiners and cokes the moment the cameras have ceased turning on the day's epic. Now that the Samburu people of Kenya had become chosen – selected to appear in the Panavision viewfinder of a Hollywood movie – they would naturally wish to confirm their membership among the elect by conforming to the Fairfax Avenue gastronomic ritual. The fact that the Samburu are vegetarians was neither here in Hollywood, nor there in Kenya. What the hell – extras can't be choosers! In the event, they didn't have to be. The culturally myopic attempt at franks-across-the-sea allowed Barbra Streisand one of the more incisive moments in her role of movie producer. On location some two hundred miles north of Nairobi, the indignation showed. Her slightly diagonal eyes were blazingly attractive but with the emphasis on the adverb. She had heard about the sausage consignment and declared the idea to be 'tasteless and humiliating'. The hot dogs stayed where they were.

It would have been better had the unit stayed where it was – Hollywood – too. And better if Barbra had exercised more clout throughout the making of her debut as a First Artists producer. The hot dogs were symbolic. Confusing life with art and possibly reality, the production half-ignored Carl Laemle's ageless precept: 'A tree is a tree. A rock is a rock. Go shoot it in Griffith Park.'

Like virtually all of the films to come out of the First Artists' stable (Newman's *Pocket Money* and *Judge Roy Bean;* Poitier's *Warm December;* the late Steve McQueen's *The Getaway), Up the Sandbox* failed to win, place or show in either the box-office or critical stakes. Barbra was bitterly disappointed that her first venture into production should largely have flopped. The fact that it now enjoys a rather more vigorous television 'half-life' than many of its contemporaries is not consolation enough. She knows that it is not merely a question (as director Irwin Kershner would claim) of the movie being ahead of its times and the times having caught up. For all its incidental felicities, *Up the Sandbox* is a seriously flawed film.

Its story revolves around a young, thoroughly intelligent housewife who is obliged to subordinate her own career, and instincts toward self-expression, to the support of her husband, a middle-status academic, and young children. As such – from Blackheath to Brisbane to Brentwood – it is almost *the* story of our times. But Kershner's reflections went far deeper than being a glib cop-out. 'Remember', he told us, that '*Sandbox*

came out when women were standing up for their rights. They were saying that women will never be completely liberated until they no longer have to bear children. Until they start coming out of test tubes. It's all bullshit but that was the popular notion and, interestingly enough, whenever Hollywood gets involved in anything that has a topical tone to it they take a popular position. The picture took an unpopular position because she wanted to be liberated but not liberated from a man, not liberated from her children, and doing well by them and raising them wonderfully. It was an unpopular position at the time.

This was no *Diary of a Mad Housewife*. Instead, like the great silent majority, she fantasised. It was, in its incursions into fantasy, depicting her wishful thinking, that the film most erred. In his own analysis Kershner uses the word 'excursions' and perhaps more aptly.

The book that it was based on had many fantasies and in the narrative of a book you can move a story forward despite excursions. In a film, a drama, it doesn't work, and this is the fight we had right from the beginning – how to make a story move forward and yet stop once in a while for a fantasy. Now, if the fantasy is on-going and continues to reveal more about the character, then it moves the story forward. But these fantasies didn't. They were never integrated.

In fact here Kershner is being somewhat less than candid. Since it has come of relative age, film has explored the perpetually shifting opposition between reality and fantasy to produce – in films such as *Sherlock Junior, It's a Wonderful Life, Les Belles de Nuit* – some of its finest, most perceptive moments. Fantasy can illuminate and extend if properly deployed. In *Up the Sandbox* it was not. Daringly, interestingly, Paul Zindel's adaptation of Anne Richardson Roiphe's original novel asked for a seamless transition from reality to fantasy. The audience would be asked to worry over, work out for itself, the degree of interpretation of the two states. Fine. In theory. In practice, a basic shortcoming was to create confusion rather than complexity. Kershner's honourable career has offered some superb screen performances, some first-rate story-telling, some disquieting analyses of contemporary attitudes. But, to overstate, he works in terms of words not images. At home in inner-urban New York – he shot it in quasi-documentary style – he could find no pictorial equivalent for the fantasy sequences. Fantasies, except for a schizophrenic, do not look like reality to the mind's eye. To audiences, they risk appearing contrived, more fake than fanciful.

The African sequence is perhaps the most glaringly obvious example of visual nothingness. Although the backdrop to one good line – the isolated heroine is told: 'You are as safe here as you would be on the streets of New York.' – it comes up on the screen as very much a poor man's Griffith Park. The arduous trek into the bush and the film's production budget seems ten times more unthinking when it is remembered that the endeavour was to capture not the 'reality' but the *unreal* (fantasy) version. Kershner now handsomely admits and accepts responsibility for the error of judgement.

It was like being on the back lot at Universal. When I came to Africa a village had been built for me. It was totally wrong and I had to scrub it and get another situation going and try to go more and more primitive because I wanted to deal with primitive instincts in her. What they had built was a sort of sophisticated East African village. What I didn't realise until we came to Africa (because the research hadn't been done properly) was that we had no dancers, no musicians. The East African dances and music are of a very simple nature that don't lend themselves to anything. It's not filmable. It's standing and jumping. I shot stuff and then cut it out. We had to import the Senegalese dancers – which was ridiculous. Why we went to East Africa I have no idea. To this day. When Hollywood goes to Africa, Africa washes away and Hollywood takes over. I think it was an error of judgement on my part – completely – and I would take the blame for that.

But the question immediately suggests itself that if, wearing her First Artists' hat Barbra was the prime mover of the film, should she not be held basically responsible for the mess? The answer is, simply, 'no'. Far from behaving like the possessive mother of popular Hollywood legend, she entrusted the nuts and bolts of the production to Irwin Winkler and Robert Chartoff. On the release print they receive credits where credit is due. They must also accept the obverse. Barbra, once committed, rolled with the punches and revelled in the exotic compensations. The National Dance Company of Senegal were a revelation in themselves. Internationally famous, sophisticated globe-trotters (their accustomed London address is the Dorchester; in Paris they favour the Georges Cinq), they proudly saw no reason why they should cease being the aristocrats because of a new environment. They found the Kenyan hinterland tiresomely hot and dusty. The gawping onlookers, who jostled for a glimpse of unscheduled breast-baring, were just plain tiresome. This was White Man in hired safari suit looking for vicarious thrills in Darkest Africa. The fact that some of these oafs mistook their impeccable French for Swahili roughly indicated the level of this peeping tomfoolery. The dancers lit out to Nairobi whenever the schedule permitted. They had as little rapport with the indigenous Samburu as they had with the invading Californians. The exception was Streisand. Barbra, always the insatiable explorer, had left her preconceived notions and attitudes back home. Everything about Africa, the smells, the colours, the strange melancholy of the music, the high-pitched harmony of the women's voices over the beat of the drums – excited her.

Barbra was fascinated by the costumes and exotic make-up of the ultra-beautiful Senegalese women. At one point she asked one of them to put some of the dancer's blue eye makeup on her own eyelids. 'She broke a twig from a tree,' Barbra said later, 'took a long thread from her husband's skirt, made like a Q-tip, broke off a piece of soft-blue rock, spat on it and put that on my eye with the Q-tip. Now I put all my eye shadow on that way.' One thing led to another. Streisand and the dancers did what most women do in similar situations. They gave each other the freedom of the wardrobe. Streisand, as excited as a child, allowed herself to be costumed, necklaced and turbaned in the style of an African princess. Her own Nilotic features clinched the Nefertiti cliché. Good manners obliged Barbra to offer the Senegalese troupe reciprocal hospitality. 'Help yourself,' she smiled. To her considerably qualified amusement, if not amazement, the prima ballerinas assaulted her collection with a laconic efficiency that left her speechless. Since it was not a loan-out but for keeps, no point in beating about the bush. They arrowed in on her *haute couture* models with a discrimination that showed their days in Paris had not been spent touring the Flea Market. The ladies from Dakar were not into thrift shops that year.

Away from the home patch, Barbra found a considerable degree of role-reversal occurring. Here she was the rubber-necker. As Kershner's plaintive pleas hovered on the African air, she took endless pictures of her supporting cast. 'I always ask them first,' she told us. 'They might not like the idea. I know I don't like having my picture taken.'

Throughout, the Samburu remained wary of the heavy-duty Hollywood hardware being dragged across their stomping ground. But Barbra's request was always granted. Her ear and facility for language helped her establish a genuinely warm rapport with them. Not that her ability to assimilate languages is on a genius level. In one scene of the movie, trapped in a pit and threatened by spears, she had to beg for mercy on the grounds that she was pregnant. A chance to display her new learning! During rehearsal she shouted *'tatu nutay'*, Samburu for 'I am in child.' The surrounding Samburu women cracked up. So did Barbra. 'In', 'with', what's a preposition between friends?

The fledgling producer in Barbra observed an instant by-product of the descent upon Kenya of the Hollywood gestalt. 'It's very interesting,' she said. 'These people are used to walking five miles a day; but after three days with us they've asked for a bus to take them back to their villages.'

Flaws aside, Kershner did achieve some first-rate performances. As the husband, David Selby competently and unselfishly threw away a role essentially written – it is

Up the Sandbox and Barbra tries out a
Samburu costume

another weakness in the film – as a stereotype. 'Mine was a pretty passive role. When Barbra is on a film it tends to emphasise the woman's role. True of most of her films. All I know is I got a fair shake. Everything that was in the script I played. Whether the character gets a fair shake in the script is something else. I went in and out and that's about it.'

Jane Hoffman's role as Barbra's mother ('Move to New Jersey. The air is cleaner and nobody writes "Lesbians Unite" in the elevator') is finely portrayed. As (in the fantasy) she chomps through the chain-lock on her daughter's front door with the most over-kill pair of wire-cutters a girl's mother ever toted, it is impossible not to detect an echo of Barbra's earlier life. Her interest in the property surely links back to those teenage days when she first translated herself to Manhattan and there, outside her door, wielding over-kill jars of chicken soup, was her own mother.

Barbra's own performance is quite superlative. She has said, 'I wanted to play a part where I did nothing, where I was just a human being. This is the most natural role I've every played and the most rewarding as an artist.' It shows too. The brief scene in which, despite her physical revulsion, she contrives to eject a cockroach from her kitchen shows Barbra acting with all the brilliant control needed to recapture the 'natural'. The deeply felt love she has for her children is beautifully communicated in the casually primordial way she handles them. The film's wisdom is implicit in the aura of contentment the children create around their mother. Her performance is also, finally, unselfish. Barbra Streisand is submerged in Margaret Webster.

Kershner has stood up to be counted among the clear majority of directors who have declared working with Barbra to be, however strenuous, a pleasure and a privilege. We invited him over to expand on it: 'I think that she's creative,' he said at once,

> to the point where I would call her obsessive. Which I happen to appreciate. Because immediately she starts doing something she does it 'no holds barred'. And I love that. I think that her judgement of the things she does herself can be very good, but I feel that she's often affected by the people she works with and the people around her and sometimes she can lose her way. The environment is very important. She has to be in a supportive environment. People think that she's competitive or she's bitchy. I never found her bitchy. I never found her competitive. I find that she fights to maintain her artistic integrity, right or wrong. This is what she feels has to be done and she'll fight for it. But she's not a vicious person in any way. It was impossible for her to ever fire anyone who was really doing something terrible to her. She couldn't do it.

That was Kershner being a happier and wiser man after the event. Before, he must have had his tremors anticipating the gossip columnists' scenario of braying tantrums and locked egos. He elected to meet trouble half-way.

> I told Barbra right at the beginning of rehearsals: 'I've heard things about you – that you're tough, that you can be a killer.' I told her exactly what I'd heard and what my fears were. And she laughed, and said, 'Well, I don't think I'm

those things. I have nothing to say . . . don't know what to say.' But I'd cleared the air in some way.

He certainly had. The 'Matthau factor' was totally absent from the production.

I looked forward every day to working with Barbra. Because you can have the opposite – when you don't want to go in to work in the morning. I really looked forward to going to her trailer, sitting down and having coffee, laughing and talking about what we were going to do. I'd have done my homework so I could lay out what we were doing that day. She'd sit there knitting away. She'd have these little parties on Friday nights for the crew, and have all this beer and whisky and she'd made cookies for everybody. I tell you – she was marvellous. And people don't want to hear this. People don't want to hear this!

No. On the whole they do not. But it also has to be said that, on the whole, people did not want to go see *Up the Sandbox*

For the fans (as opposed to the cinema enthusiasts) Barbra's 'low-profile' characterisation of Margaret Webster was too much. Or not enough. A rather after-thought theme tune 'If I Close My Eyes' did nothing to counter the general sense of disconnection. This was not Barbra belting, or wisecracking or, in capital letters, acting. 'I mean, jeez, she's like, ordinary. Don't bother . . .' It needed the sale to television for *Up the Sandbox* to cover its relatively small production costs.

Barbra learned several lessons from the experience; among them was the conviction that in future if she was going to be in the driving seat of the production then she was going to have a decisive influence on where the vehicle was going. (That conviction, three movies along the road, was to have a profound effect on several people's lives.) Another lesson was to have an immediate effect upon her own. She had proved what she had always known, that she was not a one-style, loud-mouthed Brooklyn broad. She could act. Up, down. Bernhardt as well as Brice. The word had been put around that, after the commercial failure of *Up the Sandbox,* she swore never to try anything as experimental again. This is hard to believe. Whatever her degree of vulnerability to self-doubt, she must have known she had delivered a finely achieved performance. She had always pushed herself a little further into new territory. The truth was, she was prepared to let the money men keep their vigil outside the box-office. To her, *Sandbox* represented a modest but expert climb to base camp. From there she could see the route to the highest peaks.

Barbra returned to Hollywood via Tel Aviv. It was not merely to demonstrate that she had nothing against Hebrew National sausages *per se*. It was to meet Golda Meir. The two ladies got on famously (the Israeli leader could have been Barbra's cousin from Milwaukee) and, of course, both by word and deed, Barbra has never since attempted to disguise where she feels much of her political and spiritual allegiances lie. More short-term, on her return to Los Angeles she immediately plumped actively into George McGovern's Presidential campaign. One of the 'Four for McGovern' (the others were Carole King, Quincy Jones and a piquantly new-born star, James Taylor), she appeared in April 1972 at a fund-raising concert at the Los Angeles Forum. It may have been good politics. It was bad music. Barbra was (as always) scared to death. More to the point she was ring-rusty, in poor live-performance condition. A record was cut and released but, given the 'hurry-up' circumstances of the concert, it is kinder to forget it. The detractors – 'all she can now do is holler' – had a field-day. Her political affiliations having been established publicly, Barbra was now officially numbered among Richard Nixon's long list of political enemies. She was *persona non grata* at the White House. Maybe, then, the concert was not such good politics. Maybe being in such radically chic good company she just didn't give a damn. After all, there was no virtue on any level in denying her own inclination towards a more liberal America. Certainly not when the peak rearing up on the immediate horizon was the role of radical Katie Morosky in *The Way We Were*.

FIFTEEN

When I came in to take over the Studio I thought I was going to get a disaster in the first big project, seeing them spend all this money on a picture with Barbra Streisand – not only was she not going to sing a note but she was going to play a Jewish Communist. I couldn't figure out what the hell was going on.

FOR MANY people, recollecting in tranquillity, *The Way We Were* remains Barbra Streisand's best film and her depiction of the 'Jewish Communist' her most achieved, her profoundest performance. The executive who admitted with engaging candour that he was totally unwise before the event is Al Hirschfield, the then (1972) new man in charge (along with David Begelman) of Columbia Pictures. His attitude was neither so surprising nor so foolish. He had every reason to play safe. He had inherited a studio in the direst straits. Following a string of bad and financially disastrous productions, Columbia at that time – before the first oil crisis, the soaring of inflation into double figures – was some $200 million into the red. Real, not Monopoly money. Hirschfield as a businessman was required to administer rather more than a band-aid. And here he had the use of possibly the world's most popular singer who wasn't scheduled to sing. He was aware, too, that virtually no American film with a serious political theme – serious, that is, beyond the 'pie *à la mode*' world of Capra – had proved a commercial success. Communism, McCarthyism, seemed like two strikes out before the first frame of Shot One, Take One. No doubt, too, Hirschfield had forgotten who Barbra Streisand was. Or, more properly, had been. The uneasy deprivations of Pulaski Street, the tradition of her father's fierce, self-demanding intellect gave her an instant affinity with an indignant political activist. That such a relatively radical, racially vulnerable character should then be juxtaposed with the dubious capitalism and Lamborghini liberalism of Hollywood made perfect her casting as Katie Morosky. If, that is, she chose to accept the role.

It must be the cause of the greatest admiration for Barbra Streisand that, confronted with a part she knew was potentially contentious, in a movie that, on precedent, could die at the box-office, she grabbed the part without hestitation. The safe, money-spinning move, after her last three so-so films, would have been to revert to the solid gold of a re-vamped funny girl. She chose instead to widen her range, deepen the demands made on her. Whatever Columbia might hope for, she wasn't going to play it safe. When Arthur Laurents sent her the first draft of his screenplay she got back to him on the phone in nothing flat. 'You've got it,' she said. 'That's me!'

The Way We Were was Laurents' original conception but its birth as a motion picture brought him the acutest labour pains – frequently, in his opinion, inflicted by others. The genesis, in fact, involved two thoroughly refined and intelligent talents at odds with each other and not quite able to agree to disagree. The second talent was that of director Sydney Pollack.

Pollack, with such films – among others – to his credit as *They Shoot Horses, Don't They?*, *Jeremiah Johnson* and more recently *The Electric Horseman*, is a director of genuinely durable reputation. Thoroughly American, his films, whatever flaws they may have, reject the surface flash and filigree touch of the more conventional, self-effacing directorial approach. They emerge that much more profound and intelligent. So too were his observations on the making of *The Way We Were* and on Barbra Streisand, in the interview he gave us at the Warner Studios in Burbank. The flat, sun-baked studios in the dust of the 'Valley' are hardly a source of inspiration. But readers may consider, as we do, that Pollack's analysis of both movie and star displays a rare, and most articulate, perception. Clearly all the peripheral areas of the film's production were shot through with disquiet and unpleasantness. Nobody had told him – then! – the parlous position of Columbia's overall financial position.

The picture was going over budget, not radically but a few hundred thousand dollars over, because of shooting in New York and overtime hours. The pressure I was getting was just unbelievable. There's always panic when you talk about millions of dollars but in this case it was excessive. 'Hurry up! Hurry up! You can't do this! You can't do that! Hurry up! Get it done! Cut this, cut that! Don't do it with more than one car! Shoot up angles so you don't have to fix the streets . . .' Truthfully, nobody had any faith in the picture. The script had been turned down by lots of other studios as being talky, political McCarthyist, boring. We went ahead and made the film and, even during the editing period, it was a very depressing time for me because the sense I got from the studio was one of great trepidation and fear. Nobody knew how it was going to come out.

The initial responses to it in rough-cut were not good. And then what happened was – we went up to San Francisco for a preview and did something I had never done before which was that we scheduled two previews, one on a Friday night and one on a Saturday night. At first the film was going very very well, until we hit a spot in the third act where we just lost the audience completely. And I went up in the projection room with Margaret Booth (there was no cutting room), taking a razor blade with me because we didn't have all the trims or out-takes and in this answer-print I made a cut of about eleven minutes. It was a whole sequence where she was being named as a Communist which was then going to precipitate the break-up. The problem was that the break-up was inherent in the picture right from the beginning. But the audience was not of a mind to sit still for another complication, and this one was so complicated politically because they could see that the two people loved each other but weren't able to have any kind of rapport together. So it was not necessary to do this curlicue or detour for this new development. When we cut this piece out and previewed it the next night the audience absolutely loved the picture. All of a sudden everybody was ecstatic about it, and morale turned around. We started getting good reviews, the word got out about the picture, the film began to make money and it did, in fact, turn Columbia around.

Over-simplifying, *The Way We Were* works on two levels – as a love story ultimately more bitter than sweet; and as a recapitulation of certain political attitudes that may or may not belong to history. Certainly it was the former, the love element that made the film such an immediate success. The opposite magnetic pole in that love element was, all importantly, Robert Redford. What Pollack has to say on the casting of Redford must surely give the lie to the suggestion made before, and since, that Barbra Streisand was that kind of Crawfordesque superstar bent on cutting her leading men down to size. We had reminded Pollack of Laurents' remarks regarding the casting of that leading male role:

Ray Stark got Robert Redford whom Barbra had wanted from the beginning. That was the start of my troubles. Redford does not want to be an actor, he wants to be a 'movie star'. The way I'd written *The Way We Were*, it was Katie Morosky's story, but Redford wanted it slanted toward Hubbell Gardiner. I knew it couldn't be done, so I refused. I was taken off the project and they brought in no less than twelve writers to reshape it, including Dalton Trumbo and Francis Ford Coppola. I took my screenplay, started reworking it as a novel and forgot about the picture.

Pollack's reaction to this, while not insensitive to Laurents' attitude, made clear he felt that there was another, a *deeper* point of view; in a sentence, that the picture would not be stronger for being, at whatever single depth, a one-woman vehicle.
'Ryan O'Neal was mentioned,' he recalled,

also a new fellow named Ken Howard who has a series now. Four or five people were mentioned. And I say this without wanting to denigrate Ryan O'Neal or anyone else – I could never entertain the picture without the concept of Redford. And it was the single toughest act I ever had to do to convince him to play the part. I spent literally eight months beating him to death in order to get him to do it. His basic objection was the story was written as a woman's piece. It was not a question of ego. It was the question of not wanting to spare the time to play a weak, spineless male sex object. It was suddenly a reverse prejudice from the situation that women have had most of the time. Now, that's not the picture that emerged. That was what was written originally. The re-write work that I did on it to try to get him to do it was in complicating and strengthening his role so that even though he was not the committed person that she was, he still had a point of view which was valid. I kept saying to Bob: 'Hubbell is an existentialist. Hubbell sees the long view. Hubbell knows that for all of this passionate rhetoric, twenty years from now the guys who are putting these other guys in prison are going to be working together with them.' Which is in fact what happened.
Bob's original objection was: 'I don't want to go through a picture where all I say is "Okay, stop doing that" and I have no point of view of my own. And all I am supposed to be is this blond, blue-eyed hunk of romance that all the girls go crazy over, and I have absolutely nothing else to do in the picture.' And of course, at this same time, Arthur was very upset that Redford was unhappy with the screenplay in terms of his role. And Arthur was doubly

upset when I put two other writers on, which Arthur felt was at Redford's urging. In other words I went to Albert Sargent and David Rayfield, two people I work with a lot, to come in and take over Laurents' original screenplay and essentially strengthen the Hubbell Gardiner character. Laurents got his nose out of joint and understandably so because he felt (a) an actor was dictating what would and would not be contained in a piece of 'literature' which he had written, and (b) I think what got him angry was he never had a face-to-face confrontation with Redford. So he felt he didn't get his day in court to defend what it was. It was all done through me, in a way. I called Arthur and told him I was putting Rayfield and Sargent on for a while. He was very upset and blamed it on Redford. He said, 'That goddam actor who has so much control over everything – firing a writer – I never heard of an actor being able to fire a writer – what is Hollywood coming to . . . ?' It was that kind of situation. He loved Redford as an actor but his position was that he was being fired because of an actor's dissatisfaction with his role. I think it's safe to say that Arthur identified more keenly with the Streisand role. He felt that to strengthen Hubbell as a character would be reducing the clarity, significance and correctness of Katie's character.

So finally Ray Stark, who is a very proud man, said: 'Look, I'm not going to wait any more. I'm not going to be pushed around by Robert Redford. We'll get Ryan O'Neal or so-and-so, or so-and-so.' Without wanting to seem one of those 'I told you so' guys, I knew I was right in this case, so I kept saying that the picture would not be right without Redford. It literally wouldn't work. Because up until that point Barbra had never worked with a really strong leading man. All of her pictures had been Barbra Streisand vehicles – all of them. I did not want to do a Streisand vehicle. Not because I don't love Barbra – I do. But the essence of this picture really had to do with the relationship which required equal footage for both characters. The picture required political foils or you had nothing. So I kept saying the only guy I know of who could stay toe-to-toe with her, is Redford. Because he has a strength and intelligence on screen which does not rely on histrionics or what's in the role. It's something he brings in his persona like the old-fashioned movie stars. Like Cooper did. Like Tracy did. They come on screen and you read in a past with them, you read in more than what's there, somehow. So I kept insisting to Ray that at all costs we must get Redford. I must say my greatest ally was Barbra who felt the same way. I needed the strength that Redford brings on the screen and Barbra understood that.

These may grate somewhat on the ears of Messrs Sharif, O'Neal and Montand. But the immediate compulsion most audiences found in *The Way We Were* flows directly from the tense electricity between its two main characters. Pollack, of course, was totally aware of the project's potential resonances:

I'm not stupid enough to assume – ever – that I know what people want. That way lies death. The only thing I could go by – and it seems arrogant but it isn't – is to assume that, if *I* like it, I can make somebody else like it. Because my passion for it will somehow get on the film. I must say I owe a deep debt to

Playing opposite Robert Redford in *The Way We Were*

Margaret Booth [the editor], because the morale factor was enormous. I loved those characters. I saw them in my mind and I was touched by them, by their courage, their problems and their decency to one another.

Redford, of course, had come to trust Pollack's ability during the making of *Jeremiah Johnson*. They were buddies. But Pollack and Streisand? New to each other, what of the potential for *angst* and misunderstanding there? We asked Pollack the obvious question: had he, prior to shooting, confronted her eyeball to eyeball in Kershner fashion and asked her if she was a killer to work with, a right royal pain in the ass? Pollack's answer was as disarming as it was civilised and illuminating:

No [he said], I'm too dumb to do that. It would never occur to me to say that to anybody. I never felt threatened by her right from the first meetings I had with her. Because I was so impressed with the way she was thinking about the part. When I hear an actress talking to me with an understanding of a role that's so close to my own understanding – that makes me feel confident that we're not going to have a problem. And we didn't. As far as Barbra is concerned the least of my problems was Barbra, funnily enough. I had only one problem with Barbra – and it wasn't a problem, it was a challenge in my mind – and that is I wanted Barbra in this picture to really act. I did not want her to rely on any of the Streisand mannerisms which theater and musical comedy and nightclubs can instil in a performer. When you get insecure you tend to fall back on mannerisms, line-readings, mugging, bits of behavior which pull you out in a nightclub act. I had some of her films that she'd done and I really wanted to get her back to a kind of simple truth in her performance which I knew she was capable of. That was not a major problem but it was the only one I had with her because Barbra is like any other enormously talented person. They're never a problem if you can create an atmosphere of trust. They're always a problem if they mistrust you. If they feel, Barbra or Jane Fonda or Burt Lancaster or Robert Mitchum or Al Pacino or Robert Redford or any of these people I've worked with, that I'm in some kind of ego contest with them, well, that would be disastrous. With Barbra, I spent enough time with her prior to shooting to let her know where my head was, to listen, interestedly and concernedly, to what her fears were and what her problems were, and to discuss out in the open where we were going to have trouble, what this picture was about, what was moving to me and what was moving to her . . . and I think it's safe to say that she trusted me. Now, that's not to say we didn't argue occasionally. But those arguments were healthy arguments. They were never ego arguments. She called me around eleven o'clock almost every night. And I loved her for it. I mean, she called out of compulsive worry, the way I'm a compulsive worrier too. If I had some mentor around, I'd call them eleven o'clock at night. As a matter of fact, when she gave me a gift at the end of the picture, she wrote on it: 'FOR ALL THOSE ELEVEN O'CLOCK PHONE CALLS'. She knew – Oh! my God! Every night! – 'Should I do this? What d'you think if tomorrow, I . . . Suppose, maybe I should wear my hair down? When we get to the bed scene, what might be nice, suppose I feed him – some grapes or bananas or something . . . ?' I'd say, 'We'll try it.' None of it was silly. None of it. Or she'd call and say, 'Listen, I was reading back five drafts earlier and I found this line . . . what d'you think of it?' And she'd quote an old line that maybe we'd cut out, and I'd say, 'Gee! that's not bad!' Or I'd say, 'No, Barbra, that does not work because what we have is better for the following reasons . . .' and she'd say, 'Right – it was just an idea.' It was all pushing and testing and trying to cover every base and being a perfectionist, being totally thorough about it, worrying it, worrying it, worrying it . . . that's the way she works. She's that way with her records too. Robert Redford's a little like that too. This isn't a problem really. It is just time-consuming.

A fine example of Pollack's intelligent teamwork is demonstrated by his choice for director of photography on *The Way We Were*. The great Harry Stradling having died during the shooting of *The Owl and the Pussycat*, it was his son, Harry Jr, who now re-established a Stradling connection. 'It seemed a good choice,' Pollack said.

Barbra felt quite comfortable with Harry. She has one of the most unusual faces which does not conform to plain, flat-looking photography. One has to be careful when one gets that many planes and lines in a face. Every time bones and skins change angles you create shadows and light and these create effects that are different from reality on film. We were aware of it. So was Harry.

The cameraman enlarged on the problem. The son had no reservations about his late father's regard for Barbra. 'He liked her very much,' he said.

He liked working with her. He thought she was a fantastic woman. Brilliant. I'd talked to my father a great deal so it was almost like I knew her. I would do it the way he did it. He used to talk about her a lot. He'd say how soft she was; how fast she would pick things up; how she'd ask why aren't you doing this, why did you do that? He said most of the times she was right. And he'd been doing it for what? – forty years. She's a very intelligent lady. He was very good with women. He hated working on exteriors. Inside you have control of the light, but outside you have changes, you get all ready to go with the sun and then it goes down, you've got to change . . . you're at the mercy of Nature. On women: he made them look good. He did pictures going way back with beautiful women like Marlene Dietrich. That was *Knight Without Armour*. He did *Suspicion* with Joan Fontaine. Like Sydney Pollack told you, there isn't any special trick. You've just got to make them look good. You've got to fool around with them. You've got to want them to look good. You've got to get them in there. You've got to be a pest. You've got to say: 'Hold still for a second so I can look at you.' You've got to experiment and then you see. They're not all the same; what you can do with some ladies you can't do with others.
The Way We Were – hell, I was very apprehensive. It was a big movie. Naturally I wanted to do good because my father had worked with her so

much and naturally I couldn't help being a little apprehensive she might not like what I did. That was the only thing to be afraid of. There was nothing else I could screw up except that she didn't like the way she looked. I knew she wouldn't hold back on telling me if that was so. She's not afraid of feelings. She would say things to me . . . !

But I tell you what kind of lady she was. We had a thing where the editor who works with Ray Stark called up and said to Ray Stark that she thought Barbra looked awful, that the film was terrible. I felt awful – this was during shooting – we were back in Schenectady in New York. And she was seeing the film in the studio. I hadn't seen it, so naturally I didn't know what to think. Sydney Pollack wanted a kind of over-exposed kind of look which I was doing for him. He saw it and he said, 'That's what I wanted her to look like.' That was that. And then another time we were working at night on a thing and again someone said, 'I didn't think Barbra looked good.' Streisand was at the Sherry Netherland or some place. I was in another hotel. And she went to the trouble – and she didn't have to do this – she called me ten o'clock that night and she said, 'Harry, I saw the film and I thought it was very good.' She didn't have to do that at all. She could have said it the next day. She need not have said anything.

She only likes you to photograph the left side of her face. Always automatically, even when they start to rehearse a scene, when the director's looking, she'll get herself into a position where only the left side of her face is showing. And another thing, you can never photograph her outside. You have to build something over. Like if she's coming in close you kind of build a house that she walks into and then you light it with a light . . . with daylight coming down on her nose, it looks awful . . . so you shade that all off, and light it. It's very difficult to do. Like when you're doing a long, long shot and she runs from across the street into a close shot and you've got to kind of build the thing. There's a mental strain there. At the end of the day you're exhausted. But that's what you're there for. And that's what she's there for as well.

The world knows what happened at the end of the day. Barbra won golden opinions and another nomination for an Academy Award. There were glowing reviews but the nomination did result in a piece of Monday-morning quarterbacking from Laurents. In conversation with René Jordan he delivered himself of this viewpoint:

'When we ran the first roughcut, the Redford group hated it,' Laurents is reported as saying.

They thought it was a bomb and the worst movie he'd ever made. Everyone was called in for retakes and I advised Barbra to insist on redoing the telephone scene, the one in which she breaks down and begs Hubbell to come back and talk to her in the middle of the night. She should do it again, more frantically. Her eyes were not red enough for a woman who has been weeping for hours and she kept covering her nose with her hands to stop the sniffing. She was surprised at my suggestion and said, 'But I look so beautiful in that scene.' It was never reshot and – if done properly – it would have won her the Academy Award. She is disliked in Hollywood but they would never have denied her the Oscar if she had really let go in that scene. It was a set piece for her from the very first draft of the screenplay. She did not grab the chance and it was her loss. She was just worrying about her looks.

Pollack puts the charge into a perhaps more persuasive perspective:

> I can't think of a single time when Barbra came back from the dailies and said, 'I don't like the way I look.' As a result of that I was not anxious about it. Sure I was aware that she needs reassurance – absolutely. But again, it was not any more reassurance than Faye Dunaway needs, or more than Al Pacino or Natalie Wood. It's an occupational hazard. You're making your living off the impression you're creating on a screen forty-feet high, where every imperfection, every flaw is magnified through a microscope. It's hard. I did one film as an actor, and I'm no Redford. I couldn't bear to watch it. I wanted to hide. I would have wanted to commit suicide if I had to stay in a career like that. If I thought I really looked like that, I wouldn't go out in the street.
>
> As to that telephone scene, I can tell you for a fact that it was done in one take and she was really crying, and there was no attempt to hide the fact that she was crying. Nor was there any attempt to dramatise or glamorise the crying. I didn't know how far the tears would go. I set it up in one shot so that I wouldn't have to cut because of the emotional line of it. I didn't want to have to stop in the middle and then crank it up again. So, for her sake I set the whole shot up. She did it on one take. She asked to do another take, just in case. She did a second take but the take that's in the picture is Take One, and the tears were really there . . . and her eyes were plenty red. Maybe we didn't have a pin-light picking it up because it was a dark night scene.

In fact neither Barbra nor Laurents nor Pollack nor *The Way We Were* gathered in an Oscar that year. The 'Best Actress' Award went – unexpectedly – to Glenda Jackson, for providing a stolid façade against which George Segal could bounce his deftly comic touch of class. The poor publicity flacks were left to spread the word that the hard core of the film was the love scene between Katie and Hubbell – Streisand and Redford locked in erotic fulfilment of ten thousand watchers' fantasies. As a 'hype' the suggestion may have had commercial value. Put forward as the *raison d'être* of the film it is, of course, nonsense. Pollack was under no illusion what weight to give it visually.

> I'm a bit of a Victorian about these things. I've never really had graphic nudity in my films – I don't even use much bad language very often – I don't like it. So I have a problem every time I come to a scene like that because I'm not a kid and I know you can't lie about it – cut to rain on the window or whatever – but I have no real interest in a lot of graphic sex. I don't find it erotic, I find it, as a rule, distracting. So I had to find a way to not cop out and still make the love scene belong in that picture, which was after all a period picture. It wasn't

set in the Seventies where you could show everything. It was the late Forties. More than anything, without sounding sophomoric, trying to be true to the scene. The scene is not just about Streisand and Redford being in bed. The scene is about a woman who's had a fantasy and a dream all her life, coming true – and she can't believe she's there. She cannot believe it. Like anything that's delicate, where something you've wanted for so long is happening, there is this sense that, if you breathe, it will go away. I wanted to stage it in the most simple, careful way, so that her whole attitude was 'I mustn't breathe, I mustn't move . . . or this will all go away.' In other words, it had to be shot from her point of view. Here her fantasy was coming true. A god, literally out of a dream, is coming down, and is now in her bed – moving over her and going to make love to her. She can't believe it! So. I didn't do any cutting, I just held still, still, still. I picked a neutral simple angle. We suspended a camera straight over the bed and just dealt with it that way. I sent everybody away – everybody. Stradling, for example, did the operating himself. I didn't even let the camera operator stay – just to keep them from being self-conscious, particularly Barbra. It's very tough for a girl. It's eight o'clock in the morning, there are electricians all around. I just put some screens round the bed. They're almost nude in this scene.

It took two days to get it. He falls asleep on top of her and her last line, 'Hubbell, it's Katie. You *did* know it was Katie?' She was afraid he didn't know it was her! And she did it beautifully. I actually had a zoom lens on the camera, and very imperceptibly kept tightening during the whole scene but you couldn't see it, you weren't aware of it – it just got closer and closer till finally at the end you just see her face and part of his back and you see him relax and fall asleep. And she goes 'Hubbell?' and you hear him '*zzzz . . . zzzz*', snoring and she says, 'You *did* know it was Katie?' Then it dissolves to the next morning. She's very self-conscious. Doesn't know if he'd known, or remembers or was too drunk or whatever, because when he came in he was sick immediately and she was making some tea for him. And when she comes out she sees his clothes strewn on the floor and she doesn't know what to do. Should she get into bed with him? He's lying there clearly sleeping. So she gets in bed with him and thinks 'This is going to be a fantasy, he's never going to wake up' and she just kind of slides over and thinks, 'My God! I can't believe I'm here' – and slowly puts her arm around him and all of a sudden he starts to move towards her – that's when she just freezes and wonders what's going to happen now. He rolls over on top of her. Makes love to her and just falls asleep.

The aftermath of the scene very much foreshadowed the same 'morning after' sequence between Redford and Jane Fonda in a film bearing more of Pollack's influence as a writer, *The Electric Horseman*. Here again, after the ultimate intimacy the woman is highly self-conscious. But Fonda's sharp citified role in the later film allowed her to punch, so to speak, her sexual weight with Redford.

The gossip columnists tried, but failed to make stick, the suggestion that Streisand was having an affair with Redford. They were not even 'good friends' but – far stronger – mutually admiring, utterly professional colleagues. Nevertheless, in

Redford and Streisand

the early Seventies Robert Redford *was*, though he fought continually against the bankable type-casting, the blond, god-like sex figure, the fantasy male for tens of thousands of feminine bedrooms. Barbra had broken the ice, and her screen virginity, on nude scenes in *The Owl and the Pussycat* and Pollack had conducted this sequence with impeccable decorum. Yet once she had been 'crazy Barbra'. And here was Redford. They're almost nude and in bed. At eight a.m. – with the giant Panavision monster suspended overhead, the zoom-lens scanning every move, nuzzle or twitch – a physical frisson would be unlikely if not unprofessional. But *intellectually* the thrill of it all must have existed. If not then, surely on the way home, when realisation dawned . . . They had danced around jeering the ugly duckling on Pulaski Street, but she had since come a long way, baby . . .

The Way We Were has been successful enough commercially. But it is not a picture one would include in a shortlist of all-time greats. The shortcomings are not hard to find. Pollack himself, objectively lists them:

I think it is a picture that is severely flawed. And it is saved, really, by the two performances. It's a picture that has structural problems. These are the problems that worried me from the beginning, but I was never able to solve them for various reasons – mostly my own fault. Also there was resistance from the studio, resistance from everybody to making a real commitment to deal head-on with this McCarthy issue. I wanted to do the picture, begin it at the trials. I wanted Hubbell on the stand. And I wanted him to be testifying and then I wanted the whole picture to be in flashback, constantly coming back to that trial. The reason is that, for me, it was a little bit like two people living next door to Dachau and watching the people being led into the ovens and then having a domestic squabble. It does not directly touch their lives. The audiences wanted to see their love story. They didn't care about McCarthyism. They'd paid their five dollars and they wanted to see Redford and Streisand fall in love. As a result we had to emasculate the picture by taking out an awful lot that was political in it that was quite good I thought, but boring for the audience. I'm not apologising for the picture – I think it worked for a lot of people – but if you want to be a purist about it, it did not successfully blend politics and love story to the extent it should have, or could have. Of course the studio never came around and said *I* was right, *they* were wrong – nobody ever says that. But the new management were terribly pleased about the grosses of the picture. The film did eventually between forty and fifty million dollars. In those days that was a lot. You have to credit Barbra with going a long way to saving Columbia's bacon – putting it politely – single-handedly. There are so many things that are special about her. She has a passion, that you can hear in her singing. And her musical talent extends right directly into the acting – I'm talking about rhythms, and hearing even a choice of words that's better than another choice of words – a way of saying something that's better than another way, that's essentially musical. But you sense in her singing a passion and a well of emotion that makes this transfer over into acting in a curious way. She's not a big girl, but she has this ability to create the impression of being much bigger than she is, on-screen, which happens to a lot of stars who're special like that. She's original. There's not anybody like Barbra Streisand. You can't compare her to anybody. That's a blessing and a curse for her. Makes it tough to cast her, but when she's cast properly . . . I mean, there isn't anybody else who could play that part – with the same power and impact. She's funny, she's touching, she's real – all at the same time. She has a wonderful sense of comedy which we've all seen. But beyond that she has a well of emotion that she can tap, that's just extraordinary. And she cares so much about the work – she drives you crazy, beating at the work. She's a workaholic; a maniac for work . . .

When you told me that Minnelli gave her a picture of Sarah Bernhardt, saying, 'You're the only woman who could play this role,' I thought that Vincent had got it exactly right. I think she's the most gifted actress we have in this country. The most talented. I think there are other great actresses. Jane Fonda, I think, is an extraordinarily good actress. But there is something Barbra has that goes into this combination of singing, and comedy, and serious acting all rolled into one, combined with this original look, this original style of hers, that makes her a dynamo of talent. Of course a dynamo hooked up wrongly is dangerous. There are dangers with a talent on that scale. I think the biggest danger that happens to people like that is that there isn't anybody for them to listen to. And if they listen only to themselves, they'll get into trouble. That's what's happened to people, like Brando, whose careers have just gone away. That's understandable you know, because ninety-nine per cent of the people Barbra Streisand deals with are inferior to her in terms of talent. It's very hard for her really to be given guidance. And once you're in a position where people, for one reason or another, can't give you guidance, you lose a kind of rudder. You drift. Make wrong decisions. I think that if there'd been somebody around to really challenge her on some of the films she's made, she would have been better and the films would have been better. That's true with everybody. Everybody needs to check themselves out and have someone they can listen to.

The problem, when you're that talented like she is, and like Brando is, who *do* you listen to? They can listen to some directors but most people are not as talented as they are. That's what happened to Brando. He finally took a look at all these people who were telling him what to do and he knew, like any genius knows, that in his little *finger* he knew more about acting and theater than these people who were ostensibly telling him what to do. Well, that not only makes you cynical, but it makes you tough on the other people and tends to insulate you from growing. Now I'm not saying that's going to happen to Barbra. But that's the danger – that's what you have to look out for. You have to keep growing – you can't let that kind of talent stagnate because it's so enormous, so powerful, that it can feed, turn in on itself.

We're actually very close friends and talk all the time, she and I, and I think I can say this without her feeling bad about it – she'll call and we'll talk for an hour and she'll say, 'What am I doing? Why am I not working? What am I saving myself for? This is stupid. I should be out there, Sydney. So every picture won't be great. I mean I haven't done a picture in so long . . . I just sit and wait and wait and wait . . . for what? For Chekhov to come along? For Shakespeare to come along? I'm getting older, there's a million things I want to do – what am I saving myself for? And yet I say to myself, why would I want to go and do something that I'm not *really* stimulated by?' And then she says: 'And then I argue with myself. I talked to Truffaut once, who said, "You do your work and at the end you have a body of work and some of it is good and some of it is not good, but the stuff that's good will override what isn't good – and that is what a body of work is. You can't just sit and wait for the perfect thing to come along."'

Now I don't have her kind of talent and don't pretend that I do, but I understand her dilemma because I do the same thing myself. I read script after script after script and I keep saying no, no, no, no. Then after six months I say – the hell with it! I've got to go out and do something. So it's not great, I'll do the best I can with it and maybe the next one will be better. It's more important to keep working because it's the only way you can keep growing. So she faces that problem all the time and she deals with it all the time. And she's bothered that people are scared of her. She knows people are scared and she doesn't understand it. She says, 'What the fuck is he afraid of me for . . .?' And it does bother her. You know, she's a very sweet girl. I know it sounds a silly thing to say about Streisand. I have to tell you that I love her. I don't mean that I love her like a lover – but there isn't anything I wouldn't do for her. I'm very moved by her in a peculiar way which I can't explain. I think that inside, if you get through all the fears, the insecurities and the defensiveness, she's a good person. One senses that in her singing and her performances. There's a goodness there that I'm very touched by. She was so young when she got so successful. They ran out of superlatives when they tried to describe her when she started singing. She was twenty years old – and my God! when you heard her singing you went crazy! And you said, 'What kind of talent is this!' And then you saw *Funny Girl* and you said: 'She can act too, be funny too, and be touching and pretty, and sexy and attractive, and weird and strange-looking' – and it was too much! You didn't know what to make of this creature. Well that's not too easy to deal with for anybody. But I would offer that ninety per cent of the problem in dealing with her is the person who's dealing with hers problem, not hers. Because when you face that kind of talent, all of your own fears come to the surface. You're measuring yourself against her. And that's why people get into trouble with her. As long as you're comfortable with yourself and you know what you know, then she's not a threat to you and you have no problems with her.

That was the way it had been with Irwin Kershner, and the way it was with Sydney Pollack. Other top directors have talked about the great players they have worked with – Tracy, Dietrich, Hepburn, Stewart, Bogart, Grant and Gable. But none can recall a performer who has sought, picture after picture, to be locked in so intense a wrestling match with the director, as Streisand; a protracted battle 'to the death' just to bring a characterisation to life. Those eleven o'clock calls were not ego-boosters. They were made in the pursuit of excellence. Tracy is on record as having admitted that he rarely played anybody other than himself. Bogart, Wayne, Boyer were also welded to their public images. The Lisp, the sailor-roll walk, the smouldering Great Lover look – why buck a winning streak by stepping out of character? This luxury is denied Barbra Streisand. As an actress, her characterisations are not linked by a unifying charisma or star sheen. There is no such thing as a 'Streisand picture' as there was a 'Crawford picture', a 'Lana Turner picture', even a 'Newman picture'. But the effort of going back to first principles for every role cut deep psychologically. It was hard on everybody's nerves including her own. And the phone bills didn't come cheap either. It had been her good fortune that Pollack, shrewdly recognising the nature of the beast, was able to emerge from it all with himself, Barbra, and the movie, all intact.

It was a high-water mark in Barbra's career. Unfortunately the finger was about to be pulled out of the dyke.

SIXTEEN

No OSCAR came Barbra's way for *The Way We Were*. Ultimately, that was of no significance measured against the sheer accomplishment of having given the performance. The professional in her will know unerringly which was the more lasting reward. That same professional, several years later, can acknowledge that, for timing alone, *The Way We Were* struck at a definitive moment in her career. Judged by the highest standards – hers – the projects she was associated with in the early Seventies were, qualitatively, more set menus than *à la carte*. Remove *The Way We Were* from the list and the remainder – *Up The Sandbox, For Pete's Sake,* and *Funny Lady* – reveal that we're in the kind of territory for which Paula Prentiss, Stella Stevens or Debbie Reynolds are rightly remembered. 'You are only as good as your last . . .' Barbra's unflagging enemies no doubt gleefully awaited the day when she would be playing a singing Mother Superior.

Nor was this indifferent patch much enhanced, let alone redeemed, when two weeks after the premiere of *The Way We Were* Barbra's fifth special for television – her first in five years – was transmitted. Often a calculated put-on of her own musical past, 'Barbra Streisand . . . And Other Musical Instruments' was a pretentious mis-hit. It elicited this comment from John J. O'Connor of the *New York Times*:

> The program is well-made and it certainly is expensive. But it is overproduced, over-orchestrated and overbearing to the point of aesthetic nausea . . . In a large studio with multi-level platforms the star is reinforced with a full orchestra plus a slew of international musicians playing their national instruments. That much is fine. But what is supposedly meant to be an 'album of international music' turns out to be little more than a labored gimmick.

When Dwight Hemion and Joe Layton reunited to do it again for Barbra and came upon the '. . . Other Musical Instruments' concept, it would have seemed like a great idea. Barbra in an almost infinite variety of ethnic costumes, to a backing of stringed, blown and thumped instruments . . . A grand gala round the world in sixteen minutes to 'I Got Rhythm' . . . The finale would be 'The World Is a Concerto', an opus conceived and written by Ken and Mitzie Welch. The instruments in this case were ordinary household appliances – orange juicers, steam kettles, sewing machines, a doorbell, electric shavers, hair dryers, you name it. Well, the world may be a concerto but it is not a very good concerto. Nor was it a very good approach to a television special. It is easy to understand a couple or more guys getting hyped up on the idea in a spitballing session around a piano. But that kind of enthusiasm needs examining in the cold light of an executive producer's eyes and here the executive producer was Marty Erlichman who was going to be featured playing, perhaps appropriately, the washing machine. The fans were not amused and for once their herd instinct was right. The joke they were finally being asked to share was tedious, pretentious, condescending. They made their opinion felt in the nicest possible way. They turned the other way to make Barbra's single of *The Way We Were* number one in the charts.

Tough luck, erring judgement – the same perhaps could have been said of events in Barbra's personal life around this time, mid-1973. There had been a brief, conspicuously unpublicised association with a businessman for whom Barbra, according to her friends, displayed more than ordinary affection. The romance struck a reef. Barbra's hurt and unhappiness was a pointer to, for her at least, the depth of the relationship. Bitter, let down, she turned to the infallible bromide of work. But choosing movies, like new boy-friends, on the rebound, can be hazardous. Not wanting to get trapped in another offbeat piece of unfilmable whimsy she opted for her most blatantly 'formula' movie to date. And her worst.

For Pete's Sake stands in direct lineal descent from those Sixties movies in which the scientists of Cape Hollywood tried to land a man on Doris Day. Nothing overt ever happened in that sub-genre and, despite the more permissive context of its times, nothing explicit quite reached the screen in *For Pete's Sake*. Which is surprising. The basic plot of the movie is that, to help her husband's finances, a housewife gets in hock to the Mafia and to work off the debt (for Pete's sake) . . . goes to work in a cat-house. It never comes down to the ultimate. Fate intervenes to keep things cosy before titillation takes over. Buñuel in *Belle de Jour* and Giles Cooper in *Everything in the Garden* employed variations on this premise. *For Pete's Sake* is nowhere in the same league as it pursues its arch, whore-with-a-heart thesis. Despite an adroit, personable, equal-time-claiming performance from the neglected Michael Sarrazin as the husband, the most interesting aspects of *For Pete's Sake* were the events occurring behind the camera.

The director originally pencilled in was the master of closeups and incredible shooting-to-editing ratios, Milos Forman. He had to check out of the project and the eventual director was Peter Yates. The producer (with Stanley Shapiro) was Marty Erlichman. It is hard not to feel this was a reward for consistent, loyal, effective service to Barbra Streisand. Peter Yates has affectionately amused recollections of their partnership now that its fall-out has settled. A relaxed character, too successful to be afflicted by the occupational neurosis of the trade, Yates looked back with humour:

> Marty was naturally very nice the first few days, not making waves because he felt that, if the movie fell flat on its face, Barbra would probably blame him. Then he started fussing. I find it very difficult to work as a director if I have to continually refer to a producer. We argued, and one day I threw a ladder at him. But I missed. I couldn't have been trying. We started off having enormous rows and we finished up the best of friends. In fact, my agent said, just after that ladder row, it was the first time in the film industry that he'd ever known two people having a row give exactly the same version of the story to him. We've been good friends ever since. That's basically because he's an honest man and you can deal with honest people.

Yates too is firmly enlisted in the ranks of those directors who found working with

Barbra a pleasing stimulus rather than spilt blood.

'She does like to ask questions,' he admiringly recalled.

I think a lot of her questions harass a lot of people because they are very pertinent. Unfortunately she does see things very clearly. She's not befuddled by bureaucratic detail that sometimes gets in people's way when making movies. I think, now that she has a much larger knowledge of film-making, that she is in some ways easier to work with. On the other hand she's obviously much more demanding because she would demand that everyone be as quick and as imaginative as she is. She has so much talent, so much potential – I think her only danger is she might stifle herself.

No director has, to date, directed Barbra twice. Yates is obviously one, if the price and the shifting planets had augured well, who would certainly have liked to. But the planets had other stratagems. Unwittingly, the affable Peter Yates was manoeuvring a new and abrasively influential decision-maker into Barbra's life. A man who, for as long as he played that role, would determine (among other activities) who would receive the royal command to direct her future films. In this sense, Barbra's most indifferent film was to have the most profound influence on her personal life. Yates well recalls his catalyst role. 'I was responsible for her meeting Jon Peters,' he said with a smile that acknowledged the under-statement.

It was in the line of work. I wanted her to change her hair for *For Pete's Sake*. It was a light, 1950s-type Hollywood-type comedy which was supposed to, and I think did, make the star as attractive and charming as possible. That's why, when anybody asks me whether I had any rows with Barbra, I always say 'How can you have a row with anybody when you're trying to make them look as good as possible?' And she's certainly nothing else if not intelligent and appreciated what we were trying to do for her, and had lots of very good ideas of her own.

One of the things I wanted to do was to make her wear slightly tighter-fitting clothes because I thought she looked wonderful in *What's Up, Doc?* and she was quite a bit lighter then too. I wanted her to lose a lot of weight and also to have a different hairstyle because she'd used that same hairstyle in everything and I thought she might look good in a short haircut. She wasn't sure about it and said she might consider wearing a wig. I said, 'Well, why don't we find you a wig and get you tested in it and then make up your mind?' She wasn't absolutely certain. Then she called me up one day and said she'd seen somebody at a party with a short haircut which she really would not mind having at all, and she'd asked the person, who said she'd had it done for her by a hairdresser called Jon Peters. So I said if she liked, we'd make contact with him and, if possible, she could go in and see him. We did contact him and she did go in and see him. In fact he was immensely useful during the making of the picture because he persuaded her that (a) she did look very good with short hair, and (b) also she did look much better a few pounds lighter.

Enter then – and almost completely from left field – a dark stranger. As he hung in

Barbra with Jon Peters

there, hung on, hung around the *For Pete's Sake* locations, hung around the set on her next production *Funny Lady*, people went speedily from 'Who is he?' to 'Who does he think he is!' And then, when the tongues really got into their stride, 'What does she see in him?!'

The confrontation between the actress and the hairdresser took place at her house in Holmby Hills. It had all the barbed cheerfulness of the weigh-in for a title fight. Barbra, after Gould, Sharif, dalliance with Beatty and O'Neal, diplomatic high-flying with Pierre Trudeau, was back on tougher territory . . . Peters, the self-styled 'street fighter', had, like her, endured sufficient poverty to relish his millionaire status. And more than that, his independence. Barbra Streisand, weary of nodding sycophants who jumped and ran for her unasked, found Peters to be her kind of man. The versions vary as to who picked up the phone to call the other, and just how long she kept him waiting before making a regal entry down the sweeping stairway. It is scarcely significant, though their verbal shadow-boxing on the phone indicated an eager rivalry to score a points lead. Peters, who had captured most of the celebrated and powerful scalps in the town, saw shrewdly that to have Barbra Streisand among his clientele was equivalent to displaying the words 'By Appoint-ment to Her Majesty the Queen' on his window. He let it be known among the 'Streisand people' that he'd like to cut her hair and would go anywhere, any time, and any place to do it – for free. The bait deftly thrown, he took himself off to Europe on a business trip, knowing that a fish of that size and rarity would only be landed with patience. Ordinary hustling would not apply. In fact, though he was not aware of it, he was pushing at an open door. Peter Yates, following through on Barbra's request, had instructed his production people to find him. The news reached Peters while he was abroad. He was not slow to call Streisand on his return: 'Hey, I'm Jon Peters, I'm back. I want to cut your hair.'

'Yeah, I know,' said Barbra.

'I'll see you at four,' Peters offered.

'Two,' countered Streisand.

'Three-fifteen.'

'Two-thirty.'

At that point, Peters stopped the bidding. He sensed, smartly, that an advantage ceases when pushed too far. At two-thirty precisely he drove up in his Ferrari and was shown into the Streisand living-room. Whether she kept him waiting thirty minutes, forty-five or, in the Peters' version, one hour, is irrelevant. By the time she was making her provocative Busby Berkeley walk down the stairway, he was standing below, nursing a fine anger and preparing to leave. 'Don't ever do that again!' is what Hollywood folklore had Peters saying to Streisand. He has since claimed – specifically to Barbara Walters – that he was too knocked out by her beauty ('She had this great, uh, ass actually . . .') to get uptight about a measly sixty minutes waiting time. Streisand looked, and liked what she saw. No question but she was excited by this darkly handsome, Al Pacino-type with a beard, lean frame, and the thrusting look of a man not given to backing off from a fight.

Peters had acquired that persona the hard way. His mother was Italian, his father a Cherokee who died when Jon was nine years old. Peters watched it happen and the shock stayed with him. That tragedy, and the volatile distillation of Italian and Red Indian blood, made Peters archetypal problem material for the streets of Los Angeles. A tearaway with a feisty inclination to disturb the peace, Peters was tossed out of several schools. (His one early contact with movies, as an eight-year-old extra riding a donkey in *The Ten Commandments*, taught him the 'Eleventh' – nobody helps a loser, buster.) Left alone, unavoidably, by his working mother more often than was safe, Peters purged his resentment, mostly at being fatherless, by picking fights with all comers. The courts ordered him to a reform school for a year. During that time he was assigned to a work-gang up in the mountains. Each night he was chained to his bed. In the mornings they sent him out to do road building like a convict. Hardly the apprenticeship for the fragrant opulence of a beauty parlour on Beverly Hills' Croesus-rich Rodeo Drive, or for that matter, into bed with Barbra Streisand. But the proving ground for a Streisand lover requires more than just two-fisted resilience and a hustler's intuition. Peters was determined to haul himself upwards. At thirteen, his mother took him into the beauty business. The effect of all this free-ranging nubility on the frisky adolescent was decisive. 'This,' he declared (anticipating *Shampoo* by some years), 'is for me!' Instantly understandable, considering the perks, he had the heady notion of starting out immediately on his own. He would have this salon and all this free action, and in between times he could do the odd cut and set. But in California they do not hand out licences to thirteen-year-olds no matter how promising the talent, or pressing the urges.

Peters took the only option. He borrowed $120 from his mother and hopped a bus to New York. His mother, family name Pagano, had given him the names of two acquaintances in the business. The introduction taught Peters a salutory lesson. Not all the young male operatives in the beauty business are solid, paid-up heterosexuals. In fact the two characters he moved in on, albeit briefly, turned out to be decidedly gay. Their admiration for this good-looking youth from L.A. signalled to their newly acquired room-mate that a *ménage à trois* threatened. One night when they thought he was taking a shower, Peters split out of a window to find less attentive landlords elsewhere. Persistence, and a neat line in self-projection, got him a start in beauty salons unknown to fashion magazines and high society. These were the all-night parlours where off-duty prostitutes had their hair dyed to match their poodles. And sometimes the other way round. So what if the ambience was seamy and seedy and now and again a pimp would arrive to haul off a trick with her hair still in rollers? Young Peters was learning his craft, and a harlot's conversation was often more stimulating (as he was to learn) than the blue-rinsed babblers of Beverly Hills.

During the day, Peters attended beauty classes to refine his skills. To pay for them, he augmented his earnings at the all-night salons by boxing professionally in backstreet rings. That experience – a touch of the *Golden Boy* scenario – processed Peters into material of rare, and raw, potential. It was brawling, bruising stuff, risky too for a young man who needed the gentle touch of a Vidal Sassoon, not the hands and dented nose of a pug. But Jon Peters was a hustler in a hurry. He wanted everything now, or sooner if he could grab it. Hence his marriage at fourteen to a girl just one year older. He had moved now to Philadelphia, again working in a salon on the tougher side of the town. For the ambitious Mr Peters, Philadelphia was just a holding pattern in his fight to better, bigger things. So too, in effect, was his marriage. It ended after five years, with both parties amicably accepting that fourteen or fifteen is no age to make that kind of commitment.

At twenty, and a bachelor now, Peters was back in Los Angeles where his flair for sweet talk backed by muscle landed him a job as a nightclub bouncer. Here Peters is dead on course for the triumphant dénouement. Determined to start his own salon in the area where it really paid, Peters borrowed $100,000 from a friend in real estate on the promise that he'd return double the amount within a few months. He kept his word. He opened a beauty parlour in the San Fernando Valley which, after Philadelphia, was an ascent into class. And, as Peters was swift to notice, it was only a couple of snips over Coldwater Canyon to Beverly Hills – and Babylon. In making the trip, from the Valley to Rodeo Drive, Peters acquired more salons, and another wife, actress Lesley-Ann Warren. At twenty-six he was a millionaire tycoon in the beauty business, a father, sharing with Lesley-Ann the good life and the same gestalt therapist to whom, later, Streisand was to turn. According to Jon Peters, by the time he was kissing customers on Rodeo and before he met Barbra, he was earning $10 million a year. That astronomical claim acquires credibility when it includes two beauty supply companies, a wig factory in Hong Kong, and a reputation for being as good a stylist as any of the fancier fraternity crimping into the gossip columns. By the time (1973) Peters combed his way into Streisand's life, he had already been divorced from Lesley-Ann Warren. They had been together for a total of seven years producing a son, Chris.

So the man who drove up in his Ferrari to talk hair with Barbra Streisand was a hustler sure, but one who had made it in the Streisand manner, on his own terms. He was in the head-hunting business like all the others, but with Streisand it was the legend he wanted to capture, not the money. (Hadn't he said, anyway, that he'd do it 'for free'?) Barbra, more immediately concerned with getting Peters to do her hair for the film, must have had more than a passing curiosity in the man she tactically kept waiting. Though Peters was not source material for Warren Beatty's film *Shampoo*, he has conceded there were plenty of similarities.

His attitude to the free-wheeling 'cut 'em and lay 'em' school of hair-styling, is clear from interviews he gave (to girl writers) at the time. His vocal manner is straight Cagney. His staccato sentences match the brevity of his urchin-cut hair styles. 'When I was a young person in the beauty business and I came off from the street, from jail and all that, I'd go into the salon and see the ladies with diamonds, sophisticated people from good families, the whole thing. I used to throw up before work every morning because I was so frightened.' But that fear faded rapidly when he discerned how the 'beautiful people' were excited by the reform school toughness behind his salon manners. He enjoyed it, and many of them.

> I liked the identity. I liked that I was nothing and became somebody. I liked that I could take your hair and change it and you'd kiss me and be thrilled. If you are a heterosexual hairdresser in Hollywood you are living in a playground of promiscuity. I used to get so excited each morning because I knew that if I was working I would fall in love with maybe four women that day.

He did not fall in love with Streisand, that day at her mansion in Holmby Hills.

Instead, he has since said that he fell 'in energy with her'. But judging by the speed with which love followed, that 'energy' was well over peak intensity. It was not the attraction of opposites. It was the instant recognition of two of a type. Though their styles were different they were cut from the same bale. A psychic read-out on the one would fit just as neatly on the other. Both were perfectionists, volatile, driven characters with the outer aggression that conceals the inner insecurity. It was a recipe for no ordinary relationship, no conventional affair. Drawn powerfully towards each other by need, they inter-reacted like two unpredictable explosives erupting into what the experts call 'sympathetic detonation'.

But it involved a progression of time and changing locations. For the moment, Jon Peters was Barbra Streisand's hairdresser on a 'special' for Peter Yates' film, *For Pete's Sake*. But it was more than the lure of hair that had him constantly in the wings of Barbra's next film.

'In *Funny Lady*', Barbra Streisand is on record as saying, 'I was trying to *act* the character of Fanny Brice. I also sang Jewish songs like she did in real life. In *Funny Girl* I didn't have to act the character. I *was* the character. Her essence and my essence were very similar. That is a little spooky, you know.'

By appearing in *Funny Lady* Barbra was redeeming the last quarter on the four-part marker Ray Stark had held her to when she had signed several millennia ago for *Funny Girl*. That is probably the most positive thing that can be said about the 'son of' sequel. It's an indifferent movie. Promoted from choreographer to director, Herb Ross turns in a pedestrian performance – never more so than during the dance and water ballet numbers. But he is not the central villain of the piece. As with the girlish original film, the true minus is the screenplay. Or, if you prefer, reality. The cosmetic face-lift that was required to elevate the Brice–Rose relationship to the level of a bitter-sweet bio-pic involved layers of incredulity and indifference that made one feel that seventeen straight choruses of Billy Rose's booster-rocket, 'Does Your Spearmint Lose Its Flavor on the Bedpost Overnight?' would be preferable. Fred Ebb and John Kander, covered in plaudits for *Cabaret*, wrote five new songs for *Funny Lady*. They are all eminently forgettable. Rose's own best tune, 'It's Only a Paper Moon', was not enough to run a musical on and served only to remind people that the director of *What's Up, Doc?* had gone on to direct something rather better with the film's other star.

In *Funny Lady* the almost totally up-and-come James Caan played opposite Barbra. Like Barbra he turned out a good honest job in a losing cause. His reminiscences echo almost to the last comma the overwhelming response to the inevitable question 'What's it like working with her?' 'The most important thing to me,' he said,

> is that I have a good time when I work – that I can laugh. If I'm not going to get along with someone, it's really not worth being miserable three or four months of my life. You hear all kinds of funny stories about Barbra and it's all a lot of garbage. I don't know why so many people have thorns in them about Barbra. From the first day on I was yelling at her, putting her down and calling her a spoiled rotten thing, and she would call me this or that and we'd carry on

and we'd laugh. We laughed so much, three or four days we couldn't even shoot. It's not hard to get bad words out of me because I'm very opinionated, and if I don't like somebody I'd sure say so. There's nobody like Barbra. She's talented, she's fun and we had a terrific time.

The laughter on set must have cost Rastar a five-figure sum but it continued all the way to the bank. *Funny Lady* was sufficiently able to hitch a box-office ride on the success of its predecessor to return the same sort of tidy profit at the box-office that *For Pete's Sake* had managed.

The point would not be lost on Jon Peters. Indeed, haunting the set during the shooting of *Funny Lady*, he was missing very little as he watched all kinds of points.

Funny Lady, eventually selected for the British Royal Film Performance, brought Barbra to London again and a celebrated exchange. When, after the mandatory long wait in the line-up of the stars, Barbra was finally presented to the Queen, she reacted with an excess of determined-to-be-an-individual, adrenalin-induced *chutzpah*. Having curtseyed decorously, Barbra asked point blank, 'Your Majesty, why do women have to wear gloves to meet you and the men don't?' Queen Elizabeth, it is alleged, missed a fractional beat and then came back with the diplomatically bland non-answer, 'Well, – I'm not really sure. It's just tradition, I believe.' She moved on. Barbra turned to Jon Peters and said, 'Well, I guess I still don't know.' Now it is one thing to be curious, another to level your query at the one person not expected or required to give an answer, off the top of her crown. Clearly nobody advised Barbra that Queens of England, in formal contexts, are restricted to the straight lines only. In private, Queen Elizabeth II is one of the wittiest one-liners of the British monarchy. But she chooses her occasion. A Royal Film presentation, with its subtly-defined protocol, is not one of them.

As Jon Peters re-styled Barbra's hair, and his future along with it, one thing would not have escaped his professional, girl-oriented eye. The Barbra Streisand of *Funny Lady* emerged as a dangerously conventional type – a great shape and all that – but too much in the Brooklyn/Fanny Brice mould. Streisand the 'today' star was risking type-casting by association. *Funny Girl. Dolly. Funny Lady* – the flavour of schmaltz which is rendered chicken fat lay too heavily, in Peters' view, upon this vastly untapped talent. This, combined with the seductive notion of becoming a big wheel in the movies, started the countdown on his launch-pad. We have Sharif's opinion that entering upon a relationship with Peters had made Barbra more mature. She became, he says, a totally different individual. Many of those who observed it – their enemies, that is – were not impressed. These were the bad-mouths who were to nominate Peters as 'worst influence of the year'. Their hysteria was fuelled as Barbra and Jon plunged into the celebrated/notorious production whose shock waves jolted many lives and careers, not least their own.

SEVENTEEN

Out of the differing dreams, the struggle and conflict of personalities, accidents and quirks of fate, moments of rage, disappointment, cowardice, arguments, mistakes and sometimes sparks of brilliance struck off each other in the heat of battle, a picture has emerged . . .

Frank Pierson, director of
A Star Is Born

THE SUN Devil Stadium at Arizona State University, outside Phoenix, is aptly named. On that day in May 1976, upwards of 40,000 locals, fans, extras, newscasters, journalists, disc jockeys, PR men and organizers are scorching and it is still not noon. The scene, a vast outdoor rock concert featuring Santana, the L.A. Jets, Montrose, Graham Central Station and Peter ('the face') Frampton, is for the climax in *A Star Is Born*, featuring Barbra Streisand and Kris Kristofferson in a rock-'n'-roll version of the story. Because filming requires lighting, rehearsing, staging, and sound levelling the crowds have a lot of waiting around to do in the grilling heat. So, too, do the film's controversial stars who have come through their own separate battles to reach this mutually nerve-shredding sequence in the film. Kristofferson – having quarrelled with Peters and Streisand, his latest album panned – is nursing his fury with tequilla washed down with cold beer. Barbra Streisand, who has wept tears and bayed to the moon on this Byzantine nightmare of a production, knows there's a crowd of 40,000 outside and a job to be done. She is rehearsing with the band, and the session is over-running; Kristofferson decides he's been left no time to rehearse. Blowing hot, he refuses to come out of his trailer: 'Goddamit! I've got to go out and play it in front of 60,000 people [his figure] but she doesn't give a damn' are his reported words. 'She' does give a damn in fact and with the director, Frank Pierson, tries to explain a minor change in the scene.

But Kristofferson has had all he can handle, which may also include the tequilla and cold beer. He explodes. So does Barbra Streisand. They are screaming at each other. And also to anyone with normal hearing within a radius of about five miles. The mikes are open. The Streisand–Kristofferson clangorous fracas is going out 'live' over the sound system. On any other, by which we mean normal, production the incident would have surprised as much as stunned all those within earshot. But on *A Star Is Born*? Considering the mayhem and the mortality rate on the movie even before Day One of the shooting, this brief, but amplified slanging match over the limpid air of Arizona comes almost as a welcome diversion. Seen against the earlier birth-pangs which convulsed this $6 million enterprise, it is just a minor bellyache between two over-achievers. Jon Peters is to say when the battle was finally stilled: 'I know I am not an easy person to work with. I know what I want and since it's my money I'm going to get it. I was terrified but I couldn't show them [the crew] that, could I? I had to get things done, I was the producer . . . so I walked through people. I had to.' The Gospel according to Peters. Genesis had dawned more gently.

At one p.m. on 1 July 1973 in downtown Honolulu, the husband in that talented writing partnership, John Gregory Dunne and Joan Didion, turned to his wife and said: 'James Taylor and Carly Simon in a rock-'n'-roll version of *A Star Is Born?'* Sixteen words which he was to regret with increasing intensity as, in the months and years that followed, celebrated egos savaged each other, as claims and counter-claims rocketed over the battlefield. John Gregory Dunne's idea was based on the pulling power of a legendary title. Two previous versions – Janet Gaynor and Frederic March in 1937, Judy Garland and James Mason in 1954 – won Oscar nominations. That famous last line, 'Hello everyone, this is Mrs Norman Maine,' had passed into legend and, in later years, into the camp routines of gay cabarets. Warner Brothers who owned the property smartly latched on to the idea. They saw themselves getting their production costs back from the earnings of the soundtrack album alone. Anything else that came from the picture would be gravy. Dick Shepherd, then head of production at Warners, wondered why no genius in the backroom had thought of it before. He gave Dunne and Joan Didion the go-ahead.

They had never seen the previous versions and were determined not to. What was the point? This was to be an updated tale, capturing the hard, sex-driven milieu of the rock-pop world. Instead, the two writers launched themselves on a three-week tour of one-night stands which Dunne, retelling the adventure in his book *Quintana and Friends,* described as 'the armpit auditoria and cities of the land.' Within six months they had delivered the first draft of the screenplay under the title *Rainbow Road* to the producer John Foreman. After six months of endless commissary lunches and 'creative conferences' they had delivered a second draft. They were also 'thoroughly sick of the whole idea'. Suggestions as to who should direct the picture were tossed to Warner's and summarily tossed back. Warren Beatty, Mike Nichols, Peter Bogdanovich were names that were raised. Bogdano-vich, for one, read the script and didn't like it. Dunne's crisp response was: 'His opinion of the script matched ours of his pictures.' Another director made a brief appearance in the arena. But he seemed to have had personal problems. As related by Dunne, 'he was going through a messy divorce. He was trying to put his mother into a tax-shelter condominium in Florida and, as he was interviewing UCLA housekeepers who didn't wear brassières . . . his time was fragmented.' By now *Rainbow Road* looked very rocky indeed and Dunne and Didion wanted out.

Oblivious to all these initial skirmishes, the love affair of Barbra Streisand and Jon Peters was gaining a fair head of steam. Barbra was moving more and more out of Bel Air ambience into the street mode and manners of Jon. With her hair flowing down her back, into health foods and rock-oriented lifestyles, she found Peters' funky ranch on Malibu a refreshing change from the manicured uniformity of Beverly Hills. A $25,000 sound system, which Peters adroitly stacked with Streisandia, added a stereophonic touch to their love-nest.

Meanwhile 'The Project' was still short of a director. The sometime actor Mark Rydell came aboard on a ninety-day test flight. He was given that time to punch up

With Kris Kristofferson in *A Star is Born*

the script and cast the film and transplant the heart of the story – spectacular concert scenes – into the body of the picture. If all went well he would get to direct. Richard Perry, the music producer, was brought in. He was lukewarm on the script which he saw as being too cliché-laden to work. Rydell's ninety days were running out fast and he had not yet cast the film's two leading players. He pushed for Carly Simon and James Taylor. They turned him down on the grounds that the story was too close to their 'personal relationship'. Diana Ross and Alan Price said 'no thanks' too. Warner Brothers wanted action and impatiently started pressing buttons. The original idea didn't seem to be getting off its butt. At last they hit on a name for the male lead: Kris Kristofferson. The role was of a rock superstar dying inch by inch as his career collapses, while that of his girl's zooms. The choice of Kristofferson seemed dead on target. An Air Force captain, Rhodes Scholar, Golden Gloves boxer, football player, songwriter-poet, singer . . . the combination of muscle and music had a charge to it. Everybody agreed that the Streisand-Kristofferson chemistry would 'blow the mind'. Kristofferson was resisting. He wanted to read the script. That caution was to be the least of the unit's problems with him. A key figure in the saga was to record: 'I take Kris to dinner. We get drunk. He tells me about his life; it's the old story – a short-haired, clean-thinking patriotic helicopter pilot split open by drugs, booze, sex and music to release a free spirit.'

Meanwhile back at the ranch, still blissfully untouched by it all, Peters was working with Barbra recording her *Butterfly* album. He was also working on Barbra. He wanted to change her image from the schmaltzy dowdiness (as he saw it) of Fanny Brice to the groovy world of tight-crotched Levis, David Bowie and all. The metamorphosis was slow. Pulaski Street personas die hard.

The summer of 1974 and the ninety frantic days of Mark Rydell were over. And out. Mr Rydell, like Dunne and Didion, would look back with no pleasure at the genesis of and his exodus from *A Star Is Born*. (There was a reported unpaid bill of $147 for research materials and commissary lunches which Rydell's lawyer had some trouble in collecting from the studio. In view of the money that was about to be expended on a whole sheaf of writers, one wonders about this tardiness in paying Rydell his paper-clip-and-pastrami money.)

Enter Jerry Schatzberg, the director, whose Warner's film *Scarecrow* had won the Cannes Film Festival. This move had encouraging implications. He had worked with the Dunnes before on his vivid *Panic in Needle Park*. A youngish director with a feel for the destructive, 'grass'-rooted drama of the rock scene, the idea of their movie appealed to him. He was given a 'development deal', the trade's euphemism for the proving ground between seduction and consummation. The thinking of the chieftains at Burbank was that if anyone could get this damn property off the ground, it was Schatzberg. As his star shifted incandescently into the foreground, other celestial influences were at work. A copy of the script was sent to the powerful Hollywood agent, Sue Mengers. She despatched it, and her incisive thoughts on the subject, to her most valued friend and client Barbra Streisand. Since Peters now enjoyed a lover's rights, this also implied advisory status. It was now the moment for these two leading protagonists in the tale to march down from the hills of Malibu to take hold of *A Star Is Born*. By the throat.

The astrological forces, which ordained on that July day in Honolulu that John

Gregory Dunne would make his sixteen-word statement, were now about to leap and weave into more spectacular mischief. Peters saw this vehicle for his prestigious housemate as a story of 'two singers trapped by their money and success, trying to relate to each other and really get into their feelings'. Since he was, with Barbra and his former wife Lesley-Ann Warren, into psycho-therapy he may have felt well qualified to discern the deeper motivations of the characters and the plot. But hold it there; subtle changes in syntax were filtering into Mr Peters' sentences. He was talking about 'our' concept, 'my' feelings. He also wanted to change the script. Barbra, impressed by the speed with which Jon could grasp the story and come up with racy improvements, agreed he should have a say in it. Like, become the producer. What Lola wants . . .

The top brass at Warner's scrutinised the fine print and noted that Miss Streisand had contractual clout of real substance. Moreover, getting her to sing in a musical was virtually a licence to print money. *For Pete's Sake* may not have been a great movie but it had brought in a fat profit. Streisand herself had grossed $12 million from her movies. She was not just as 'bankable' as Fort Knox. She was a multi-national corporation as powerful in her own right as anyone in the studio boardroom. From where they sat, at the wrong end of the option, it was a case of 'What's so wrong with having Peters as producer? Foreman can move up one, we get Streisand and a chunk of money.' Schatzberg's views were canvassed. His response, as he later told us, was: 'It was all right with me. I met Jon Peters, he seemed fine. He's very personable, a seducer, he knows how to get you and talk to you, and everything was fine.' Then. Warner's self-soothing rationale however, was one thing. Hollywood's reaction was another.

The sour, hysterical chorus, unleashed by Peters' appointment as producer, achieved a new record in cocktail-hour malice. A summary of the complaints, written and verbal, synthesised into: 'Here's this young punk who only knows from cutting hair going over to trim Streisand's wig and ends up the producer of a $6 million production. What the hell does he know about movies anyway?' Gibes like 'opportunist creep' and 'arrogant smart-ass' added further grace-notes to the recital. Jealousy and prejudice are blind to logic. They also tend to induce amnesia. It was forgotten that Goldwyn, the former glove salesman, had proved that almost any entrepreneurial road can lead to the producer's chair. Some of the other earlier bosses were merchant adventurers, commercial pirates, hustlers, manipulators, maverick Hungarians, opportunist Germans. And while it may not have been prudent to buy second-hand cars from them in the earlier days, many emerged as Hollywood giants. Some displayed surprisingly good judgement, even taste. As Barbra herself was to say resignedly to Roderick Mann: 'They keep going on about Jon having been "just a hairdresser". In fact he was a very successful businessman. They keep forgetting this business was built by men who were junk dealers. So what's so odd about having been a successful hairdresser?'

Back to Jon Peters, The Producer. Storm clouds gathered over the production as Peters began to view the story in terms of his own relationship with Barbra. Ringsiders later described that relationship as a rampage of fights, vaunting personality clashes, interspersed with much sweetness and light and ecstatic peace-making upstairs and down. It was a boisterous co-existence of Flatbush Avenue and Juvenile Hall. The trouble was, while it may have been all good fun in

Malibu, neither the Dunnes nor Jerry Schatzberg saw their project as a $6 million home musical called *Barbra and Jon*. Moreover, any notion they might have had that Peters would play it cool as the producer, leaving the big decisions to them, faded fast. As Schatzberg remembered it: 'We loved each other at our first meeting. I went out to his ranch; he showed me where he was putting old wood everywhere; the outdoor Jacuzzi . . . we had a good meeting. I didn't see any books but . . . I went back to New York with the idea that we were going ahead with the project.' The big basket of fruit from Barbra and Jon waiting for Schatzberg and his wife when they arrived back at the Beverly Hills Hotel augured well. But minor irritants emerged backstage, such as whether Kris Kristofferson – he had not yet signed – would share above-the-title billing with Streisand. And if the negotiations broke down, who else could play the male lead? That question was answered by a short leap into exhilarating, mind-boggling madness. Let Schatzberg tell it:

> I received a call from Barbra. She asked, 'What do you think about Jon for the part?' I said, 'What part?' She said, 'You know, Kris's part.' I couldn't believe she was saying this. I said, 'No . . . come on!' She said, 'I can't talk to you now, I'll call you later.' She called me back next day. I'd forgotten about it. I thought it was a joke. 'Well, what do you think?' she asked me. 'About what?' 'About Jon doing the part?'

Schatzberg now realized Barbra Streisand was not kidding. 'Where are you now?' he asked her. 'At the ranch,' she said. 'You stay there, I'm coming out to talk to you.' Schatzberg continued: 'I got John Foreman and we went out there and she knew I was ready to quit there and then. They were trying to convince me that the world wanted to hear the Jon and Barbra story.' As the argument developed Schatzberg raised the lethal question: 'Can Peters actually sing?' 'No,' conceded Jon, 'but you can shoot around me.' And Schatzberg laid it on the line – Jon Peters, the hairdresser turned record producer turned film producer, would not make his debut as an actor.

There were other areas of disagreement with Schatzberg, notably over the choice of the production manager. Peters had one man in mind, Schatzberg wanted him to hold off until he'd seen all possible candidates. 'I called Foreman and said I wanted a meeting with him and Peters. So I went over and we had it out. Sometimes I have difficulty in speaking. When I'm really hot I can scream. I stopped in the middle of my screaming and said, "See, I can scream,"' That discovery, while interesting Schatzberg, did not insulate him against further unpleasantries. 'The next big thing we had was they called in a writer without letting me know.' It seemed that, unknown to him, Jon Peters the producer was discussing the script with writer Jonathan Axelrod, stepson of screenwriter George Axelrod. Jon called Schatzberg to his office for a meeting with Axelrod. 'I arrived,' Schatzberg said, 'and Peters said, 'Jonathan, tell Jerry some of your ideas.' I said, 'Who's Jonathan?' Jonathan knew I wasn't interested in his ideas or in talking to him. After fifteen minutes he said, 'Maybe I'd better go.' I said that was a good idea. He left. I said to Peters, 'Jon, don't you ever do that to me again – ever.'

Another name now entered the scene, John Calley, new president of Warner

Brothers. Dick Shepherd, the studio executive who had been master-minding the project, had left. Ted Ashley, the president, had also resigned, and the squawking infant of a movie had been left on Calley's doorstep. The Dunnes, having delivered their third draft screenplay, departed too, having joyously received their pay cheque of $125,000 plus a percentage. Peters took hold of the third draft, and decided he was going to run away with it his way, whether Schatzberg liked it or not. Schatzberg did not. 'I called them next morning and said, "Okay, I quit," and that was it.' Farewell John Gregory Dunne, Joan Didion, Jerry Schatzberg. In the end, Dunne and Didion made a chunk of money to soothe their ruffled feelings. Schatzberg did not. 'I could have hung out and done that whole number but I don't care about that. It depends on where you've come to in life.'

Peters raced on, interviewing other directors. But who could come up to Jon's concept of the movie, interpret it, direct it *his* way? Why, none other than Jon Peters himself. With Barbra's smiling endorsement the hairdresser, turned record producer, turned film producer, now pushed himself as director. Those who had come to sneer remained to jeer. 'A director yet . . . do you believe it!' The tremors were felt from Burbank to Ma Maison. But with the project moving more and more under Barbra's (First Artists) control, the groundswell did not disturb cigar ash at Burbank. Director-designate Peters began interviewing other writers. Jonathan Axelrod? . . . Gone. He had written pages which Barbra and Jon initially loved, but a new phase was opening up. Farewell, Mr Axelrod, it was lovely having you. According to reports, one television writer cut Peters short, muttering away from the meeting that he wouldn't be caught dead writing for Jon even if it meant passing up a Barbra Streisand credit. From the words to the music. Composers came and went with rhythmic regularity.

It was bad news all round as Peters, pressing buttons in his 100-acre Malibu ranch, came on like the producer, director, the hustler and self-styled ass-kicker. But God was on the mountain and a *Star* would be born. Yet hardly painlessly. The mere mention of his name brought gales of laughter from those who would not come to terms with the notion of a producer who cut hair. Barbra and Peters were resigned to the certain knowledge that a sizeable section hoped Peters would 'fall on his ass.' It was nothing new to Barbra. Her 'people who don't have success hate success' applied the maxim even more forcibly to her lover. Barbra and Jon should worry. While gossip writers sniped, they were laughing all the way to the ranch and corporate bliss.

The ranch reflects their vivid life styles. It is the Ultimate Dream, with one subtle touch of reality. Barbra has secretly stuck price labels underneath the more valuable items. One day that dream might evaporate, 'so how else is she going to remember what everything cost?' The ranch is Tiffany's and Second-Hand Rose. It is macrobiotics and *My Fair Lady*. Barbra's feather boas, beaded bags, *Funny Girl* hats, satin shoes, stake their claim against the more conventional items of a superstar's lifestyle. There are tennis courts, and an art deco swimming pool. The whirlpool bath was designed with tender loving care by Peters so that Barbra can bathe *al fresco*. Outside Peters has planted a thousand pine trees. 'To get rid of his hostility,' Streisand diagnosed. The powder room has marble counters. Beneath the cathedral ceiling a fur lounging bed with antique pillows doubles as the living-room couch. Their bedroom is the essence of conjugal furnishing. The pillows and quilts are home-made. So was Barbra's step-down private bath, the old stones personally assembled by the loving hands of Jon Peters. There are nude statues, stained glass and antique fans. It is beautiful, it is sexy and it is fun. Streisand, in fact.

If their Doberman, which is programmed to attack on a signal, intrudes a menacing note, well – this is Malibu and she is Barbra. Even the electric fences, close circuit television and direct line to security patrols do not allay lingering fears of kidnapping. With each film Streisand becomes a richer and maybe more vulnerable target.

Work concentrates the mind wonderfully. She was as keen as Warner's to get *A Star Is Born* away and shooting. The pressure was on everyone, most of all Jon Peters. Against the ropes, the one-time professional boxer was picking the brains of anyone around who was generous or prudent enough the help him. And why not? Be nice to the parking jockey, says the gipsy's warning, tomorrow he may be running the studio. But Peters was finding that it takes more than fast footwork and smart listening to be a producer. Being Barbra's lover was an engaging occupation but not essentially a full-time job. Producing the film, supervising the script, organising the varying talents harnessed to a major musical does not permit you to cut hair between conferences. Thus the day arrived when the bearded boss of Jon Peters, Inc. stood before his assembled employees and told them that, as from that day, he would be devoting all his time to producing a film. Within two years of his first meeting with Barbra to discuss hair, he was producing her film, changing her style, calling the shots and pouring her breakfast coffee. The unseeded player had won Wimbledon. Wash, set and match.

But *A Star Is Born* was still without a director. Now the planetary forces that induced John Gregory Dunne's brainwave in Hawaii cast a major character for their ultimate mischief. Frank Pierson had not directed a film before. He was, however, a writer of the highest calibre. A reporter and film correspondent for *Life* from 1950 to 1958, he later wrote for both television and films. His scripts for the TV series *Naked City, Route 66* and *Have Gun, Will Travel* (which he produced) were universally admired. He had written several major films, and his *Dog Day Afternoon* script was to win the Academy Award of 1975. Warner's asked him to do a rewrite of *Star*. Pierson 'in a moment of mad ambition' accepted on the condition that he directed it as well. He discovered that six writers and three directors had all abandoned ship, many in the middle of lunch. (The nautical analogy is his; the movie, he was to declare later, was the *Mary Celeste* of the Hollywood seas.) He moved into the store and discovered a pile of unused scripts weighing forty pounds. He learned why Jon Peters abandoned the idea of directing the picture almost as soon as it was suggested. According to Pierson, Jon explained: 'How could I direct her and keep our relationship? I had to decide which was more important, our love or the movie. I'm here to expedite. You need somethin', I'll kick ass to get it.'

'Kicking ass' was no substitute for casting. They still didn't have a leading man, Kristofferson not having approved a script and signed a contract. Barbra wondered about Brando. She had always wanted to make a movie with him said she. The notion had Jon leaping out of his corner. As Pierson recalls it, Jon said, 'The son of a bitch, he was right here! He wanted to f . . . Barbra – I was ready to kill him. I take him off and I kiss him. He's beautiful! Right here! I love him, the bastard!

They'd make a great pair. Imagine. Streisand and Brando!'

It is necessary to dwell awhile on the source of this intelligence. On 22 November 1976, when the dust had settled and an uneasy peace had been restored, Frank Pierson wrote a now notorious article on his experiences for the prestigious California-based *New West*. In it he gave a vivid, at times blistering account of his ill-fated experiences on the movie, under the title 'My Battles with Barbra'. Barbra and Peters were outraged. Hollywood, not unfamiliar with 'startling revelations', was nonetheless astonished by the scale and scope of Pierson's disclosures. We asked him whether he had any second thoughts about them. He said he had none and that, apart from one detail he had asked to be deleted, he retracted nothing. He added that he wished both parties well, but had seen little of them lately . . .

Pierson's Day One. He had never seen a Streisand picture before so he did so now, secretly. He discovered her to be 'a primitive force and an elegant delight' and was 'humbled and amazed'. They launched themselves into redrafting the script. There were arguments, and heart-to-heart talks. Squeals of delight when the words looked right, icy silences when Peters didn't buy them. As the project careered onwards, one of the songwriters, piqued by criticism, refused to take calls. Some of Peters' frustrations at the way things were not going rubbed off on to Barbra. 'She was upset with me,' said Pierson who recalled her words. ' "I don't feel you really want to love me. All my directors have wanted to make me beautiful. But I feel you hold something back; there's something you don't tell me. You never talk to me." I realised she was serious. "I love you," I said "but I'm really not the demonstrative type." '

There was a dialogue about Jon who, Pierson says, Barbra claims she leans on 'because he's so strong . . . and I never had a father.'

So Barbra was leaning on Peters who was leaning on everybody else. 'The arguments were long, exhausting and angry.' There was a brief and blessed respite for Pierson when Barbra and Jon took off for New York. The report that Jon had been in a fight there (he punched a man who heckled Barbra at a TV telecast of a Muhammad Ali fight) filtered back to the coast. The incident induced the thought in Peters' mind that Barbra's vulnerability as a 'star' was a quality 'we gotta get into that picture!' Now there was a row over Kristofferson's choice of music. Pierson told of Kris leaping to his feet: 'Who shall I say says my music isn't rock – Barbra Streisand's hairdresser?' Jon screamed back at him: 'It's shit. I don't care who says it.' The fact was, Kristofferson was probably not happy with the music either. He was also terrified of Barbra. The stress of trying to match her, punch for punch, was getting to him. No newcomer to the bottle, he stocked up sufficient tequilla and cans of beer to get him through each day. Now and again, he was to admit later, 'I was a little crazy. I found myself shouting at the top of my voice in front of 300 people.' He reinforced this, months later, with, 'Sure there were times during the making of this film when Barbra and I would have killed each other if we had had the weapons at hand . . .' At one time he threw such insults at his co-star, Peters her champion stepped in and insisted, 'You owe my lady an apology.' 'My lady' scarcely cared about such chivalry. Caught in the harangue between Peters, Pierson and Kristofferson, her concern was to keep the movie on a set course, away from disaster. Intuition, and memories of *Hello Dolly*, convinced her that, whatever the public's response to the film, the press would be waiting in back alleys carrying blunt instruments.

Barbra meanwhile, was puzzled by Kris's fear. She said she liked working with him. 'He's frightened a lot of the time, but that's part of the role. He has a macho femininity about him. He's what a man should be.' Kris's 'macho femininity' seemed fine in the abstract. Barbra was less sanguine about it when the time approached for their nude scene together in a bath. Barbra took Pierson to one side: 'For God's sake, find out if he's going to *wear* something. If Jon finds out he's in there with me with nothing on, naked . . .' Pierson got the point and ordered flesh-coloured shorts for Kristofferson, who thought they were chicken. 'What the hell are they scared of?' he scoffed. For 'they' read Jon Peters, and for 'scared' read jealous. Peters did not relish the notion of the lusty stripped-to-the-buff Kristofferson and his undressed woman playing love-games in a bath. So prudence rather than prudery persuaded Pierson to put flesh-coloured shorts on Kristofferson while Barbra did likewise for herself. Not that Peters stayed around to ensure both participants were suitably fig-leaved. Someone else did that for him. He just could not psyche himself to view the sequence with a producer's detachment. 'You think it's easy,' he asked Pierson, 'some dude making love to your woman?' To offset further trouble, Pierson rehearsed love scenes with dressing-room doors open. But the bickering and the discord racketed on. Peters quarreled with Kristofferson, with Barbra and with Pierson. The language, Peters' at least, was Big Shot vernacular. Pierson was discovering, too late, that Barbra and Peters had cast him more as an interpreter of their ideas than as the conventional director. In fact, according to Pierson, she was to tell him after an argument, 'I should have a co-director credit. I have directed at least half of this movie.' Anger seems to have been the dominant emotion against a dark backdrop of apprehension. How would it all come out? Pierson, looking back at the casualty list behind him, must have wondered about his own survival. Peters must have wondered if he was in over his head.

The rock concert, played out in the desert around Phoenix, Arizona, was the torrid climax to both the film and the battle. The Sun Devil Stadium was jammed. The big-time rock groups were there, actually in Phoenix. And the word was that Barbra was going to sing. Everybody was 'hanging loose' and the 40,000 kids were loving it. The smell of sweat and grass hung heavy on the air. Helicopters were dancing around overhead with cameras focused on the crowded stadium. The audience would be in the film, the groups would not. They were there simply as crowd-pullers. Showers were set up around the stadium and the progressively unclothed kids stood in line to cool down. The Streisand-Kristofferson shout-out, which had a brief stereophonic life over the amplifiers, was forgotten. Barbra moved out front to give her audience the thrill they'd souped themselves up for. Writer Lee Grant, observing it for the *Los Angeles Times,* captured it well:

The crowd had become irritable, impatient, wanting more music, more concert, less filming, less take after take of Kristofferson's song. Finally Streisand ventured out to quiet them, tossing a few profane words out tastelessly in an attempt at identification, at 'getting down'.

'Hey you, mother-f—s, are you having a good time?' appears to have been Barbra's verbal warm-up.

One way to quiet them, she decided, was to sing. It worked, miraculously. The songs were recognisable. 'The Way We Were' and 'People'. The throng settled, action on stage halted, the crew, Pierson, Peters . . . listened. The voice took over. That voice, that Streisand voice, sailed over the stadium, inducing shivers. It caressed this boogie-oriented, raucous, rock-'n'-roll audience. At the end, they delivered her a standing ovation. Cradling it, smiling, at home here on stage, she told them: 'Thank you. You're my first live audience in a long time.' It was Central Park come to Arizona.

But the Streisand magic was for the moment. In the days that followed, argument, apology, rage and drinks all round, continued to beleaguer the production. One night while they were shooting a scene on a parking lot, Pierson heard in a bar that he'd won an Oscar for his screenplay of *Dog Day Afternoon*. It was a fortuitous boost for a first-time director notably duelling with a first-time producer. But a couple of nights later, at two a.m. in Pierson's hotel room, Peters was back into the attack. It was a verbal *Blitzkrieg* in which the producer angrily catalogued his criticisms. The following morning the shouting continued. As Pierson saw it Peters yelled finally: ' "I'm sick of you. I'm waiting until the production finishes. Then I'm going to punch you out." It was a nightmare that had no end.' The effect on Pierson was traumatic. The gilt was flaking fast from his Oscar. Finally, like a particularly painful and protracted pregnancy, the film was finished. The crew exited from the studios like soldiers from a battlefield. Perfunctory goodbyes were exchanged by all parties. Only Kristofferson seemed contented. The movie had given him a salutory insight into his personality. Watching the daily 'rushes' it dawned on him that the character's blind, self-destructiveness bore too close a resemblance to himself to be safe. The Rhodes Scholar-turned-song-writer, who had created hits like 'Help Me Make It Through the Night' decided that 'forty was long enough to be a fool.' His intake had been around a bottle and a half of hard liquor a day. Some days before they 'wrapped' shooting on *A Star Is Born* Kristofferson wound up his 90-proof lifestyle. A doctor's report on the state of his liver sealed his decision. It enabled him to confess unequivocally: 'I was so drunk at times, if I had been Barbra and Jon I'd have fired me.'

This generous admission by Kristofferson shows that, whatever crosses Pierson and Peters felt they carried, Barbra Streisand endured her personal calvary too. Her title 'Executive Producer' in the credits was more than just a means of 'upping the ante'. It was her movie and in the three years gestation, from inspiration to exhaustion, it drained her more than it did the others. What did they, Peters and Pierson, have to lose anyway? If the picture flopped, Jon – constructed to bounce on falling – would spring into something else. Pierson, now an Oscar winner, would have enough substance on film to prove his capacity to direct. But Streisand in a $6 million disaster, and one that had had the worst pre-publicity of any film since *Cleopatra*, could expect scant sympathy. That, in fact, was what she received. The film opened in December 1976 to some of the most scathing, even vicious notices ever. How much of this was due to genuine critical evaluation or media prejudice would be hard to determine. It cannot be overlooked that Pierson's article was published in *New West* on 20 November, a couple of weeks or so before the premiere. Media backlash or not, there could have been few critics or commentators who would not have been influenced, at least subliminally, by Pierson's version of the affair 'Top Oscar-winning writer tangles with ex-hairdresser producer and his live-in superstar . . .' was the flavor if not the text of the average, untutored reaction. There can be no doubt that Pierson's summation of the events was the way he genuinely saw it.

> Years ago, or so it seems, I drove up that sun-dappled lane to the ranch; we had a dream of a picture then, each of us with a slightly different view. Out of the differing dreams, the struggle and conflict of personalities, accidents and quirks of fate, moments of rage, disappointment, cowardice, arguments, mistakes and sometimes sparks of brilliance struck off in the heat of battle, a picture has emerged . . .

And having emerged, was Pierson justified in impaling it on the barbed wire of his post mortem? Maybe the 'pro' inside Pierson made it impossible for him just to 'take the money and run'. The strongly supported rumour had it that, when he was signed, an executive told him, 'Your job is just to make sure you're not fired.' Playing it cool was not Pierson's style. But not every director, placed in the same position, would have taken the same action. Jerry Schatzberg, who had no call for fond memories of his brief encounter with the production, argued nevertheless: 'Once you take on an assignment you've got to live with it. You can't go around saying it was their fault and all that. They can fight you all along the way, but after it's over you're responsible for it.'

Barbra's reaction to Pierson's article was predictably more a sense of injustice than anything else. She felt he'd betrayed the necessarily private relationship between director and actor. No doubt that she was deeply hurt; no doubt either that she felt his timing would crucify a barely finished picture. As she said in interview for *Playboy:* 'No other article has ever touched off this deep sense of injustice in me. I felt totally helpless and impotent knowing so many people would probably believe what they were reading. It was a field day for critics to take that article . . . and review the movie from it.'

Her indignation is understandable, but critics of calibre do not operate that way. *A Star Is Born* failed entirely on its own de-merits. *Newsweek* declared: 'Streisand's constant upstaging of Kristofferson often goes beyond the bounds of run-of-the-mill narcissism . . .' adding, however, 'Streisand is so overwhelmingly a presence that she can probably get away indefinitely with making movies as slipshod as this one. But it would be a shame if she were to settle for that.' *Rolling Stone* was typically terse: '*A Star Is Born* . . . dead on arrival.' Judith Crist got closest to the film's fatal flaw: 'The latest remake . . . is an exercise in superstardom and the power that goes with it. If the result isn't what its director, Frank Pierson, predicted would be a "home movie" it is at least a vanity production and at most a bore.'

Well yes, but given its brawling, Byzantine formation, and its enormous economic success, *A Star Is Born* has to be regarded as a major work in the Streisand canon. Judged simply as a film it is a frail work whose uncertain parentage shows at all levels. If in *Funny Girl* we see a species of fantasised home movie, then Barbra Streisand in *A Star Is Born* dangerously follows suit. Frank

Pierson handled his first feature very much as one might predict a talented writer would make his directional debut.

We can forgive him the perfunctory handling of the Sun Devil concert. Logistics were clearly against him. Mark Rydell (who put his ninety-day run at the controls to later copycat use in *The Rose)* fared no better. The rock concert sections of *A Star Is Born* look like fugitives from television coverage. It's all been done before and done better. But where one can find deepest fault with Pierson is in the small scenes, the crucial nuts and bolts exposition that carry the narrative along. Few films budgeted so highly can have had such obvious blemishes as boom-mike shadows, dirt on a lens, a fill light reflecting back to camera; but even these are not important. The film is fussy, both over-made and under-made at one and the same time. Arguably the best scene in the movie occurs during the break in the born star's rehearsing of a television special when Paul Mazursky, adroitly accurate as John Norman Howard's manager, offers an ambiguous apologia for withdrawing his support from the rock idol with feet of clay and cocaine sinuses.

As the downwardly doomed star, Kris Kristofferson is considerably more than adequate. With undertones both in voice and looks of an unreconstructed Jack Palance, he conveys the burnt-out case history of Howard with an impressive throw-away control. The hurt is allowed, just occasionally, to surface from beneath the posture of indifference. And the disdain. The major single flaw in the film is that, given the tawdry appurtenances of rock-idol success. John Norman Howard's turning his back on them seems the most mature, well-adjusted attitude on display. The suspicion lingers that he commits suicide to escape his co-star's performance.

Here, Barbra Streisand's central performance is an embarrassment. It is unforgivably self-concious. Given the ghosts that must have hovered about John Norman Howard for her (for failed star read failed would-be star read Elliott Gould; for self-built Arizona ranch house read Ramirez Canyon), it may well have been next to impossible to exorcise a sense of self. But her delivery of every other line throughout the picture is 'cute'. She acts each one, by God how she acts! She utterly fails to rise to the two set-pieces written for her at the end of the movie after Kristofferson's death. Both with the corpse that she cannot believe is dead, and the posthumous cassette of his voice she blunders upon, she sinks to the occasion. A neon sign reading 'Set Piece' flashes out from between the lines of the radically chic soliloquies. And the film's conclusion is a straight steal. After the ghastly, overly sentimental key-signature of the audience turning itself into a candelabra in memory of the late great husband, the 'art and emotion triumphing over death' affirmation, celebration, is a re-run of the 'My Man' sequence in *Funny Girl.*

Esther Hoffman in *A Star Is Born* is essentially the straight man's role. Barbra Streisand's uncharacteristically unevenly pitched performance derives not only from the lack on the set of a tough, objective father figure prepared to tell her to go back and get it right, but from an attempt to soup up into pole position an inherently subordinate role. During the whole fracas of the pre-production an idea arose giving Barbra the key role as the falling burned-out rocket. It might have worked supremely well.

Judith Crist concludes her mordant appraisal with: 'But as a man from Warner's said, "Let Barbra sing six songs and it's $60,000,000 in the till." ' The figure can be revised. Takings on the film and the album exceeded $100 million. Attacked by the press, the critics and the director of the film, Barbra found unexpected allies – the people. They stood in line to see her film. She received thousands of letters of support. The album sold 5,000,000 copies, millions more than any previous album from a movie score. Everybody with a 'piece' will go on making money through 2001 and beyond. Notably John Gregory Dunne and Joan Didion. We come back full circle to the dawning *Star*. It was Dunne, you recall, who suggested to his wife as they passed the Aloha Tower in downtown Honolulu: 'James Taylor and Carly Simon in a rock-'n'-roll version of *A Star Is Born*!' How does he view the monster he sired now? With noticeable magnanimity considering the battering he received in the eliminating bouts. 'The notices were absolutely vicious,' he said,

> but everybody connected with the picture made money, so what the hell! Jon Peters was not all that easy to get to but I quite like him. He has this street savvy which I got to understand. In the credit arbitration there were eleven other writers up for credits. Now and again when Barbra and I meet and look over all those writers, I tell her she should have stuck with us. You have to understand the way she saw it. It was her life on the line. If the picture went down she went down with it. She just had to do what she thought was right.

But at what price? Playing the generalissimo over the heads of the powerful studio brass, the writers, the entire production, made tough demands on someone who, in between, had to find time to act, and sing in front of the cameras. Not much scope, meantime, for the no-less-demanding role of being Jon Peters' woman. She well knew the image her 'executive producer' status had fixed in people's minds. She had said, 'If a man did the same thing I did, he would be called thorough – while a woman is called a ball-breaker.' It is fair comment and reveals the extent to which Barbra Streisand is concerned by other people's evaluation of her. John Gregory Dunne offers fascinating confirmation of it. Not long ago he was in a restaurant when Barbra walked over to his table. She smiled, then asked him, 'What do you really think of me?' Dunne was astounded. The question, in that crowded restaurant, was not 'table-hopping banter'. It was a genuine enquiry by a seeker after knowledge. Dunne told us, 'Even though I am constantly astonished by her I was completely taken aback. I said, "I've known my wife since she was sixteen and she's never asked me that." ' Barbra shrugged and returned to her table. Don't see why a guy – a writer yet! – can't answer a simple question!

But of course it isn't that simple. A woman who is also a powerful multi-national corporation is, necessarily, part female, part fortress. It is the sort of combination that tests friendships, pushes the tolerance threshold beyond saintly limits. It is significant that Streisand's friends are happy to bite the bullet and stay with it, like Marines joking their way on to an enemy beach. 'Listen, she's a wonderful kid, but it helps if she and you can forget she's Barbra Streisand,' said one veteran of the Streisand camp. Her name is Muriel Harris and when we spoke to her, she, Barbra and Peters were no longer friends. The catalyst to the unhappy rift was Streisand's zealous Doberman, 'Big Red'. He took the sort of bite at Muriel which only lawyers could heal.

EIGHTEEN

WHILE THE Streisand–Peters ranch on Ramirez Canyon, Malibu may have been constructed out of love, its architectural ambivalence is plain to see: part stockade, part House Beautiful. There is honeysuckle around the electric fences; the sigh of the gulls and chirp of the lesser marbled godwit are malevolently up-staged by the howl of a watchful Doberman. On a clear day you may see a security guard go by intoning, perhaps, 'Gate to Control – Number One and party of two on way up in convertible, all checked, over and out.' An intruder has no chance of getting into this trysting-fortress overlooking the Pacific undetected; he would have been spotted on several TV monitors even before he paused to read, 'DANGER, BEWARE, GUARD DOGS TRAINED TO ATTACK'. Invited to state his business on the two-way microphone at the gate, he would require all the bona fides save a saliva test. Once through, a glimpse of the six-feet high fence, the two German Shepherds and the Doberman, would warn of the consequences of ignoring the welcoming procedures. At the time – the post-*A Star Is Born* hiatus – there might also have been Barbra Streisand's personal bodyguard on hand, who for speed of reaction probably had the edge on the Doberman.

Closely-guarded estates in Malibu, or Beverly Hills, are no novelty. But that conceded, the sophisticated electronic hardware assembled to protect the privacy and high-decibel intimacies of Barbra and Jon could show a trick or two to Fort Knox. Ask Jon Peters and he will tell you that it is the least a concerned lover could do. Moreover he scarcely needed America's powerful TV inquisitor, Barbara Walters, to announce on her show that Barbra Streisand was the biggest female box-office draw in the world. Jon would also explain that he was coping with something considerably more complex than the familiar movie star apprehensions. Streisand's chronic fears *need* the elaborate security systems, the armed guards and the dogs. She hired Joe Amsler as bodyguard after narrowly escaping injury from a falling flower pot in some public place. According to a security officer, Barbra suspected that the incident might not have been an accident. (The bodyguard was introduced to her by Ryan O'Neal who had worked with him on *Love Story*. A more practical gift to Barbra than candy or perfume.) One of Streisand's worst nightmares reveals her terror of being abandoned in a crowd.

She dreams she is driving alone and is suddenly taken ill. She needs to get to hospital. People press in around her. 'Please help me,' she begs. But the response is, 'Hey you look like . . . aren't you . . .?' She feels she is dying, they gawp and do nothing. 'Gee, wait till we tell 'em back home we saw Barbra Streisand!' That terror of recognition was brought to a fine point one morning in the waiting-room of dog-trainer Michael Kamer. Barbra had been waiting there with four or five other clients. 'Suddenly there was a pounding on the door,' Kamer said, 'and Miss Streisand was yelling for me to let her in. She was shaking. When I asked her what was wrong she said she had to get out of the room because the other clients had recognised her.' No one had actually approached her. It was enough that their eyes carried a flicker of recognition. The stage, the film set, the public auditorium, or the private waiting-room – the place hardly matters. Fear is the dominant emotion. Attempting to conceal it, Streisand resorts to defensive needling or, though she's often astonished when told of it, downright rudeness. Sometimes it's a game of brinksmanship, seeing how far she can go in the game before blood is drawn. At other times it is Streisand determined to state her mind, rather than sustain relatonships on bogus values. She has been called one of the rudest women on earth. But the director who said it reflected that a great deal of it is accidental. 'She's often sincerely upset when she discovers what she has done.' The writer Rick Edelstein saw the other side of the coin. During a rough period in his life, he found himself broke with four hungry children to feed. Barbra heard about it and the cheque for $7500 was in the post almost before he'd put out a feeler. A year or two later he was directing a play he had written. Barbra and Jon came to the opening night. The following day they took out a full-page ad in one of the trade papers declaring how much they'd enjoyed it. 'Once you are Barbra's friend,' he says, 'she makes you very much part of her life.' There are several friends who will gladly testify to this. If one piece of evidence is more persuasive than others, it is because the attractive divorcée, Muriel Harris, can still root for Barbra despite the row which blew up when the Doberman took an unsolicited bite at Muriel's arm. The dog, 'Big Red', meant well. He even sent an apology to her pinned to a life-size effigy of himself constructed entirely in flowers. Fairness demands that Miss Harris's version of the affair is seen in the context of her understandable indignation. Although this does not detract from her admiration of Barbra, it should not be supposed that the same magnanimity extends to Jon Peters. 'He knows I can't stand him,' says Muriel, cheerfully, 'and he can break my knees for it, but I have to say what I feel.'

Muriel Harris's apartment in Beverly Hills reflects the taste and flair for interior design which she and Barbra had in common. Ivory is the dominant colour; antique silver, pastel silks and fine ornaments are the fruits of their many shopping expeditions together. Friends for seven years or more, Muriel, formerly married to a veteran Hollywood producer, was one of those friends who could make Barbra forget she was Streisand. A few minutes into Muriel Harris's recital of her rough-with-the-smooth friendship with Barbra, and you get a clear vision of Streisand with her hair down. Shopping for gifts, baubles, bits and pieces, together; going to health spas; chewing the fat over the unintrusive mid-afternoon soap operas – this was when Barbra could forget who she was, forget that she merely needed to snap her fingers and producers, writers, bankers and 'gofers' would all come running. Listening to Muriel Harris, one can see the two of them lying prone under adjoining masseuses, comparing midriffs or indulging in 'girl talk', the verbal blood sport which Hollywood women have raised to Olympic status. But that afternoon, over tea with Muriel Harris, the talk was all about Streisand.

Maybe I was a kind of mother image to her – I don't know – but we were very close. My husband had been a producer for thirty-five years. Jon Peters, who was living close by to us in Malibu at the time, was a hairdresser and wanted to learn all about the business. So they'd go for walks talking, and I'd sit around

Barbra with her mother, Mrs Diane Kind, and her stepsister, Rosalyn, who has a singing career of her own

with Barbra on the deck looking out on the ocean. We'd exercise together and go to these health spas when we thought we were getting too heavy. You know Barbra goes for very funky clothes, but she's very hard to fit. She cannot go in and buy a conventional dress unless she's been exercising. Men don't see it but a woman would. She is extremely short waisted with these long legs, so she can't just step into anything fitted. Mind you, she's got a wonderful bust, beautiful shoulders and a marvellous skin. But if she wants something out of a store it's got to be a funky thing that would fit anybody. If she sees something she likes she goes in and buys it for her friends as well for herself. She really is a great girl and I like her a lot.

I sympathise with her fears of being alone, though I don't happen to be that way myself. It would be very difficult for her if she didn't have Jon. I mean, who's gonna call her and ask her out? Who could have the nerve, I mean – Barbra Streisand! She needs protection and support round the clock. Where do you get those things? From Ray Stark who is married to somebody else and has his own family? From her secretary who has her own life? From Jason, who's too young? From her help? From her mother who's a nice little Jewish lady but . . . typical, you know, a martyr! A nice lady, but you know there are these special mothers who can never show you they eat with the rest of the family. The table could be groaning with food but she'd take this little bowl with hardly anything in it, then go over into a corner on her own. It used to drive Barbra insane!

She knows she's wealthy but she never flaunts it. Sometimes she'd go to Tiffany's and buy something for me just because I'd admired it on her. But she has this guilt thing about money. She never forgets that she was poor for a hell of a long time. So maybe she'll go and buy Jon a present of a Corniche costing $100,000, but then, like once we were in the car and they were playing a record of hers. 'My God, I'm getting a penny every time that plays!' she said, and here she was counting pennies. She knows she could look beautiful but she's never absolutely sure about it. If I said to her, 'Gee honey, you look lovely in that dress,' she'd go back into the shop and buy three more, and maybe others for her friends. At Christmas she would often send money in my name to my favorite charity, CONCERN.

Of course her big love is Jason. She worships him. Sure she loves the house but it's all very kitsch. I mean *he* [Jon] built this sunken grotto with flagstones but she said her ass was always ice cold from sitting in the thing. It is beautiful, it's sexy, but no doubt it's cold on the ass. Where was I? Yes, Barbra loves Jason. She has such patience with him. The studios and everybody can put the pressure on but she never lets them take away her time with the boy. Luckily for our friendship, I had nothing to do with the business. I couldn't have cared less about the legend, the whole charisma bit. And that's what she liked. Once we were in a big store together and we'd see a whole crowd of people rushing along the floor. I'd say, 'What's wrong?' And Barbra would answer, 'I dunno, what d'you think is wrong with those people?' Then we'd both look at each other and I'd say, 'My God! – it's *YOU*!' It hadn't dawned on her, or me. We thought maybe someone had fainted in the store.

We hardly ever talked movies, but now and again they'd send a script over to the beach or to her town house, for her to read. Afterwards she'd give it to me and ask my opinion. I'm not a professional but I'd tell her the truth about it as I saw it. Then she'd go to the studio or whoever, and say, 'Muriel didn't like it.' And they'd say, 'Who the hell is Muriel?' It became a funny thing. She was always asking me my opinions maybe because I was old enough to be her mother. I think she had very special thoughts about her father and maybe that is why she never talked about him.

Sure she talked about Jon and other men she knew before him. There was one man – she never told me his name – who she had known before Jon, but I understand he was married. And of course she never really cared for Ryan

O'Neal. She always dismissed him as . . . well, you know. Most times she talked about her relationship with Jon who, of course, I'd known before through my husband. He's enthusiastic, he's protective, and one hundred per cent behind her. I think they need each other, and for whatever reason, it works. They do fight. I've witnessed many of them. I mean, *I* wouldn't put up with it but I don't have her fears. Whatever else, he protects her and that's vital. The relationship goes much deeper than it appears. But those fights could be something! You have to know that they loved each other, or else you'd think . . .

Well, one afternoon they were sitting in my living-room on the beach. There was an argument about buying a house or something, anyway they got into a terrible argument. They really went for each other. She was here and he was there and they were fighting, knocked over a couple of pieces of bric-à-brac, broke a table, and I didn't know who was going to kill who, so I put my lighted cigarette against his *tush* [backside] and burnt him. He thought it was Barbra but then he saw I was the only one smoking. Next thing I know they're out the back and it's blowing into something really big. Just a nice little average fight – it's their kind of togetherness.

Anyway, you wanted to know about the Doberman. It was January I think, and I was wearing this leather jacket, a sweater and a skirt. I drive up to the house and sort of put my arm out of the window. The dog sees this and maybe is scared, anyway it clamps on to my sleeve and won't let go. Jon Peters comes out and grabs the dog which has torn my sleeve – and look at the scar here – and I am really shaking. Jon hauls the dog off and I go with him to the house. The leather jacket is torn and I figure I need shots for my arm. Of course everybody wants to cool it on account of the publicity. So I get into my car and drive to the nearest hospital but I'm so shook up that I turn into a wall.' [It was Muriel Harris's complaint that she was left to go alone to the hospital instead of being taken there if not by Barbra – 'I understood how scared she was of the public' – then at least by Jon Peters. Jon could equally have argued that he didn't care to leave Barbra alone at night with a nervous Doberman on her hands.] By the time I hit the wall with the car I'm really angry; I was also, I guess, temporarily insane. I'd just been divorced, I wasn't aware of how much money I had, didn't even know whether I could cover the cheques I signed. Well, it's all over now but it took a letter from my lawyers to get payment for the damage done to the car and the sweater. They each sent me a cheque finally for $750.

Muriel Harris paused, then shrieked on a laugh, recalling a straight *Goodbye Columbus* sequel to the drama: 'The next day a florist in Malibu sends me a great flower arrangement in the shape of a dog. It was made entirely of chrysanthemums, dark burnished blooms, with ears and a tail, and eyes yet, a dead ringer for their Doberman. With it there's this note, from the dog: "Dear Aunt Muriel, I'm sorry I bit your arm. Big Red." '

Unhappily for the friendship with Barbra the incident was not resolved by the floral Doberman. As of this time, girl talk and calorie counts have ceased between Barbra Streisand and Muriel Harris. 'But I miss her,' says Muriel. 'We had great times together. She has her hangups, but she is a good person. You can't help loving her.'

But, love Barbra love her dog, says Muriel, is something else again.

Coming up from the dangerous cross-currents of *A Star Is Born* Barbra and Jon needed the controlled transition of a decompression chamber before again being tossed back into the deep end. Streisand, who had considered herself to be the prime target, watched as Peters now drew the fire. Two major factors worked against him as far as the anti-Peters lobby was concerned. He had actually had the gall to bring the picture in under budget and just one day over schedule. Worse, the movie had confounded all the sour predictions by foreshadowing huge profits at the box-office. The bad-mouth mutterings against 'Barbra's boy' continued with unremitting ferocity. Though it was manifestly untrue, they saw Peters as a Svengali with street-urchin manners. Not instantly lovable – hustling is not an endearing trait – Peters was swiftly acquiring the persona and abrasive language of the fast-footed producer. Lean, bearded and bounding ever forward like a confident boxer, he was determined from the start to prove he was no Svengali, or 'Mr Streisand' either. If now and again his punches were off target, well, hit or miss is the name of the game. Just occasionally even Jon wasn't ready for the counter-punch, as evidenced by this renowned exchange between himself and Dino de Laurentis whose gigantic *King Kong* had opened before *A Star Is Born*.

PETERS: I bet my picture will outgross yours.
DE LAURENTIS (mildly): It's possible, My monkey doesn't sing.

Not built of the stuff that makes friends and influences people, Peters launched himself on the other tack of proving he didn't need them. He had already demonstrated with Streisand's *Butterfly* album, which went on to be a gold disc, that he could produce records. *A Star Is Born* proved he could put together and mastermind a major multi-million dollar production. On the personal level he had wrought an impressive metamorphosis on the Streisand image: goodbye Fanny Brice, enter Dylan. He had also scored the additional coup of being the man she had chosen from many to be the lover who turned the lights out at nights.

If Peters had been cynically concerned to hitch a ride on Barbra's coat-tails or, to switch metaphors, milk the coconut for all it was worth, he, and Barbra, would have pitched into another commitment immediately after *Star*, In fact it was Peters who advised her to take some time off to enjoy a 'bit of living'. Peters came on the scene in a supporting role when Barbra's confidence was way down on the scale. It is unlikely that the song 'Evergreen' for which she and composer Paul Williams shared an Oscar, would have emerged if Jon hadn't told his faltering love-mate, 'You can achieve anything you set your mind to.' For Barbra, enjoying a 'bit of living' meant getting to plant trees, learn the Latin names of scores of plants, and nibbling her way into health foods. It was a curious conversion to 'whole earth thinking' by these archetypal urban mavericks raised on lox, bagels, burgers and fries. Pulaski Street 'knew from nothing' when it came to the classification of foods on the principles of yin and yang: whole grains and hazelnut surprises. Weaned on chicken soup, raised on salt beef and potato pancakes, Streisand's brave new macrobiotic world on Malibu would have had her old immigrant neighbours in Flatbush murmuring the all-purpose put-down, 'Feh!'

Barbra's spiritual explorations were no less fascinating. The traumas on *A Star Is Born* had bitten deep. Confusion about who she was, what she had become, where she was going, induced considerable turbulence in Barbra. Up there in Ramirez Canyon, the quiet, the away-from-the-Beverly-Hills-circus tranquillity gave her time to organise her mind. She studied meditation, and practised it. Any cult, science or ritual that slowed you down, lowered the reading on the stress scale, was given a hearing. Peace and perfectionism do not sit well together. Not the perfectionism, at any rate, of movie and recording stars. For a while, Barbra Streisand studied the spiritual teachings of the Indian mystic, Krishnamurti. Other tormented celebrities, notably the Beatles, had followed similar routes. They, like Streisand, were to discover that 'supreme and lasting happiness' is no easier to find in the Himalayas than it is in Hollywood.

Meanwhile, the actress-singer who could now tell which type of cactus was the *Opuntia* and which the *Pereskia,* still had half an ear to the ground, and the future. She endured the dichotomy of being afraid to take on another major film, and being scared at not doing so. Remember her words to Sydney Pollack: 'What am I doing? Why am I not working? What am I saving myself for?' One answer at the time was an understandable reluctance to risk another *A Star Is Born*. A bigger danger she faced was her awareness that, whatever she said 'Yes' to, the studios would go into production on. 'Just tell us how much you want, honey, twenty million, thirty, forty . . .?' Privately they could grin, and say, 'What do we care if it's a big piece of crap? With her name on it, singing maybe a couple of songs, we're in profit from Day One.' But Barbra Streisand cared, and saying 'No' became easier than saying 'Yes'. If in doubt, pull out. Ingmar Bergman sent her a script of a projected movie, *The Merry Widow*. She read it, liked the first half, had doubts about the second. She politely enquired whether the distinguished Swedish film director would care to rewrite it. He refused, either out of a genuine difference of viewpoint, or, perhaps, he was not going to be told by any actress, even Barbra Streisand, which way a script should go. But if she were going to play the lead, shouldn't she be permitted to put her artistic ten cents into the discussion?

This flirtation with ideas which were not ultimately consummated had begun earlier. Tantalised by the character of Sarah Bernhardt, Barbra had also long nurtured the idea of playing Juliet on stage. She gave that serious thought too, as she chewed sunflower seeds up on the ranch. She got as close as discussing it with the Royal Shakespeare Company in London and with its counterpart in Connecticut. But the old tremors intruded. Going on stage doing the things she was superb at, still made her sick to her stomach. Playing Juliet with at least half the media gloatingly anticipating the prat-fall of the decade, would be masochism on the grand scale. During these kinds of deliberations, Jon Peters was more sounding board than ringmaster. He had now set up his own outfit, the Jon Peters Organization. Flexing his muscles, he later opened offices in Burbank, vast and opulent enough to house his empire-building dreams. Several magnificent portraits of Barbra Streisand exercise dominant priority over the art deco ornaments and mirrors, and the mogul furniture. Nothing apart from a series of disasters will stop

Jon Peters becoming an entertainments tsar of real power. He already has so many projects in preparation that people don't make snide jokes about him any more. Professionally, the 'smart-aleck crimper' has made his critics eat their own abuse. Privately, playing Barbra's unofficial husband is not one of his favorite roles.

Peters is on record as saying he has proposed marriage to Barbra – and been rejected – at least three times. Her reasons for saying 'No' (as of early 1981) are her own. We can speculate that her objections are on religious grounds though Streisand has never seemed a candidate for this kind of orthodoxy. If she has not married Peters by the time these words appear, it will not be because of some ethnic aversion to standing under the marriage canopy alongside a half-Cherokee half-Italian Catholic. The subject arose one afternoon when Muriel Harris was over at the ranch. The usual rumours had been circulating and had reached Jason's ears. 'Jason turned to Barbra and asked, "Mother, are you marrying Jon?" Barbra replied, "If I were to marry Jon I would have told you. No, I'm not marrying him." ' In the opinion of Barbra's once-bitten friend, such a marriage is unlikely. 'Why? Because,' laughed Muriel, 'she's too smart!'

Barbra's comment to her son Jason, reveals, perhaps, his crucial status in her deliberations about remarrying. It is not merely a question of an ideal husband, assuming she was prospecting for that phenomenon. The man who would play second father to Jason would clearly have to be made of the fine textures that she thought had characterised the late Emmanuel Streisand. Born hustlers often make great lovers, even good husbands. But everything in the way she and Elliott Gould have orchestrated young Jason's life shows that they want something more for him than a blinkered world which extends no further than the Beverly Hills city limits. Hating violence on television or in movies, Barbra rarely watches TV at home and encourages Jason to discern junk from quality on the several channels. She is not playing mother. She is living it, Jason being, if not her whole life, then at least the part of it that really matters. She took him once to a special screening of the Robert Altman film, *The Long Goodbye*, which starred his father, Elliott Gould. Jason was five years old. There was a considerable amount of violence in the film. Finally Barbra decided it was no entertainment for a five-year-old. She took Jason's hand and walked him out of the screening room. When a star of Barbra's calibre makes that kind of exit at an important 'opinion searching' preview, shock is the immediate reaction. Altman was angry. A couple of hours later Barbra phoned him to apologise, explaining her reasons. But she thinks he never forgave her. There may be even longer goodbyes in Streisand's relationships. Her credo goes beyond the 'win-some-lose-some' shrug of resignation. She does what she thinks is right for her work, for herself and for Jason. She has a total vision of an acceptable lifestyle and standard of work. If either, or both are invaded, nervousness turns, on automatic reflex, to aggression. No offence is intended. But if taken, she'll sigh, wish the victim well and 'don't let's make a big thing out of this, huh?'

Barbra's obsessive perfectionism is frequently offered as part cause for the abrasive confrontations in her career. The charge oversimplifies. Debating it with Barbra Streisand will produce a spirited rebuttal, citing evidence of other seekers after excellence from Chaplin to Sinatra, Kubrick to Sydney Pollack. Asked to define perfectionism to *Playboy*'s Lawrence Grobel, she produced this gem:

Perfection is like a wine-velvet snapdragon, or a tuberous begonia, the smell of a gardenia or the texture of a just-ripened avocado. A Gallé blown vase. A piece of Walter or Argy-Rousseau *pâte de verre* glass. A painting by Van Gogh. A child when it's born. Perfect is too small a word for it, it's a miracle. It's God. It's mind-blowing. It's more than perfect. And yet it shits and it pisses. There's no such thing as perfection, because everything seems to fall apart sooner or later.

Son Jason

NINETEEN

THE EXQUISITE torment which passed for the professional and personal life of Barbra Streisand, both supervised by Jon Peters, had everything except its quieter moments. Jon Peters as a lover is not in the Rossano Brazzi school of wooers. Barbra Streisand, as the loved one, is hardly in the lie-back-and-think-of-the-Republic category. With both partners fervidly capable of being alternately irresistible and intractable, the affair, at times, had all the tender overtones of a Chicago abattoir. Muriel Harris's emergency antidote – a lighted cigarette-end placed on the guilty buttock – was, however, not needed a second time. Somehow, when they finally called it a night and went to bed, both were temporarily able to forget that First Artists was snuggling up to the Jon Peters Organization, Inc. More eager than ever now to prove that his hairdressing triumph was just a holding pattern for the future, Peters took on the production of *The Main Event*. Non-event would be an apt verdict upon this disappointing effort. The most incisive post mortem on this return to the screen by Barbra Streisand after three years' absence, came from David Denby, movie critic of *New York*. He wrote:

> The last time that Barbra Streisand functioned as an actress and not as a movie-pulverizer was in *The Way We Were* over five years ago. In her recent pictures and particularly in two she has produced with Jon Peters – *A Star Is Born* and the new romantic comedy *The Main Event* – she has been so brazenly self-promoting that one could not possibly react to anything in the movies but *her*. We have to decide every time whether to adore her or reject her, and I, for one, can't even work up the energy to *think* about her anymore. I wish she would just go away until she settles down. Yet she seems eager to see how far she can push us. In *The Main Event* there's a scene at exercise class in which Streisand, in her two-tone leotard, stretches and spins and finally bends over and puts her head between her legs, rear in the air. Now, there's no reason for the scene to be shot in the exercise class (it could just as well be at her office) except to give Streisand the opportunity to show us that, although she's in her late thirties, her thighs haven't gone flabby. How nice for her! But couldn't we have noticed this in passing – do we need her bottom stuck in our faces? The scene says, 'Love me totally!' – and that's all it says.

The camera's preoccupation with Streisand's backside induced similar reactions in Richard Schickel of *Time*. He gets around to it slowly:

> Were she not an unquestioned star one should suspect *The Main Event* of being a vanity production, the sort of thing ageing screen queens sometimes get their wealthy admirers to buy for them so that the camera may once again be permitted to adore them. In particular, this star seems to labor under the delusion that it is not so much her face as her bottom that is her fortune – so

many low angles of it upturned and bouncing about are featured. It is not a bad bottom but you can't really make a movie of it.

It is difficult not to agree with both assessments. The film was a woefully lame piece, indifferently structured. The emphasis, throughout the film, on the Streisand seat end, is in direct line of descent from Kristofferson's observation (also repeated) in *A Star Is Born* that 'You got a great ass.' And that, of course, echoes Jon Peters beaming reaction to their first meeting. There is also a hint of autobiography – Peters' – as the film homes in on a green young boxer. In fact, the truer title for *The Main Event* might have been 'The Prizefighter and the Lady'. But whereas such a title would promise a crackling Forties-style battle of the sexes, the *de facto* title, *The Main Event*, results merely in television sit-com writ not much larger. The premise – 'upmarket perfume manufacturer finds herself with only one remaining tangible asset – an out-of-condition feckless hack fighter' – comes laden with the advance *ennui* of remorseless predictability. This, in turn, is loosely tacked to total incredibility. The plot mechanics whereby this non-rated fighter lands a major bout are so awkward that disbelief, far from being suspended, asks to be held aloft like an iron-pumper's clean lift. And a comedy set in never-never-land is gutted of its deepest laughs. Without relevance to a world we identify with, all the piece has left are superficialities, sight-gags, put-downs and misunderstandings.

It is true that, physically, Barbra in *The Main Event* is in good form. She looks trimmer, younger than she did three years before as Esther Hoffman in *A Star Is Born*. And just once, in a deliciously played instant, when under duress she signs away her perfume business with the physical pain of someone lancing their own carbuncle, she achieves high comedy. For a split second Edith Evans lives. But that is the sole touch of class that *Main Event* manages. Instead of wit there are gags. Instead of the (genuinely erotic) banked-down sexuality implicit in the clash/ attraction of opposites, there is a demi-explicit, so to speak, handling of the goods in public. There is Streisand's 'great ass', Ryan O'Neal's hand on it and a fair flurry of tasteless dialogue. The idea of obtruding Barbra upon a boxers' gym – 'All those men, Barbra, with muscles! and you'll look so good in those silk shorts!' – is milked for its lowest level of potential. Add a plot that is not particularly sequential – scenes are there because they provide good 'bits' – and Peters' enthusiasm for the movie seems misplaced.

Nor, in this instance, can Barbra claim (as with *Sandbox*) that she kept away from the in-fighting that characterised the production decisions. Scenes, she has stated, were rewritten up to and after the first 'takes'. Whitman Mayo, one of the co-stars, has reiterated the by now familiar anthem:

When we first started shooting there was resentment among the cast and crew because Barbra interfered in everything. She's a fighter. She is very aggressive and she get what she wants. Actually she's a workaholic. I couldn't believe how much energy she had. Each day was like a boxing match, and as it went on you caught different aspects of Streisand. I saw her as a woman, a young lady, and as a child. But I don't blame her for feeling so intensely. She's a perfectionist and likes to have things her way. She genuinely feels her way is right.

'Welles disease' as their respective detractors would say. Impressed, or disgruntled veterans have remarked that, if she had total command, Barbra Streisand would project the reels and sell popcorn in the theater. But perfectionism has no value with imperfect material.

Much of the element of unbelievability in *The Main Event* stems directly from the casting of Ryan O'Neal as the fighter. A John Garfield he is not, though his star value is undeniable. Once a Golden Gloves boxer and part-owner of prize-fighter Hedgeman Lewis, O'Neal is no more a contender for Sugar Ray Leonard's crown than he was for Cary Grant's. Kristofferson, too, had Golden Gloves experience but he retained his muscles, moving from ring to stage. Thick-waisted, limp-armed, O'Neal in the midst of a bunch of genuine boxing pros would not even convince as a has-been. Los Angeles playboy-bland, he has the jabbing impact of a cream-puff. Since covert autobiography appears to have been the name of the game, Peters himself might have been more convincing opposite his lady. Whether or not he can act – on the screen – is an open question. But given his background as a gritty waif and stray, an ex-supporting bout fighter, he might have brought to the part something more than the graceful prat-falls and pleasing underplaying that is O'Neal's best contribution to the movie.

The Main Event is a blemish in the Streisand career. In retrospect she may feel it convicts her of a rare charge in relation to her work – intellectual and professional laziness.

Barbra Streisand's surprisingly long withdrawal from the screen after *A Star Is Born* did not effect the flow of her records. There were always, of course, the soundtrack albums. But other than milestones, mementos of an occasion, none of these are memorable. Stage or film, none of Barbra Streisand's musicals can claim distinguished scores. Fanny Brice, musically, loses in a shoot-out with Annie Oakley. *On a Clear Day* is not even a *Perchance to Dream*.

In 1976, the same year her Esther Hoffman, rock singer, belted on to the screens, *Classical Barbra* was released. It was an attempt – the Columbia Symphony backing her claim – to capture the salons and concert halls of the *Lieder* singer. Instead of Styne, Arlen and Mercer she had the less commercially-driven Fauré, Handel and Wolf penning her tracks. In the event, the suspiciously slow tempo, the comfortable keys, the heavy reliance on legato, suggested that the effort would have been better left to Victoria, rather than Barbra de Los Angeles.

As with her earlier albums, the sleeve of this one has a 'name' drop in with an eye-catching hyperbole. Leonard Bernstein in this case, with: 'Barbra Streisand's natural ability to make music takes her over to the classical field with extraordinary ease. In her sensitive, straightforward and enormously appealing performance, she has given us a very special musical experience.' Yeah, well. Another concert pianist, Glenn Gould, was already on record as saying that he ranked the Streisand voice alongside Elisabeth Schwarzkopf's as 'one of the natural wonders of the age, an instrument of infinite diversity and timbral resonance with the fastest vibrato in the West and the most impeccable intonation this side of Maria Stader's prime.' Yeah – well, again. It seems not to have been a universal opinion. The record was a commercial failure perhaps because subject matter apart, there seems to be such a lack of rapport between orchestra and 'up front' singer. There is the feeling that this is an example of recording to backing tracks, cold-blooded, in a sound studio. However, the disc, whatever its final level of performance – good, bad, 'interesting' – does represent an attempt to widen repertoire and horizons. The Barbra Streisand who has consistently shrunk from churning out Xerox copies of herself, who has persistently gone out for a more daring, a different shot, can at least claim: 'I gave it a whirl.' Still, the classical 'experiment' has never been repeated.

The same spirit of innovation exists in the non-show, 'mainstream' evolution of Barbra's recordings. Her albums have increasingly reflected current modes, looking to the present rather than the past. Cynics might argue this is a blatant commercial pitch to mount a maximum appealing package. Much of it continues to derive from the 'singer in search of a style, a look' phenomenon. Lacking a single-career singer's repertory, Barbra's choice of material has always hinted, and probably always will, at a lack of lived-with commitment. But there's the advantage that occasional discs, rather than endless gigs, have given her scope to range more widely.

By 1969 Barbra Streisand was a big enough name for her to drop on to the back of her then new album *What About Today?* With embarrassing self-consciousness, however sincerely felt the compliment, she wrote: 'This album is dedicated to the young people who push against indifference, shout down mediocrity, demand a better future and who write and sing the songs of today.' In retrospect, the message seems unfortunate. It reads too much like an attempt to hitch a ride on the Joan Baez, Pete Seeger bandwagon without suffering the physical and economical deprivations their active 'pushing against indifference' had brought to them. But the dedication is an accurate key-signature for the album's spiritual contents. Now, where there had been Arlen, there was Paul Simon; where there had been Styne, there was John Lennon. It was, all things considered, a change for the better.

To begin with, it exorcised the ghosts of all those – Tormé, Holliday, Eckstein, Fitzgerald, Vaughan – who did not act but, simply singing for their suppers, haunted her earlier recordings. Now, taking on material less obviously hand-me-down, Barbra avoided having her 'My Funny Valentine' run an inevitable bad third to Fitzgerald's and Sinatra's.

The Sixties had seen the powerful flowering (or reborn) species of thoroughly talented songwriters and poet-lyricists. Lightfoot, Lennon (plus or minus McCartney), Dylan, McCartney with or without Lennon, Buffy Saint Marie, Carole King . . . the list grew honourably longer by the month. Two strains, amid many, could almost always be discerned in their work: the folk idiom and its more urban cousin, the Brel, Brassens *chansonnier* style. If we are honest, a third strain was very often evident too. That in the recorded voice. Nobody has trouble with knowing how to place Dylan's 'Blue Moon' as against Mel Tormé's. It is fairly universally recognised that very few of the Sixties recording superstars could sing well. It scarcely mattered. Part of the compulsiveness of Bob Dylan was the cracked 'ordinariness' of his voice. Gordon Lightfoot's light-voiced thinness was an important contribution towards making his beautiful poem-songs seem as if they belonged to everybody. The hoarse urgency of John Lennon's twisting and shouting vocals perhaps touched the heart. Interpretation is all.

In fact, falling between two stools, *What About Today?* is a less than completely successful album. The tracks of less familiar songs (like, 'That Is a Fine Kind o' Freedom') sound like an under-achieving melody portentously in search of significance. The Sixties standards – 'Until It's Time for You to Go', 'With a Little Help from My Friends' – suffer from the overmannered, too-tugged-about effort to step out from the shadow of the original. The chamber-music strings, for instance, in the Buffy Saint Marie song, the false overdone weight of emphasis on the word 'Start' are pieces of flashy, inappropriate decoration designed to disguise that the edifice is fundamentally the same structure as one already erected. The 'sign-off' ending to the Lennon/McCartney 'Goodnight' is Barbra at her most coy.

The album overall, however, was a pointer in the right direction. Two years later she produced what remains arguably her best record, *Stoney End*. It was, in fact, technically produced by Richard Perry and is a magnificent example of the finesse that can be achieved in a modern recording studio. It is also, more than any other, the album where Barbra Streisand allows her self-consciousness to take a back seat as she just gets on with singing a straight-down-the-middle version of each song. They are exceptionally good numbers. The listener can relax into enjoying her singing that, even when at its most on-driving and diamond-hard, is still itself relaxed. Whether the man in the street ultimately prefers 'If You Could Read My Mind' as sung by Lightfoot, Joplin, Streisand or Marian Montgomery, is now a matter of subjective preference. Like the other singers, one feels Barbra is here experiencing the song directly.

Unfortunately, despite the continuing presence of the same producer, the next album, *Barbra Joan Streisand*, represented a lapse back to bad habits. Stephen Holden of *Rolling Stone* latched on to the problems, the strengths, the weakness. 'The whole,' he wrote,

> turns out to be an uneasy mix. An unqualified bummer is Barbra's rendition of John Lennon's 'Mother' in which she belts out the primal scream. A mechanised shriek that has all the humanity of a police siren, it makes an embarrassing mockery of a great song.
>
> The point of the album, the Bacharach–David medley, is pure vintage Streisand. A duet with herself, she croons it like it is for all the male models and Marjorie Morningstars of this world with kleig lights in their eyes. Everything works together to achieve the ultimate in pop professionalism. More than Dionne Warwick even, Barbra would seem to be the singer best suited to record the complete Burt Bacharach–Hal David songbook. It would be the crowning achievement of her career. As for the Carole King or John Lennon songbooks, God forbid!

The tendency in the studio albums that followed over the years has been to fail to analyse the reasons for the aesthetic success of *Stoney End*. Perhaps the phenomenal sales success (five million plus) of the *A Star Is Born* album seduced Barbra away from a sagacity in her projection of material. With a second Oscar in her trophy cabinet as co-composer of 'Evergreen' (she is said to have received more pleasure from that than her 'Hello Gorgeous' first), she may have felt that her *ad hoc* instinct had the edge over experience. Wrongly. The impression strongly remains of a supertalent in search of a style.

From time to time – in the occasional duets, for example with Neil Diamond, Donna Summer – the talent is confined within the framework of the song and both become the stronger. But the feeling persists that it was commerce rather than a seeking of a 'control' that induced the pairing. Indeed, without a vocal identity of her own, with no chance to evolve gradually at a singer's naturally developing pace, Barbra Streisand's recording moods throughout the Seventies seemed to follow, guardedly, changing trends. After soft rock there were bows in the direction of Motown, and latterly of a disco sound. The duet with Donna Summer on the aptly named *Wet* ('Come Rain or Come Shine' encapsulates all her worst failings) was given the PR hype of being a duet in the studio, a shoot-out between two mean, deadly lady gunslingers. In fact, they collaborate superbly on the best track in the album; but the clear winner is neither. The rhythm track romps away with the honours. It makes the latest in the line of LP's, the Barry Gibb-produced *Guilty,* seem correctly named. With its sub-disco orientation, it is probably the weakest album musically Barbra Streisand has ever been associated with. That it has slain them in their millions and that 'Woman in Love', the single spin-off from it, achieved number one poll status on both sides of the Atlantic, is a bleak reminder of the gap between public taste and artistic substance.

The production of one LP crystallises the unresolved embarrassment of riches that resides in the voice of Barbra Streisand. Dating from 1974, the disc in question is the famous *Butterfly*. It marked the active intervention of Jon Peters into her professional career – and in a characteristically brash and abrasive fashion. A veteran engineer, Al Schmitt, began production of the LP, but after three cuts Barbra informed him that she did not like the sound of the end product. Schmitt was let go and Peters took over. The new result was a fine technical sound. But it was a record playing its reggae and country-and-western ends against its Paul Williams middle. Something for everyone, folks. And a lot you'll be happy to pass on. Nobody admiring the straight job she does on David Bowie's brooding 'Life on Mars' will fail to be acutely embarrassed by the overbearing, look-at-me-I'm-lilting of 'Since I Don't Have You'.

Infinite variety and eclecticism become irrelevant; talent runs away into a wasteland without a unifying personal stance and style. Experiment, improvement, yes. Changes of pace and direction, by all means. But grafted on to, stemming from, an authentic individual voice. Streisand as a singer has an utterly identifiable voice, an unmistakable personality. She is not an individual voice in a higher artistic sense.

The constant refrain from all who, from the very beginning, have worked with Barbra Streisand, is the unremitting level of her perfectionism. The charge is confirmed by the evidence. If genius is the infinite capacity for taking pains, she is a genius. But not, in terms of her discs, if genius also involves seeing the wood for the trees. On the playback context of a recording studio she can be a four-letter-worded tiger as she frets over a guitarist's late entry or lack of attack. But in an overview sense, she has been peculiarly careless. She has denied herself a body of work, a core, a tradition from which she can regularly derive fresh artistic nourishment. Her working practice is to visit songs from the outside. When she puts them on she cuts a dash but is seldom at ease. Neither is the song. To be a singer in the Holliday class, Barbra Streisand needs to work the same material over and over again (and in public) until all the meretricious ornamentation has been polished away.

Perhaps she will never do this. Consequently she will remain, at bottom, an amateur – as she correctly said those two decades ago – 'an actress who sings.'

That analysis, as she advances into the Eighties, begs the question: could the same charge of being ultra-gifted but essentially amateur be levelled at her as an actress?

TWENTY

BARBRA STREISANDS'S relationship with the media at the close of the decade deteriorated in inverse ratio to her soaring power and influence. Unable or unwilling to arrive at the truth, there was a heavy reliance on rumour, half-truths and barefaced invention. The frustration of chasing, in vain, this steely will o' the wisp, is neatly reflected in this item from the *Los Angeles Herald Examiner* (28 January 1980):

> Barbra Streisand evidently still hasn't accepted the full measure of fame that is hers. The star of stars doesn't understand why the public is interested in her private life, doesn't quite believe it when the New York *Daily News* stakes out her Manhattan apartment with a photographer to catch an exclusive first glimpse of the newest man in her life, and somehow feels she should be able to live and behave like a perfectly normal, anonymous individual.

That said, the writer himself jumped on the bandwagon, continuing:

> Barbra has been going to the theater in New York almost every night with Arnon Milchon – the man who will produce Robert de Niro's next movie. Milchon is a multi-millionaire Israeli in his early 40s with homes in both Paris and Israel. He is divorced from a French woman and has two children. Meantime Barbra insists that Milchon is a friend and not a new beau. She says that she and Jon Peters are still living together in a completely compatible and open manner. They are said to have no secrets from one another.

More than ever now, Barbra Streisand was being caught in the journalistic crossfire occasioned by the central paradox of her life. She is both a star of stars and, minor aberrations apart, a normal individual. Whichever way she plays it, she is resigned to the fact that she must lose. She knows that she can win every trophy going, except an award for popularity. The Women's Press Club, Hollywood, annually distinguishes between those stars who 'co-operate' and those (who are awarded the 'Sour Apple Award') who have better things to do with their time and talent than chatter to fawning, ill-informed interviewers. Almost invariably, the rarer the interview the more substantial is the quality of the 'victim'. The distinction drawn is between the artist, and the mere 'personality'. It is not paranoia that drives Barbra Streisand into a kind of anti-media purdah. It is a genuine nervousness, terror sometimes, of the hostile question, of the too persistent probing.

The main focus of interest, target for the attack, has always been the precise state of her love life. Since neither she nor Jon Peters have ever denied that their alley-cat fighting was basic to the intensity of their relationship, professional onlookers felt free to speculate. The *Herald Examiner* returned to the theme some weeks later: ' "No, no, no," said Barbra Streisand yesterday. "It's not true. Period," she insisted, of the stories circulating around town of her split with hair stylist-turned-movie-producer Jon Peters. Still Jack Martin of the *New York Post* told us yesterday, "If they're still together then they're together apart." Martin's story in the *Post* puts the details this way: Streisand and Peters were together last Saturday at the Bar mitzvah of Streisand and Elliott Gould's son, Jason. Since then, La Barbra's been holed up at her house in Holmby Hills while Jon's been going it alone at their ranch at Malibu." ' Here you get two professional keyhole-gazers for the price of one.

Denials? See where they get you. A star who is also a person possesses all the 'heads they win, tails I lose' vulnerability. With Peters still around – obstinately so from the gossip writer's standpoint – speculation switched to Barbra's career in her third decade in show business. The guesswork reads like a soothsayer's almanac:

> She wanted to/would definitely play the title role in the movie of *Evita* – opposite Brando's Che Guevera. 1980/81 would see her touring in a *Star Is Born* –style road-show. She would be starring opposite Neil Diamond in a film scored by the Bee Gees. She had concluded arrangements with David Begelman of MGM to 'actively participate in the development of a project concerning two women living in New York City during the turmoil of the early 1900s with the specter of the forthcoming World War in the background.'

Frequently even straight-forward, factual items bring out the worst in their chroniclers. Item:

> The UCLA School of Medicine won't have Barbra Streisand to kick around, only to sit on. Through a $500,000 pledge from La Barbra and an additional $300,000 from the Greater Los Angeles Affiliate of the American Heart Association, the Streisand Chair of Cardiology has been established.

The omission of any reference to the prodigious generosity is surely more eloquent than the item's showbiz style. The description 'La Barbra' is as dead and gone as Hedda Hopper. It is almost a relief to return to the idiosyncratic fracturing of the language by *Variety*. Whatever the syntax, here, in a column of 20 May 1980, is at least hard information and some soft innuendo:

> In a more than surprising casting change [*Variety* reported], Barbra Streisand has assumed the co-starring role opposite Gene Hackman in Universal's *All Night Long*, replacing Lisa Eichhorn.
> The romantic comedy has been lensing for five weeks on a ten-week sked . . . under the direction of Jean-Claude Tramont. Tramont is the husband of agent Sue Mengers, who apparently put the package for the film together and represents both Hackman and Streisand . . . Box-office potential of Streisand–Hackman obviously delights execs, although it's reported that Streisand's salary is $4 million plus 15% of the gross.

The fee may sound laughably excessive, but not when considered against

Streisand's box-office potential and the gigantic stipends paid to the class of Brando, Burt Reynolds, Redford and Clint Eastwood.

Clearly the cost of running the Malibu ranch and the Holmby Hills house is not an immediate problem any more than meeting demands on a charitable purse. Only Brando and Redford could present an asking price hiked so high. Possibly its stratospheric *chutzpah* reflected the perilous problem of last-minute recasting.

It was, of course, unique of Barbra to replace any actress who already had a week's work in the can. In terms of severance pay it amounted to a paltry quarter of a million dollars. Petty cash when Streisand is part of the bargain. It was also unique of her to appear in a picture without knowing the clear-cut central role. A good deal of water – not to say blood, sweat and tears – had passed under her bridge since she had hired herself out to a project she had not personally developed. But four million is four million. That's not bad take-home pay for a role in which no singing is required. The film, at the time of writing, was not ready for critical inspection. But on a surface level it augurs well from a Streisand viewpoint. Its plot outline offers scope for the submergence of self, into a naturalistic role. The story of *All Night Long* has to do with a drugstore executive who at a personal crisis in his life succeeds in getting himself demoted to the minor position of managing a San Fernando Valley drugstore. The Streisand role is of the Valley housewife who partners the hero in the affair he also manages, after quitting his wife. Playing opposite that most subtle and deeply ranging actor, Gene Hackman – *French Connection* to *The Conversation* – the hope is that Barbra will appear on the screen as housewife and not superstar.

There is an irony to the replacement of Lisa Eichhorn. It was alleged she brought disaster down upon her own head by being 'very difficult on the set, objecting to things like camera angles.' Difficult on the set? Objecting to camera-angles? Now where have we heard that before? But it is hard not to be sorry. It was left to her agent to make the right noises: 'Lisa's not bitter about the replacement,' he said deftly, 'although of course, she is not pleased. But when you're replaced by Barbra Streisand how can you fight that number?'

Barbra Streisand, as *All Night Long* wrapped and 1980 with it, inspired even more vigorous guessing by the commentators as to what would make her run one, five, ten years from now. Long-term speculation in the tinsel village being a moon-struck enterprise, the crystal-gazers concentrated on Streisand's more immediate plans. Her plans, even in a town weaned on amazement and raised on shock, left everyone in the trade agape. It was not merely that she had decided to direct her next film. Even her critics – never any shortage of these – conceded that, if Redford could do it, so could she. It was on the choice of film and the tight-money period for which its production was scheduled, that the widespread incredulity centered. It was announced that she would star in and direct Isaac Bashevis Singer's story *Yentl*. The spare ribs of this fanciful tale tells of an orphaned teenage girl (Yentl) who disguises herself as a boy in order to join the all-male Yeshiva, the traditional Jewish school devoted to the study of rabbinical literature and the Talmud. The convolutions of the story, involving Yentl dressing up as a boy and even going through a marriage of sorts, reads like a Shakespearean comedy tricked out in the black velour and gabardine of rabbinical Poland. Leaving aside its message of a bright girl's struggle for equality in an all-male world, is *Yentl* the sort of movie Hollywood bankers should invest their money in?

The rule-book answer has to be 'No' on several counts. The first can be summarised in the stock front-office jargon: 'Who the hell's gonna be interested in a story about orthodox Jews somewhere in Eastern Europe, with Streisand rigged out like a learner-rabbi, and not even singing? At least *Fiddler on the Roof* had some great numbers, and Topol and – where's the sex . . .? The Streisand fans will go bananas!' The second argument flows from the first. The style of Bashevis Singer, a Nobel Prize winner, is scarcely ideal screenplay material. His flat, primitive stories, rather like Lowry townscapes, are essentially two-dimensional. They're heavy on 'significance' and 'symbolism'. Jack Warner's dictum about 'messages' and Western Union receives a powerful boost if Singer's story is to be filmed as written. The final and most compelling argument against *Yentl* was commercial. As cinemas throughout the world, but most significantly in the U.S., studied their returns for the year, the staggering losses of several major films were plain to see. *Two-thirds* of the big budget films in America lost money. The most devastating example was Michael Cimino's *Heaven's Gate*. The most expensive Western ever made (costs were in the $40 million area) it was so savagely mauled by critics that it had to be withdrawn for another $10 million worth of re-editing. Names that had seemed as bankable as bullion, even in bad movies, failed to pull in the crowds. The public were beginning to demand 'let's see what you're offering' before moving away from their colour televisions. The uncompromising message was circulated around all the 'majors' – the recession can't carry extravagant, superstar self-indulgence any more.

So Hollywood blew cold on almost everything at the close of 1980 except guaranteed, spot-welded certainties. And it blew coldest of all on *Yentl*. The collective verdict – 'We need "Yentl the Yeshiva Boy" like a hole in the head' – would have warned off most stars flirting with the idea. But not Barbra Streisand. Hell could freeze over before she would abandon *Yentl*. Though budget estimates soared from $7 million to nearer double that figure, she swept through London, Paris, Czechoslovakia, with a brief pause for a chat with Stanley Kubrick, that equally uncompromising film-maker. Was Streisand's *Yentl* project an act of fiscal recklessness, of Flatbush tenacity, or of something much deeper? We can ignore the cynical theory that Barbra had blatantly jumped on the Nobel Prize bandwagon with Singer currently the hottest commodity in the up-market writing field. In fact, incredibly, or with incredible precognition, she has owned the screen rights to *Yentl* since 1968, a full decade before Singer received Sweden's highest honour. (Her advisers as strenuously opposed to the idea then as they were to be ten years later).

So we can look for reasons.

Its generating current goes back to the late Emmanuel Streisand, that is certain. And his presence must have hovered benignly in the foreground in January 1980 when Jason Gould, at thirteen, was bar mitzvahed in the Center which Streisand so munificently endowed. Barbra Streisand, seated in the front row of the temple, watched as her son went through the age-old ceremony, reciting the prayers, touching the sacred scrolls with the fringe of his prayer shawl. 'Blessed are you, Lord God, who has given us the Torah of Truth and planted everlasting life among

Showing a leg in *The Main Event*

us.'

So Jason Gould, Streisand's son, achieved manhood. He was acquiring an identity, not an image. Outside the Cadillacs and the 'limos' waited to take the celebrated congregants back to their palaces, pools, ranch houses and tennis games. Inside, there were overtones of Pulaski Street *circa* 1940, and tears in Barbra Streisand's eyes. Bar mitzvahs are one of the few spiritual milestones that grandparents pray that they'll live to see. This would have been a big day for Emmanual Streisand. Hard not to imagine Barbra counting the years . . . he died when he was thirty-four . . . let's see he would be about seventy now . . . not old these days . . . and he'd have liked Jason . . . There were hugs all round and cries of 'Good Luck!' That milestone passed, Barbra Streisand got back to making movies.

Personal feelings apart, one can see the force of the attraction that 'Yentl the Yeshiva Boy' has for Barbra. Unglamorously set in nineteenth-century Poland, it is, from the beginning, the story of a girl battling against the sheep and goats discrimination in the religious education of the sexes. Yentl will not take no for an answer; she will not deny the, so-called, masculine traits in her make-up – intelligence, ambition, judgement and perception.

More subtly, Yentl is by plot-definition, a virtual schizophrenic. So, in effect, have been many of Barbra Streisand's previous screen roles. In *On a Clear Day* she oscillates between the two variations (stronger, weaker) of the same self. Fanny Brice on-stage is abrasive, aggressive, extrovert; off-stage she is vulnerable, no longer dishing it out. Dolly Levi is utterly female at heart but her external, predatory behaviour is all masculine initiative. In *Up the Sandbox* who wears the pants is an essential theme of the movie. Less blatantly, *The Way We Were* also involves the heroine in the question of role definition. When Katie Morosky, Jewish radical, surrenders herself for a while to the image of a conforming Hollywood stereotype, it is for a man's sake.

All of these examples of ambivalence reflect a deeply central aspect of Barbra Streisand's being. She contains extraordinary opposites within her. Nervous of being recognised in a waiting room, she can still dominate an audience running into six figures. Conventionally ugly, she is unconventionally beautiful and then just beautiful. In her best moments on screen, or disc, much of the excitement derives from the tension generated by the sweet and sour, soft and hard elements by which the performance is driven.

In Singer's story, this paragraph occurs:

Night fell and the light faded. In the darkness they seemed to be listening to each other's thoughts. The Law forbade Avigdor to stay in the room alone with Anshel [Yentl]. But he could not think of her just as a woman. What a strange power there is in clothing, he thought.

There is indeed. Barbra Streisand, the little girl 'dressing up' in front of a mirror, has continued to do so all her life. Very often as a man. The variations on a man's outfit are – sexily – exploited in *The Main Event*. In *The Way We Were* she is briefly Harpo Marx. At the (would-be) climax to *A Star Is Born* she is dressed not only in reaffirmation white but in a man's suit. And one of her recordings, with coaxing eroticism, constantly repeats the refrain, 'Honey can I put on your clothes?' Part of the fascination for any actress immersing herself in the role of Yentl must be the awareness that her surface persona for much of the film must be masculine.

The hat, the ringlets, the features – one can visualise Barbra, the yeshiva boy. But there is more to the role for Barbra, than putting on fancy dress. In early December 1980, Barbra Streisand arrived quietly in London for costume fittings. She went to Berman and Nathan's the famous theatrical costumiers to try on for size their yeshiva hats, prayer shawls and other garments. Berman, who dressed the film *Fiddler on the Roof* and other ethnic epics, could kit out a thousand Yentls and still not have to call upon strategic reserves. Monty Berman, the de Mille of the costumier trade, received Barbra and was immediately surprised. 'She was so much more petite than I had imagined her,' he said. 'But she had this tremendous presence. She knew exactly what she wanted. There's no doubt *Yentl* means much more to her than just another film.' And then when the costume fittings began, he became oddly moved. Here was Streisand in London's unfashionable Camden Town (the costumes are housed in a repository there and not at the company's plusher offices), trying on traditional clothing, 'psyching' herself back into a nineteenth-century Polish yeshiva. As she draped the tallith (prayer shawl) across her shoulders, held the fringes whose knots symbolically bind a people to their faith, a deep atavistic resonance must have vibrated somewhere in the makeup of the $4 million-gross superstar. The commonplace of a theatrical fitting must have been replaced by a corridor of thought that drove straight back to Emmanuel Streisand's spiritual heartland. Wearing the prayer shawl, Barbra may have seen Yentl in the mirror. But it must have been her father who dominated her thoughts.

Beyond that, there is another layer of compelling attraction. For a concerned adult living in the sybaritic capital of the world – pools, guards and Dobermans – the fascination of the physically impoverished, spiritually enriched life must be very strong indeed. For all her Laliques, Klimts and Gucci pen-wipers, for all her flair with antiques and decor, Barbra Streisand embodies another contradiction. She can feel guilty about being a big spender. And even more so about being a big earner. The star Sue Mengers can promote a cool $4 million plus for, recognizes it is the idiot game all the inmates have to play. Perhaps *Yentl* is not only an act of homage to an ethnic past but an act of reparation to the countless millions from that past who did not make it to Malibu. Like the Religious Center in Venice, California, it has overtones of a world-famous entertainer from Brooklyn yearning to get back to reality. Roots.

Missing most from a life now approaching its middle years, was a dialogue with her father. The pangs of being robbed of it must have become more intense as she looked around for substitutes and found none. No fault of Mrs Diane Kind's. Barbra Streisand has been denied that dialogue when she would have relished it most. The Oscars, the Grammys, the Emmys, the string of gold discs; the ranch, the millions, the handshake with Her Britannic Majesty . . . Trudeau, Golda Meir . . . Jason. Father and daughter would not have been short on conversation had Emmanuel lived to sit front-row center over the years. Barbra Streisand has manifestly kept her father's image standing prominently in the foreground of her life. By instinct perhaps, every move she makes of any substance, submitted to the unseen scrutiny of her father.

However, no terrestial command center can change the Streisand orbit. Its direction is now fixed on the director's chair. The demon that inhabits Barbra Streisand will not let her renege on that, or the film, or the talents she was born with. Well-wishers might consider this a mistake. Their advice, citing history and Garbo, Shearer, Irene Dunne and Mary Pickford, is to quit while you're still at the top, ahead of the game, fortune made. 'Barbra baby,' the argument runs, 'take a long look at youself. Each night you go to sleep in a luxury Stalag imprisoned by the electric fence you yourself have strung. Is it to keep the world out, or you in? You've proved to the world you can do it on your own terms, the hard way, your way. Now relax. You owe it to yourself to go out and get yourself that nose job and melt into the crowd.'

That will not happen. If Elliott Gould and Jon Peters are still in the fight why should she pull out? Gould with such movies as *California Split* and *Bob and Carol and Ted and Alice* and much good stuff besides, has earned his niche in the Hollywood Hall of Fame. Jon Peters can also relax contentedly at night. Like the scrap-iron dealer, the glove salesman and the furrier before him, he has proved to scoffers that he has long left the Sammy Glicks at the starting blocks. And the Sammy Glicks never married Barbra Streisand.

Singer, actress, producer and now director. It may happen that, Barbra Streisand, thriving on the exercise of a director's omnipotence, may score another triumph. It may also happen, with the movie (as we write) not rolling, that the project may have been the first spectacular casualty in Hollywood's battle against recession. The danger is, assuming *Yentl* goes ahead, that total power might tempt her to indulge in the cuteness and kitsch that have characterised her work at its strident worst. But there is also the glittering possibility that the director, having learned a trick or two from Pollack and Kershner, will turn it to good account, add another feather to her boa.

Two diverging routes. Those who do not know, or care to know Barbra Streisand, may allow their prejudices to point her towards failure. Friends, including those close enough to the epicentre to feel the heat, will hope to see Streisand score another victory, yes, even win another Oscar. Imposing no limits upon herself, the possibilities too are limitless.

Incredible though it may seem, the interim verdict on Barbra Streisand must be that, given her talent, her will, her intelligence, her stamina, she is to date, like Woody Allen's God, an under-achiever.

BARBRA STREISAND FILMOGRAPHY

1968 FUNNY GIRL (Dir: William Wyler) With: Omar Sharif, Walter Pidgeon, Kay Medford, Anne Francis (Columbia)

1969 HELLO DOLLY! (Dir: Gene Kelly) With: Walter Matthau, Michael Crawford, Marianne McAndrew (20th Century Fox)

1970 ON A CLEAR DAY YOU CAN SEE FOREVER (Dir: Vincent Minnelli) With: Yves Montand, Bob Newhart, Larry Blyden, Jack Nicholson (Paramount)

1970 THE OWL AND THE PUSSYCAT (Dir: Herbert Ross) With: George Segal, Robert Klein, Allen Garfield (Columbia)

1972 WHAT'S UP DOC? (Dir: Peter Bogdanovich) With: Ryan O'Neal, Kenneth Mars, Austin Pendleton, Madeleine Kahn (Warner Brothers)

1972 UP THE SANDBOX (Dir: Irwin Kershner) With: David Selby, Ariane Heller, Jane Hoffman (First Artists)

1973 THE WAY WE WERE (Dir: Sydney Pollack) With: Robert Redford, Patrick O'Neal, Viveca Lindfors, Bradford Dillman (Columbia)

1974 FOR PETE'S SAKE (Dir: Peter Yates) With: Michael Sarrazin, Estelle Parsons, William Redfield (Columbia)

1975 FUNNY LADY (Dir: Herbert Ross) With: James Caan, Ben Vereen, Omar Sharif, Roddy McDowall (Columbia)

1976 A STAR IS BORN (Dir: Frank Pierson) With: Kris Kristofferson (First Artists)

1979 THE MAIN EVENT (Dir: Howard Zieff) With: Ryan O'Neal, Paul Sand, Whitman Mayo (Warner Brothers)

1980 ALL NIGHT LONG (Dir: Jean-Claude Tramont) With: Gene Hackman, Dianne Ladd (Universal)

In Preparation: YENTL

INDEX